The Real Soviet Russia

By David J. Dallin

Translated by Joseph Shaplen

New Haven · Yale University Press
1944

COPYRIGHT, 1944, BY YALE UNIVERSITY PRESS

Printed in the United States of America

The Amasa Stone Mather Memorial Publication Fund

The present volume is the twenty-second work published by the Yale University Press on the Amasa Stone Mather Memorial Publication Fund. This Foundation was established August 25, 1922, by a gift to Yale University from Samuel Mather, Esq., of Cleveland, Ohio, in pursuance of a pledge made in June, 1922, on the fifteenth anniversary of the graduation of his son, Amasa Stone Mather, who was born in Cleveland on August 20, 1884, and was graduated from Yale College in the Class of 1907. Subsequently, after traveling abroad, he returned to Cleveland, where he soon won a recognized position in the business life of the city and where he actively interested himself also in the work of many organizations devoted to the betterment of the community and to the welfare of the nation. His death from pneumonia on February 9, 1920, was undoubtedly hastened by his characteristic unwillingness ever to spare himself, even when ill, in the discharge of his duties or in his efforts to protect and further the interests committed to his care by his associates.

Preface

CONVENTIONAL truths and conventional lies may be necessary to soften the grinding of the wheels of diplomacy. They play a distinctive role in foreign policy and the conduct of diplomatic affairs. But no successful foreign policy can be based upon conventions and it is impossible to grasp the true meaning of events by proceeding on any such basis.

The wartime policies of the United States and Great Britain in relation to Russia have merely reflected the course of events. Military alliance, supply of war materials, political and strategic collaboration became natural and logical under the circumstances. Any other governments in the United States and Britain would have followed the same general course, including even the attitude on the difficult Baltic, Polish, and Yugoslav questions and the huge billion dollar credits, as well as the warm congratulations and compliments heaped upon their ally.

Unlike Foreign Offices and State Departments, the active molders of public opinion have not only the right but the duty to scrutinize and to analyze without resort to conventionalism. They fail in the performance of their duty if they do not penetrate deeper into the meaning of contemporary history, do not perceive difficulties and dangers, but confine themselves merely to "healthy optimism." From the optimistic to the ridiculous is only a short step.

Otherwise, what is the use of a free press and of free science?

In Russia foreign and internal policies are more closely allied than in any other country. Only by studying the general concepts dominating Soviet activity at home, the established social relations, the direction of internal political development, is it possible to comprehend and to foresee the evolution of Soviet foreign policy and to avoid the naïve and dangerous mistakes so frequent during the past decade.

This book is designed to serve as an introduction to the study of the real Soviet Russia. It seeks to set down some of the essential facts concerning the character of the Soviet regime, its guiding ideas, its political structure. These facts form the foundation of Soviet foreign policy.

Appreciation is here expressed to George Denicke and Vladimir Zenzinov, authorities in the field of international literature on Russia, for their substantial help in the preparation of this book. To Dr. N. M. Jasny I am indebted for advice and factual material on Russian economy. Much labor was devoted by Joseph Shaplen to helping to shape the literary form of this book. The staff of the Slavonic Division of the New York Public Library gave me invaluable aid. The charts were prepared by Alexander Dallin and drawn by W. C. Kirkwood.

D. D.

Contents

The Real Soviet Russia

I

"Klyukva"

FOREIGNERS have been discovering Russia in recent years with the same rapture with which Columbus discovered America. Nearly every month some intrepid traveler, having exchanged the edict of the King of Spain for the credentials of an American newspaper, and the wooden *Santa Maria* for a winged Douglas, produces a weighty book, containing the results of his observations in Russia. This literary output has created a very sizeable library. The authors are honest, decent folk who often do not know either the language or the country; who today are in India, tomorrow in Tierra del Fuego, and, in between, in Moscow; and who invariably try to be nice to the powers-that-be in each country. For this reason, because of their energy, American speed, and desire to combine whatever objectivity they possess with "hot news," they produce books, some of them called scientific, some political, which would justify the Russian people in exclaiming in horror, as do the Indians in a certain operetta, when Columbus comes ashore, "Woe to us, we are discovered!"

Such is the fate of Russia. A certain French traveler, upon visiting there a century ago, was intrigued by a plant which the Russians called *klyukva,* a cranberry plant used in the manufacture of a popular beverage. Klyukva grows on small, low bushes. But upon his return to France the noted explorer related how he drank tea with Russian grandees "sous l'ombre d'un klukva majestueux"—under the shade of a majestic klyukva. His report provoked laughter in Russia, and the word "klyukva" came to be used as signifying a certain kind of ridiculous misinformation.

As an example we may cite a young journalist who tries to be objective, but who apparently never saw women working in either American or Russian industrial plants. He reports that in Russia "the women are neither entirely masculine nor entirely feminine . . . They look like a mixture of both sexes, they are different from any other women."

Another writer, the editor of a New York newspaper, discovers that "the Russians rarely say 'da'—yes; they say mostly 'da-da-da.' "

One author of a widely circulated book reports seriously the alleged fact gleaned in Moscow that "only one per cent of the Russian people were literate before the Revolution." The fact is, as is well known, that the proportion was 40 to 45 per cent. But he wanted to be obliging to the government by showing the low level of literacy it had to contend with at the beginning of its rule. Another writer, for the same reason, reveals the state of education in Russia as the most extraordinary in the world: "nearly half of the people in Russia know German." In reality, only about 5 to 6 per cent are familiar with that language.

One writer, having failed to grasp the Russian word for boiled water, says it is "kippy tuck" (kipyatok); a photographer, having snapped the picture of a woman from Tambov, explains that the city of that name is located in Siberia, although Tambov is seven hundred miles distant from Siberia. Another author calls Stalin's father Illarion, although he could have learned the correct name from almost any person in the street.

In a book published in the United States by a serious and well-known organization devoted to the study of foreign policy we find the following bit of information concerning the agrarian question in Russia: "By 1914 only one-third of the peasants owned land . . . The rest were landless peasants who worked as tenants or farm hands on the estates of big land owners." All of which is pure nonsense. The percentage of landless peasants before the Revolution was negligible.

In the same book we learn that "there are about 300 million Slavs in Europe." The actual number is between 180 and 190 million.

A good many people are familiar with the "white nights" enjoyed by Leningrad, located in the sixtieth degree of north latitude. But a lady journalist, having visited only Moscow, and having heard something about "white nights," informs her readers in the United States in klyukva style: "The white nights of Moscow is a phrase that Muscovites have used for centuries, but with the war it has taken on another meaning."

In general, geography and history suffer most. Take the German town of Tilsit, for example. In October, 1943, a newspaper in Virginia published this: "In the course of the last centuries many a conference took place in Russia which decided the fate of Europe: the Tilsit conference of 1807 . . ."

The system of limited free enterprise reintroduced in 1921 in Soviet Russia was abolished about five years after Lenin's death (1924). But a military publishing house declares in a book that "when Lenin felt that the movement toward Socialism could proceed, he abandoned the NEP." The same book offers the following gem of historic lore bearing upon events of 1917: "When Lenin saw that the revolution might become a democratic or bourgeois revolution he joined with Trotsky in violent action. Civil war ensued."

It is strange that all such nonsense is written mainly with respect to Russia. No one writes that Manchester is in Ireland or Lyons in Belgium; that the Germans do not say "ja" but "ja-ja-ja," and that the Italians are all illiterate. Careful verification of facts is obligatory for all other countries. Why is the exception made for Russia?

THIS brand of klyukva attains its greatest proportions in discussions of Russian politics. The desire of various writers to follow a political line leads to most curious results.

We will not speak here of publications and writers belonging to the camp which is morally and materially obligated to eulogize everything Soviet, without exception. It would be easy, but not interesting, to cite examples of "majestic klyukva" from works of this type. But since not many people take seriously the political advertisements of any country, it is hardly worth the effort to criticize such patent ballyhoo. For this reason we confine ourselves to literature and authors that seek to explain, not to advertise.

Take, as an example, the correspondent of one of the most prominent American newspapers, who arrived in Russia in the summer of 1941, soon after the German invasion. Upon landing in Moscow in a plane from the south, he went directly to the telegraph station from the airfield and informed the

American public through his paper that everything was progressing beautifully in the Russian villages and in Russian agriculture. How did he manage to establish this fact so quickly? "From my airplane I saw peasant women working in the fields!"

The same author who quoted the statistics on illiteracy reports also that before the revolution "only ten per cent of the people wore shoes," and that now, in the midst of war, "the people yearn for minor luxuries." How did he come to this conclusion? He saw "crowded hair-dressing rooms" in the wealthier sections of Moscow, while waitresses in his hotel, occupied by foreigners, i.e., a relatively luxurious hotel, had manicured nails. That was enough for him.

Another correspondent reports that "before the war the Russians could not manufacture even a matchbox without the help of foreign engineers." He also supplies some history. In the Kremlin stands the famous Tsar-pushka, an antique gun, produced in the sixteenth century, bearing the likeness of Tsar Feodor. The Russians used this gun, he says, in defending Moscow against Napoleon in 1812. But no shot was ever fired from this gun; the barrel is so thin it would have burst with the first discharge.

To the realm of political legend belongs also the report of one author that "tea drinking has only become general among the peasantry in the last twenty years," and that "the diet of the Tsar's soldiers consisted of dried herring and a handful of kasha (porridge), which they carried in their knapsacks." Actually their diet included bread, kasha, meat, tea, sugar.

The Russian general Suvorov, born in 1729, performed his military exploits at the end of the eighteenth century, but a writer in one of the most serious American magazines devoted to foreign affairs declares that Suvorov defeated Charles XII of Sweden at Poltava, a battle fought in 1709, twenty years before Suvorov's birth.

A certain American presidential candidate, having visited the city of Yakutsk in eastern Siberia, refers to it as a place to which the poet Alexander Pushkin had once been exiled. This heightens his description of the city and adds drama to the candidate's entire journey. Only Pushkin was never in Siberia.

A former American envoy writes that before the present war there were 400,000 students in Leningrad "in the university and in the dozens of technical and scientific colleges." To lift the state of higher education in Russia to this striking level, it would have been necessary to send six-year-old children to the universities and colleges of Leningrad, and even then the total number would have been only 370,000.

A British author and "War Office official lecturer," as he styles himself, characterizes the late Prince G. E. Lvov, the first premier of the Provisional Government as "a leader of the Social Revolutionary Party." Actually he was a liberal monarchist. According to this British authority Stalin is "no more dictator than is Mr. Churchill." There were 58,500 kilometers of railways in Russia in 1913, and, according to the same author, this had been increased to 1,143,700 kilometers in 1940, a fantastic expansion. The actual figure was 84,900 kilometers in 1937, and even the third Five-Year Plan only contemplated an increase to 95,000 kilometers by 1942.

Much has been written during the war concerning the food situation in Russia, but in most instances the writers have not had the courage to tell the whole truth: that the people were fighting and would continue to fight regardless of difficulties, but that their privations were monstrous, and that they were experiencing inhuman suffering. On the contrary, the reality has consistently been misrepresented. "I had lunch in the workers' dining room . . . In addition to *shchi* with a piece of boiled beef, there was steak, fresh tomatoes, beans, fried potatoes, pastry and coffee."

What exposes the author of these lines is the "pastry and coffee." If he had spoken only of a piece of beef, we might have concluded that he visited the plant in question on a particularly happy occasion. If, in addition, steak had been served, it would have been most unusual. But coffee? Foreign diplomats had to import coffee from abroad, and each pound represents an event in the diplomatic world. But in this instance, it seems, thousands of workers of some extraordinarily fortunate plant were receiving coffee by the barrel.

Another author, however, describes the food situation more carefully: "The waiter requested me to eat in my room. He did not wish his regular patrons to see the special food that I was being served, which was much superior to the ordinary fare—probably soup, bread and tea."

What is worse than these examples, however, is the inclination of some foreign journalists to strike superior attitudes: of course, living conditions are bad in Russia, and it would be difficult for foreigners to endure such conditions; but "the Russians are used to suffering," "they need little," "even children can do with cabbage and rye bread." The usual Moscow fare, reports one journalist, who apparently regards his own people as a *Herrenvolk*, consists of "vegetable soup with black bread; occasionally they have cereal and now and then a piece of bread." Fortunately, it appears that "this diet, meager as it would be to an American family, seems to agree with the Muscovites."

In fact, according to this journalist, who supports his statements with the alleged testimony of some doctors, the food situation is so satisfactory that "there is very little disease."

Forgetting, however, the testimony of these remarkable doctors, the same writer tells us, in connection with another matter, that "doctors maintain that most adult civilians have lost about fifteen pounds in the past year." "The four-year-old Anatole had lost ten pounds since last year, his curly blond hair was beginning to lose its lustre, and he was no longer the gay, active boy his mother wanted him to be."

The same principle of drawing a distinction between Russians and others leads another writer to the conclusion that the mediocre, official Soviet press is quite adequate for Russia, for "a controlled press is the ideal means of rallying a country like the Soviet Union"—but not America!

The extremely difficult housing situation in Russia, aggravated by the rapid growth of the city population, is a matter of common knowledge in informed circles. Articles and even books have been written about it. But one journalist reports in something of the manner of a child's fairy tale: "A worker in the Soviet Union has living quarters from one to three rooms, depending upon the size of his family; he pays rent on the basis of his earnings; he has education, recreation and medical privileges . . . and when his days of work are over he can look forward to a comfortable pension as long as he lives."

But another visitor to Russia strikes a blow for the facts by reporting bluntly: "Most single-room apartments house at least one family and sometimes two."

THE most widespread and the easiest method of coloring reality at present consists of a simple arithmetical operation. Some eight years ago the Soviet currency was stabilized at the rate of about five rubles to the dollar. Ever since then there has been a great rise in prices, with resultant inflation; but officially the rate of the ruble has remained unchanged. Completely ignoring this basic fact, some writers have informed their readers abroad that a Russian worker receives 1,000 rubles a month (for an eleven-hour day) and earns the equivalent of $200! A ballerina receives 4,000 rubles or $800.

With respect to more complicated questions we get some rather surprising answers. For example, what were military commissars? These commissars have been introduced and abolished several times in Soviet Russia, their function consisting of keeping watch on the morale and loyalty of officers. But one correspondent paints them as playing the role of a sort of secretary of a welfare organization: "The *polkom* today is a mixture of padre, welfare officer and officer appointed for education." Another writer describes them as executive officers attached to the military authority: "The military officer is the man who makes decisions and the political officer then proceeds to see that the orders are carried out."

A British correspondent, the author of a volume on the Russian East, uses the same idyllic colors in describing the NKVD: "The place of the NKVD in Soviet life has become something like a combination of our own war-time Ministry for Home Security and the road transport department of the Ministry of War Transport." And the journalists often discover, without the slightest doubt, that in the great purge "the Russian army was purged of fifth columnists." One reporter is certain that "the Soviets proved that Trotsky and Bukharin intrigued with the Japanese and the Germans."

However, one must not be too severe with these foreign journalists: in Moscow they live isolated from the rest of Russia, sharing in this respect the life of all foreigners, among them even the highest diplomatic envoys. If they write of things they do not understand, it is not because they would not like to understand but because they are not given an opportunity to learn. They themselves reveal that contact by a Soviet citizen with foreign journalists entails great risk; that, as a consequence, they must resort to all sorts of stratagems to meet with Russians; that a romantic relationship between a foreigner and a Soviet woman has more than once led to sad consequences for the lady; that employees of diplomats and journalists—translators, typists, messengers, even servants—are carefully and mysteriously watched. How can these journalists, most of them ignorant of the Russian language, be expected, under the circumstances, to orient themselves in complicated questions?

They are isolated from the country in which they live. Foreign diplomats in Moscow "often while away the hours hitting a golf ball against a wire screen in the back yard" of the embassy. When in need of a barber, a foreign envoy must telephone the Commissariat of Foreign Affairs to send him one, for he is not supposed to enter a barber shop. The same applies to newspapermen. Here is an example of how one of the best-known American correspondents in Russia works:

"November 7, 1942, my New York office sent me an urgent telegram asking for Soviet reaction to the African landings." What was he to do? How to learn the reaction of Russian public opinion? "I tried the next best thing, interviewing the women translators, men chauffeurs and girl messengers in the Foreign Commissariat. 'Khorosho,' meaning 'good,' was their eloquent expression of opinion. So I wrote my story: the Russian people had heard about the landings, they thought it might be good news, but they did not yet know."

Another author, one who happens to know Russian, was finally driven to desperation. It dawned on him that, having worked a long time in Russia, he had failed to see very much of the country.

"I must try to get out of this routine, for this routine of Moscow is very tiresome at times. Contacts are difficult to make, outside the immediate circle of officials and embassy people, and other journalists. The Narkomindel, and the Hotel National, and the embassy, and the Hotel Metropole, and then back again to the office, with trips to the Central Telegraph thrown in . . . And to think I was sent out here 'to report the Russian-German war.' It is important I should get out of Moscow . . .; but so far there is not much prospect."

The only contact with the people that is permitted and encouraged is going to the theater and, particularly, the ballet. Although they realize the incongruity of it, attachés of foreign embassies and foreign journalists discuss interminably the qualities of Russian ballet dancers, the performance of the principal artists in *Swan Lake,* the tenors and baritones in *The Barber of Seville* and *Aïda.* To provide entertainment for diplomats and journalists, an opera company and the ballet accompanied their migration to Kuibyshev. As a consequence, war books about wartime Russia are filled with discussions of song and dance.

It is not surprising, therefore, that the political prognostications in such books, based upon this kind of research, are for the most part superficial and worthless. Here is an example of the political prophet:

"The social regimes of both England and Russia are going to evolve and may become very similar in many respects . . . The real difficulty will be America . . ."

Klyukva!

II

The Limits of Stalin's Realism

The Advantages of a Short Memory

HOW embarrassing it would be if people remembered certain of their recent notions concerning the Soviet regime! Only ten years ago much of the general press, many of the platform orators and radio commentators had come to the conclusion, after deep consideration of the nature of Russian Sovietism, that the cause of all misfortune was Stalin. Lenin, they said, was a real Russian, who having realized, after the first years of the Soviet experiment, that Socialism could not be brought into being in Russia, turned his face to the peasantry, restored free enterprise, and would have eventually granted political reforms. But he died. And Stalin led Russia back to the path of internationalism, of social revolution, and unbridled dictatorship. If only Lenin had lived . . .!

So assiduously was this conception reiterated in the foreign press that Moscow became annoyed. With gall and ridicule, but not without justice, it was declared in Moscow in 1933 that people abroad were "trying now to picture Lenin as a national hero who had abandoned Marx and turned to democracy on the basis of the NEP, while Stalin is being presented as a dogmatic Marxist who, contrary to Lenin, is sacrificing Russia to the mad idea of world revolution."

All this is very recent, and yet it is remote. Today every newspaper correspondent knows without fear of contradiction that the opposite is true: that Stalin is a great Russian nationalist who repudiated World Communism as soon as he was free to act independent of the influence of Lenin and Trotsky. But we must not be too hard on the newspapermen because most respected authorities likewise support this conception. The British expert on Russia, Sir Bernard Pares, for example, writes:

"No sooner had Stalin defeated Trotsky and expelled him finally from the country [1929] than he switched all the main forces of the new Russia from the wild-goose chase after world revolution to the practical task of raising the level of well-being in his own country."

Summarizing this general historic interpretation, the *New York Times* declared editorially in December, 1943:

"Russia has become patriotic, nationalist, even religious. It has revived the old traditions in its history, its political system, in essential respects, its economy. In short it has finished its revolution."*

Moscow newspapers and periodicals, very sensitive to public opinion abroad and careful to follow what is being said in England and America about Russia, have never seriously commented on this view, and this was quite natural. The Soviet press could not very well confirm before the people of Russia the assertion that Communist Russia has become nationalist and religious. But neither did it repudiate the idea, because, under the circumstances, this interpretation even served the interests of the Soviet Government. Nay, more, it was with a view to cultivating this idea abroad that the Soviet Government undertook certain actions calculated to be interpreted in other countries as signifying the restoration of old Russia.

In the course of this campaign Stalin himself underwent quite a transformation in his standing abroad. Only a short while ago he had been a Caucasian hold-up man, a ruthless murderer and sadist. Now he became so gentle that a child would love to play on his knee and a dog to sidle up to his leg. Every self-respecting reporter now knows precisely what Stalin thinks, what he believes, what he understands. Like a sensitive seismograph registering a distant earthquake, the journalist's typewriter, situated thousands of miles from the Moscow scene, registers the reactions of Stalin's mind and soul. And everything always appears for the best. The Moscow leader always thinks and always decides as he should, for "Stalin is a realist." And being a realist his ideas naturally run in a proper, decent, friendly, peaceful direction. How could it be otherwise with a respectable premier of a respectable and religious state?

Misinterpretations, misconceptions, and distortions of this subject have by now piled up to considerable heights.

---

* In an address in the House of Commons in May, 1944, Churchill gave expression to the same ideas. However, as in the case of other men of Churchill's position, we can never be sure whether they say what they mean and believe what they say.

"With a Slight Exaggeration"

TAKE another recent book on Russia, one that makes some pretense of a scientific point of view, since it intends to combine sociology with political, historical, and moral understanding. According to this book, things were not at all bad in Russia before the revolution, nor are they so bad today under Stalin. Things were bad only under Lenin, in that "destructive period" when the author himself landed in jail.

Everyone knows, for example, that there was a persecution of nationalities in old Russia, but it was really a minor matter. Poles? They were first punished for rising against Russian authority, and what respectable government fails to punish such acts? And then, we are told, even "the Poles enjoyed the same status as the rest of the Russian population." Why make a fuss about the use of any particular language in the schools? The Polish struggle for autonomy? The author apparently never heard of it. Admitting that there were some exceptions to equality of treatment, he grants that the Jews did not quite enjoy the full privileges of citizenship, but on this point, too, things were not quite as bad as they were painted. By accepting Christianity, for example, the Jews could have all the rights accorded Russians. And for the rest, all the talk of pogroms was "vastly exaggerated."

Jails and places of exile for political opponents before the revolution were not at all as bad as the world believed, says the author, adding: "With a slight exaggeration one can say that the banishment and imprisonment of political offenders was more in the nature of granting them a vacation with most of the expenses paid." In this one phrase the author expresses himself completely. It may be said "with a slight exaggeration" that he has no conception of old Russia!

Then, according to this treatise, came the *bête noire,* Lenin. The author's scientific researches here led him to discoveries which have escaped all others. He discovered that Lenin "eliminated money" and had actually tried to abolish the family. At this point he writes:

"The Communist law spoke of contracts between males and females for the satisfaction of their sexual needs; a contract could be for an indefinite period; for a definite period—say a year, a week or a month; or for a single case . . . Polygamy, bigamy were quite legitimate."

All this is pure invention; the satanic picture of Lenin painted by the writer is designed only to serve as a counterfoil to Stalin. The "bloody period," according to the author, ended in 1934, and then Stalin moved from "despotism to a modicum of freedom." The mass liquidation of people holding all sorts of opinions and tendencies, including many who held most moderate views, as well as priests and theologians, is regarded by the author as merely the liquidation of Lenin's disciples.

And, of course, the progress under Stalin is depicted as proceeding from "Communist dictatorship to national democracy." Even the collectives (*kolkhozes*) are democratic institutions, with their leaders elected by the peasants. There is no Communist economy in Russia, just as there is no real capitalism in America, says the author. And, in general, there is a remarkable similarity of moral and political values in the two social systems.

Finally, should the reader entertain some doubt concerning Soviet policy, such as the attack on Finland in 1939, for example, the writer assures him that "with the accession of Hitler, Germany began definitely to prepare Finland as a base for the invasion of Russia." As the serious reader will know, the facts are quite different from these presented by men of so-called pure science.

We have dwelt at some length upon this remarkable political work because it is so typical. Its self-assured, expansive tone, its "sociocultural" attitude and pseudo-scientific aura are merely the outward habiliments of a widely prevalent phenomenon: the unfounded, shortsighted belief in the established harmony of relations between Russia and the outside world, and the efforts to make undeniable facts fit this narrow conception.

The Revolution Is Not Yet Ended

THE theory that the Soviet regime was gradually and imperceptibly degenerating into a different political system was for the first time seriously developed by Trotsky. It was his "Thermidor" concept formulated as his indictment against

Stalin as early as the middle 'twenties in public addresses in Moscow. This theory was later frequently reiterated by his followers as well as by non-Communists.

The early period of the "ascending line of the revolution" in the French revolution did have some resemblance to the course of the Russian revolution. At first came the substitution of a constitutional regime for the autocratic system; the monarchy was then supplanted by the republic; then came the execution of the king; the struggle among the republican parties brought to power the more extreme, more revolutionary tendencies. The terror grew apace, political killings and executions assumed a mass character. Economic decrees issued by the revolutionary governments violated the rights of property, introduced requisitions, and limited freedom of trade. The general uncertainty, absence of personal security, and acute political tension found their expression in the political upheaval of July, 1794, when the revolutionary dictator Robespierre was overthrown. It was the upheaval of Thermidor.

That moment marked the beginning of the "declining line of the revolution" in France. At first those who came to power consisted of supporters of the revolutionary parties, but soon they began to fade out. The system of ideologies developed in previous years appeared to remain in force for a while, but very soon it ceased to play any role. Fixed prices and requisitions were abolished; the fever of self-enrichment began. Much of the old way of life and many of the old customs were revived. Finally, the republican regime itself began to give way to the dictatorship of the former revolutionist Napoleon Bonaparte.

Trotsky applied this blueprint in his analysis of the course of the Russian revolution. He conceived of himself and Lenin as the Russian Robespierres, the bearers of the pure ideals of the revolution. Stalin's victory over Trotsky in the middle 'twenties appeared to the latter as the triumph of "revolutionists grown wise," of the practical elements, of realists who proceeded to abandon everything to which they nevertheless continued to give lip service: Communism, world revolution, social equality. Trotsky never tired of denouncing the omnipotent bureaucracy under Stalin as the party of Thermidor, with Stalin as its leader. He pictured Stalin as an intellectual mediocrity, devoid of ideas, one who had abandoned all ideological moorings and principles after Lenin's death and who was guided solely by the thirst for power.

Trotsky's supporters as well as many other Communist dissidents accepted this concept. And it did, indeed, seem easy to find confirmation of it in the evolution of Soviet society: revival of the family, veneration of parents, restoration of the old school system, privileges of the bureaucracy, introduction of ranks and decorations were some of Stalin's reforms which fitted into the scheme of Thermidor. The dissidents, like Trotsky himself, kept on repeating this accusation, so deadly to true Communism, for a period of years. But they failed to perceive that there were other facts diametrically opposed to this entire conception, that the years had failed to confirm their theory, and that, after more than fifteen years of "evolution," the world was still confronted by the old enigma of Russia—Russian Communism had not only survived this long period but had actually developed in another, non-Thermidorian direction.

There were even some serious authorities among American students of Russia who accepted the "Thermidorian" interpretation of the Russian revolution. William Henry Chamberlin, one of the best if not the best American authority on Russia, who shared this view, wrote in his otherwise excellent book, *The Russian Enigma,* that "after every revolution there must be an evolution, and Russia has proved no exception to this rule. . . . From 1934 to 1941 Russia experienced its Thermidor."

THIS view is unfounded and I believe unfortunate. There is little analogy between the Russian and the French revolutions, and still less between the Stalinist system and the French Thermidor. It is essential to make the difference clear, not as a matter of historical research but as a task necessary for understanding the policies of today and tomorrow.

"Down with the tyrant!" shouted the French crowds on the day of Thermidor. They could no longer tolerate the spectacle of executions and nightly killings. They feared the Revolutionary Tribunal. They yearned for more normal conditions of life, for security from the lawlessness of the revolutionary police. The peasants wanted an end to grain requisitions. Even in his last speech Robespierre had continued to demand a bloody "purge" (the Russian Communists did not invent this term); but those who were to have been the victims of that purge forestalled it by carrying out the Thermidorian revolt. Thermidor led to a gradual restoration of "normalcy." The Revolutionary Tribunal was first reformed and then abolished. The executions almost ceased. Political persecutions declined. The economy began to improve. And even later, with the rise of Bonaparte, and despite the severe regime he instituted, there was no such terror as prevailed under Robespierre.

Thermidor marked a relief for France after the period of revolutionary stress. Can this interpretation be applied to Stalin's Russia? Can it be seriously asserted that political persecutions have ceased, that purges are no more, that executions have stopped? Have normal conditions been restored; do people feel more secure in their lives? Do collectivization and armies of forced labor constitute normalization of the national economy? One need only pose these questions to perceive how erroneous is the analogy with Thermidor.

The revolutionary process has not yet been concluded in Russia, the "ascending line of the revolution" continues. Whether we consider this good or bad, the fact is that the revolution continues even now, in the midst of war. If Thermidor is to be regarded as an inevitable station on the route of a revolutionary train, the fact is that the Russian train has not yet reached that destination.

The accompanying chart presents a graphic idea of the inner political development of Russia during the period of the revolution. It is not a diagram that pretends to specific scientific significance. It is offered merely because a graphic presentation frequently facilitates understanding of a question.

The line begins in 1917, the period of broad liberties and expansion of democracy. In the next years the revolutionary line moves steeply upward. The oppositionist press and parties are gradually liquidated; repressions are intensified, executions are begun. Then comes the civil war, the regime grows increasingly ruthless. At the end of the civil war the Cheka is established in all cities, grain is requisitioned from the villages, the capitalist classes are ejected.

The year 1921 brings some economic reforms. On an economic chart we see a decline of the revolutionary line—Lenin's concessions to the peasantry. But the main political line does not decline at that moment; on the contrary, the repressions are intensified. Economic concessions and freedom of trade do not in any way indicate an altered Communist policy. In fact just the reverse, for in order to stress its adherence to Communist principle, the Soviet Government jails the members of all other political parties still at liberty. With the same pur-

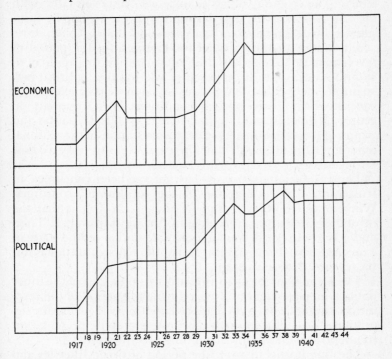

pose in mind it intensifies the antireligious and other campaigns. The line of the revolution moves upward. A measure of stability ensues for several years, marked by suppression of all non-Communist tendencies, while the Communist party continues to maintain a comparative degree of political freedom within its own organization.

But in the late 'twenties the revolutionary line makes a big leap upward, politically and economically. The period witnesses the beginning of mass persecutions of Communist oppositionists and ruthless purges, followed by collectivization with its mass repressions directed against the peasantry, against the church, and against many other groups. This continues until 1933–34.

The year 1934 brings a measure of political and economic relief. This is, however, relative. Although the peasants are no longer persecuted as ruthlessly as before, there are also virtually no more kulaks—and the stream of exiles declines. Note the very important feature of the entire revolutionary development in Russia: long and sharp swings upward, short zigzags downward which, however, never indicate a return to the starting point.

In the middle 'thirties the economic line discloses a slight relief. In 1934 the peasants are accorded the right to own small bits of land adjacent to the collectives. But the main line, the political line, soon takes another leap upward. The remnants of Communist dissident factions are liquidated. The purges are accompanied by another outburst of terror. Persecutions of nonpartisans and of priests are resumed. The country lives in perpetual fear. The line reaches its zenith.

Again in 1939 it declines slightly, when the period of repressions ceases, but without indicating any return to the point preceding the purges. There can be no toleration whatever of any opposition, legal or semilegal. Literature, art, politics, science, everything is *gleichgeschaltet*. The dictatorship reaches its apogee. There is another upward swing in economic life; a new limitation of the rights of private economy in the villages. Nineteen-forty brings a feverish mobilization of industry with a new tightening of the screw.

Soon afterward comes the war.

A Religious and Nationalistic Soviet Russia?

RUSSIAN Communism has, indeed, experienced a great evolution. But a sense of perspective in judging its progress is necessary to understand it.

What is frequently referred to as a return to the traditions of old Russia is not really a matter of just the past seven or eight years before the outbreak of war. This evolution began long before.

It began in the early 'twenties, when members of the Youth League used to discuss at meetings, heatedly and far into the night, the questions: Was it proper for a Communist to wear a necktie? Was it obligatory to wear the primitive Russian kosovorotka-shirt or should a Communist wear more modern clothes? In general, should a revolutionist attach importance to his attire in view of the fact that his task is to devote himself to fighting civil and international wars?

Very tense were the discussions among young Communists on the question of love. Was there not a contradiction between pure love and the materialism of a revolutionist? Between poetry and the Communist Manifesto? Does love interfere with work? Family responsibilities, kitchen work, and diapers make a sparrow of the eagle. Marriage ties are fetters.

There was much discussion about education. School discipline was the heritage of the old regime, sheer violence. Should the new, perfect state dictate the school curriculum and text-books? Would it not be better for the students to take these matters into their own hands? From now on there was to be only "self-government of the students." They themselves were to determine the school regime, the system of education.

Hundreds of these and similar questions stirred the minds of the Communist youth, as well as the party in general in those early days. The party as a whole consisted in the main of young people; youth was its conscience. To adopt modern dress, to embrace pure love, to have a family, to plan rigid school programs, it was feared, would be to enter upon the path of a petty-bourgeois existence, to sow the seeds of sur-render to capitalism. But how many were really prepared to travel the road of fanatical, uncompromising stoicism?

Time and nature asserted their claims. The moustacheless youths became fathers, the neophytes of Communism were transformed into veterans. The older party leaders came for-ward with the "petty-bourgeois" advice to be moderate. "Your enthusiasm is magnificent," said the leaders, "but you should apply it to other spheres—to industry, to the army, to propaganda." For those who demanded ideological explanations, it was added: "Communism is not a religious order, it is the road to a better life on earth, not in heaven."

The long series of reforms was thus the consequence of a natural, sincere evolution. "You are losing the revolutionary perspective," cried the extremists angrily. "You are traveling to Canossa, you are betraying the world revolution, as you betrayed the Chinese revolution." "You are Thermidorians," rang the cry, as sharp as a whip, in the middle 'twenties. But the opposition was in the minority.

The reformation of the way of life continued. The right of inheritance was restored. This necessarily included the right to property that a person had not earned by his own efforts. The family was strengthened, divorce was no longer encouraged, abortions were forbidden. Experimentation in education ended with a return to the old school system. Veneration of parents, insistently recommended from above, supplanted militant contempt for the "old fogies."

But this picture of Soviet society as it developed in the 'twenties and 'thirties would be misleading if we did not complete it by adding other, no less important, features. The ideology of Communism, i.e., of uncompromising repudiation of capitalism, of the bourgeoisie, of "bourgeois democracy" was intensified and became more than ever the ideology of the state. The inevitability of war between the land of Socialism and the lands of capitalism was accepted as an immutable canon. The Russian peasantry was liquidated as a class of private owners. Foreign concessionaires were expelled, Russian private trade was almost entirely abolished.

Was it possible to characterize all this as the "Russian Thermidor"? No, the entire development merely demonstrated how slight the analogy was between the Russian and French revolutions. In Russia the revolutionary process has continued for more than a quarter of a century, in France it lasted five years. For this reason some inevitable changes affecting the way of life, changes which had made themselves felt in France only after the upheaval, were effected in Russia within the framework of the revolution itself. They did not transform the revolutionists into "reactionaries"; they merely tinged the revolution with peculiar colors.

But how are we to understand the revival of venerated heroes of Russian history, of "Russianism" in terminology, the restoration of ranks in the army, of sympathy for Slavdom? This very serious and complex phenomenon has various roots.

First of all, the advent of any new party to power, including the Communist party, tends to make it patriotic *ipso facto*.

Ridicule of and contempt for "defense of the fatherland" are transformed into "defense of the Soviet fatherland" or "defense of the revolutionary land" when those who formerly did the ridiculing become the government. And, in truth, patriotism in Communist ideology is not a product of recent years, as many suppose. On the contrary, it has been dominant from the period when Lenin was waging war against the Germans in 1918, against Allied intervention in 1918–19, and against Poland in 1920.

"We are now 'for the war,' since November 7, 1917," wrote Lenin. "We stand for defense of the fatherland." In February, 1918, he wrote a proclamation in which he declared: "The Socialist fatherland is in peril! Unqualified defense of the republic!" On another occasion Lenin wrote: "Are we, conscious Russian proletarians, devoid of the emotion of national pride? Of course not! We love our language and our country . . . We are filled with the sense of national pride, for the great Russian nation has also created a revolutionary class."

Patriotism is, therefore, not a product of the last decade of Bolshevism. To be sure, it was intensified in the 'thirties; it found new soil under new conditions, and the government has encouraged it enormously. Finally it was no longer necessary to add the word "Soviet" to the word "motherland," or "revolutionary" to the word "fatherland."

The second source of the new nationalism is to be found in the stabilization and strengthening of the regime. This was a psychological phenomenon. Before the revolution there prevailed widely a primitive but extremely revolutionary attitude toward Russian history, not only in Bolshevist popular literature but also in the literature of other revolutionary parties. The entire Russian past was portrayed as a dark history of violence, stupidity, robbery, by scoundrel-tsars and idiots. Little pamphlets, published by the revolutionary underground or abroad for circulation in Russia, presented in popular form the history of tsarism in the Empire. Particular popularity was enjoyed, for example, by the little books of Leonid Shishko, which had sought to demonstrate that all the tsars "were concerned only with their power, and as for the people it was quite all right for them to die of hunger in the great state." It was all a manifestation of antihistoricity, of repudiation of the past. History begins with us!

This ideology was at first completely dominant under the

Soviet regime. It exercised its most powerful influence during the civil war, which was waged as a struggle against the "restorationists of old Russia."

Everything was still fresh and novel in the 'twenties. Every speech and every article began with a description of how miserable life had been under tsarism, and how different it would be now. The newspapers painted contrasts between the old and the new that was now beginning. Repudiation of the past was the lifeblood of political literature in the first decade of the Soviet regime. Old Russia was pictured as the springboard from which the swimmer leaps into fresh water.

Eventually all this began to sound repetitious, monotonous, banal, annoying, and unconvincing. Old Russia began to recede into the dim distance of the past; some began to forget, others had not known it at all. The new regime achieved stability, the danger of a restoration of the old had passed. A new complex of ideas gradually supplanted the old antihistoricity. The new people now sought not mere repudiation of the past but affirmation of their own place in the long chain of successive historical epochs. It was no longer necessary now to denounce Peter I as a robber and Catherine II as an immoral woman. Now it could be declared that Peter I was great for his time, that Ivan the Terrible performed mighty deeds for his country, but that Stalin was no less a legitimate and no less a great leader for his epoch. It was no longer necessary to repeat that Kutuzov and Suvorov were tsarist sycophants. No, they were great military leaders of their time, just as Voroshilov and Tukhachevsky were for theirs. His place in history is now of moment to the Soviet man. Moreover, these views fit properly into the framework of Marxist historical theory.

In just such a manner do new directors, coming into possession of a going concern, believe at first that "things will be different from now on," but very soon display their own portraits in the gallery of the founders, of the great pioneers: "You see, we are no worse than others, and we will do great things."

Communism does not cross itself out when it begins to recognize Russian history. Paradoxical as it may seem, it seeks to have its genealogy considered as beginning with Rurik and the Romanovs.

This psychological need of placing oneself within the framework of history, of becoming part of the gallery of tsars and field marshals, is so potent that occasionally it leads to a child-ish repetition of the absurd. It would have been possible for the Communists to follow revolutionary or Napoleonic exam-ples and to introduce novel decorations and marks of distinc-tion for generals; but, no, Soviet generals were given red trouser stripes, just like those of the old days. History knows a wide variety of military rewards—from the laurel wreath to marriage to a distinguished bride—but in Russia the old decorations worn on the breast and named after famous tsarist generals are restored. Napoleon invented all sorts of new ranks, but Russia now again has her major-generals and lieutenant-generals, awkward-sounding foreign ranks but taken from the arsenal of old tsarist Russia. Regiments and divisions fighting with distinction could have been given new names, but they are now known again as Guard Regiments. Shoulder straps and bars would not seem necessary to win mili-tary victories. But they have been restored in their old forms. "Privileged" military schools, traditional in Russia, have been re-established by a decree having to do with the rebuilding of reoccupied regions, and so on.

One has the impression as if a Commission of Restoration has been set up by the Commissariat of Defense for the purpose of restoring page by page the old military rules and decora-tions, and adapting all the attributes of the old army to the new.

As the Communists see it, this military restoration serves the cause of social revolution.

Thirdly, the new nationalism represents a political zigzag on the part of the Soviet Government. It is not only rooted in the new psychology but constitutes a deliberate tactic calcu-lated to achieve specific aims within a certain, definite period. Those who understand the power of the monopoly of press and speech will perceive the force of this maneuver. The widely held view that the history of the new nationalist policy be-gins with 1934 is founded upon the fact that it was at that point that the Soviet press, acting upon orders from above, had begun to cultivate intensively the use of the new terminology and ideology.

After the first year of the Hitler regime had failed (contrary to the expectations of Moscow) to bring about an internal up-heaval in Germany, it became clear that Russia had to prepare for war. The preparations consisted not only in doubling the size of the army, training the new commanding staff, and expanding the war industries, but also in taking certain ideological measures. The ideology of nationalism was one of the principal weapons at hand.

The government encouraged the patriotic participation of non-Soviet, nonrevolutionary and antirevolutionary elements. To make war and to be victorious it was necessary not only to stir the activity of party cells and regional secretaries but to enlist and move into action the dissidents, the malcontents, the formerly injured and oppressed. Above all, it was necessary to enlist those elements of the intelligentsia and government servants who would play the decisive role by holding commanding positions in the army, i.e., the new officers.

There are still in the army thousands of officers who participated in the first World War as loyal supporters of the throne. Scattered before the present war in a wide variety of government offices, they were suddenly found to be necessary because of their experience and ability. Thousands of others from the old nobility, where the tradition of military service had been handed down from generation to generation, were also welcomed as valuable military material. It was impossible to ignore such a reservoir of military leadership. It was necessary to abandon the old policy of liquidating them. On the contrary, these men were now protected, treated with kindness, and accorded material privileges. Military conditions resembling closely those that had prevailed in the old army were even fostered for their benefit.

Finally, it was perceived that the simple idea of defense of country was clearer, closer to the minds of the millions of peasants comprising the rank and file than the ideological formulas of the Communist leadership.

To the natural process of revival of national traditions was added, therefore, the artificial and artful policy of ideological maneuvers.

However, during the 'thirties, and as late as the outbreak of the war, problems of nationalist ideology and of the new nationalist policy had occupied but a small place in the press as compared with the attention given to problems of industrialization, the collectives, and administrative expansion. The schools and universities devoted a great deal more time and energy to problems of Communist science—to capitalism, Communism, the bourgeoisie and proletariat, the class war and social revolution—than was given the seedling national ideology. Fundamentally, the old system was subjected to very little alteration. From time to time the press would deliberately resort to the use of officially prescribed nationalist phrases. These were quickly caught up by foreign observers, who subjected them to varied interpretations, scrutinized them under microscopes, and drew far-reaching conclusions, failing to observe that it was often for their benefit that the new phrases were coined. Meanwhile, the Leninist ideas of Communism continued to flow in a broad stream, as before, into the party mass.

The State Does Not Die

THE state will wither away and die: once the exploiters are suppressed and re-educated to become toilers all 'pressures' by the state will disappear. The Red Army is a temporary army. It cannot be a standing army, for the civil war cannot continue forever."

This was written in 1920 by Lenin's disciples, Bukharin and Preobrazhensky, in a book called *The A.B.C. of Communism,* for years an obligatory textbook in Russian schools, and translated into many languages as the best exposition of Communist fundamentals. "When the exploiters cease to resist, the dictatorship of the proletariat will be increasingly ameliorated. The workers' state will gradually wither away."

The state is evil. For the state, as interpreted by Lenin, Bukharin, and the entire galaxy of Communist leaders of the early period, is not "a territory plus the population, plus the government," as is supposed in universities outside of Russia, but only the third element—the government. The state is the synonym of the state machine, of the state organization, of the apparatus by means of which the government governs. And the government and its machine constitute together an instrument of force; there can be no place for them in a Communist society. The principal elements of state force are the police and the army. They must disappear.

This concept differed from anarchism in that it presupposed a "transition period": the period of transition of the revolutionary government into the new system. The revolutionary government is created to liquidate capitalism, the bourgeoisie, economic exploitation. Only toilers will remain after the disappearance of the capitalist classes, and then there will be no more room for state force and violence. The anarchists wanted to begin with liquidation of the state. Lenin (in line with Marx) wanted to conclude the transformation of society by liquidating the state.

And the state of the "transition period," i.e., the temporary Soviet State, was pictured by Lenin in colors which, in the light of the Soviet experiment, now appear the extreme of liberalism and naïveté. Bureaucratism was to be rooted out radically; the entire population was to participate actively in the administration of the state. The state will "abolish the army, the police, the officialdom, and will supplant them with a more democratic state machine in the form of the armed working mass." Lenin's concept of the revolutionary state provided also for "completely free elections, recall of officials, without exception, reduction of their salaries to the customary earnings of a worker."

On the eve of the November revolution, in 1917, Lenin wrote:

"The workers, having conquered the power of government, will smash the old bureaucratic apparatus and will supplant it with a new one, composed of workers and employees, and measures will immediately be taken to prevent these from degenerating into bureaucrats." These measures were to include (1) "not only free elections but also the recall applicable at any time," (2) " a salary scale not above workers' wages." Since "all become bureaucrats temporarily it will be impossible for the state to become bureaucratic."

For Lenin the "state" was an abominable term. His state would be a "semi-state," he declared. The sooner it disappeared the better. He thought eagerly of the future that was to follow the transition period, a point which was not to be long delayed. And he painted the following picture:

"Liberated from capitalist slavery, from untold horrors, savageries, stupidities, abominations, capitalist exploitation, human beings will gradually become accustomed to observe the elementary rules of social life acquired through thousands of years of experience; to observe these rules without compulsion, without force, without subjection, without the special apparatus known as the state."

Only Communism will do away with the necessity of the state, declared Lenin, for there will be no one upon whom it will be necessary to use force. As regards the question of how to deal with "excesses committed by individuals," Lenin declared, "no special machine, no apparatus of force will be required for that, it will be handled by the armed people themselves"; moreover, he added, "the roots of the social causes of excesses are in the exploitation of the masses." With the removal of these roots the causes of excesses will begin to "wither away." With their elimination the state, too, will wither away.

"The whole of society," wrote Lenin, "will be like one single office and one plant, with equality of labor and equality of pay."

In accordance with this principle, the program of the Russian Communist party in 1919 declared, after setting forth a series of demands: "Complete and thoroughgoing realization of these measures will lead to the abolition of the power of the state." Stalin declared at the same time: "We stand for the withering away of the state . . . Higher development of the state power for the purpose of preparing for and effecting the withering away of the state power—that is the Marxian formula."

This negative attitude on the part of Bolshevism toward the state in general and toward its own "semi-state" in particular was no mere abstract theory, borrowed from Marx. It was the inheritance of the long struggle of Russian revolutionists against the old state, with its police, its Okhrana, its agents-provocateurs, and so on. The subsequent revival of all these elements under the new Soviet State had to be justified not only to the conscience of the Communists and their supporters but also to the outside world. In all of Lenin's passionate attacks against "formal democracy," in hundreds of his speeches and articles after the establishment of the Soviet regime, there was evident this need of self-justification for the revival of the power of the state in its most rigorous forms. The question of the state appeared clear and simple: Why was it necessary to have the GPU, courts, jails, etc., in the Soviet State, after the revolution had been accomplished?

For some time after 1917 the Communist view remained unaltered. Cheliapov, a Communist authority on the state, wrote on the subject in two editions of the highly official *Soviet Encyclopaedia,* in 1929 and in 1935. In 1929 he declared:

"The apparatus of compulsion, the GPU, courts, prisons, and so on, is retained temporarily, only while the resistance of the bourgeoisie continues, but these instruments of struggle will wither away in proportion as the resistance declines. The state will disappear together with the disappearance of the division of society into classes."

Six years later he wrote quite differently. The "division of society into classes" and the "resistance of the bourgeoisie" had disappeared. The landlords, capitalists, and their parties had been eliminated. The "kulaks," too, were liquidated. Stalin had already declared that the Socialist order had been realized in Russia. But why does not the state, starting with the GPU, begin to "wither away"? Cheliapov now postponed this event to the vague distant future, when "the perfect Communist society" will have been established, "when a psychological transformation" will have taken place.

Bukharin's old views, which were the views of Lenin, were now explained by the assertion that Bukharin was a potential "fascist hireling": "Contrary to what was asserted by the fascist hireling Bukharin, punitive organs and the army will be only the last to wither away," it was stated now in the *Soviet Encyclopaedia.**

The reality, indeed, did not correspond to the theory. If it is true that all opposition to the Soviet political system can be explained by the play of class interests, who are the classes that must continue to be suppressed without cessation? Are they the workers, the collectivized peasants, the toiling intelligentsia? If so, then the future looked dark, indeed.

"The function of compulsion inside the country has ceased, has withered away," declared Stalin in 1939. "The exploiters are no more and there is no one to suppress any more." But the inevitable question arising after this utterance was: But why does the NKVD continue to be so active?

The answer to this question is provided in the theory assiduously cultivated by Stalin that as long as capitalism existed outside of Russia it would seek to recruit agents among unstable

---

* The author of the article was apparently E. Yaroslavsky.

elements and to create opposition groups and movements with the purpose of destroying the Soviet State. In other words, there is no basis for opposition to Communism inside the country; the opposition constitutes merely a "fifth column."

"The capitalist world sends us spies and diversionists," declared Stalin repeatedly. The hundreds of thousands of people upon whose heads Stalin hurled his repressions constituted only an "agency of foreign capital." At every demonstration trial the government found it necessary to establish a direct relation between the defendants and the outside world, particularly with the "intelligence services" of hostile countries. It was necessary to get "confessions" from every defendant to the effect that he had acted through inspiration from outside. The theory of the "fifth column," which some foreign writers have been so ready to accept, constituted one element of this concept: that there cannot possibly be any dissatisfaction with the Soviet Government inside the Soviet land!

The state was perpetuated as an "apparatus of force." Imperceptibly, without admitting it to itself, Russian Communism began to accept the old theory of the state as a complex of population, territory, and power. The Soviet press began to speak proudly of "our great state," of "the great prestige of our state." "Service to the state" became an honorable idea, the "needs of the state" were given priority. Stalin took another step forward when he applied to his state the formerly contemptuous term of a "great power." "We have become," he said, "a great industrial and collectivized power!" How removed from the time when Lenin spoke almost apologetically of his "semi-state"!

The term "Great Power" was rapidly adopted in the press, in textbooks, in Soviet science. It was a substitute for "Empire." The point has now been reached when the proud term "Soviet Empire" could well be adopted without qualification, and it is only the old theory of hostility to imperialism which has interfered with this remaining final step. However, it is not a matter of words.

One more important element in the new worship of the state derived directly from the history of Communism in Europe. After the numerous disappointments, the unsuccessful uprisings, and the shattered revolutionary attempts in other countries, Russian Communists began to look upon the Soviet State

as one of the chief instruments for effecting Communist transformations abroad. Therefore, the Soviet "apparatus of force,"
its military and diplomatic machinery, emerged as the great
hope of Communism. The greater the new Great Power becomes, the more capable it is of substituting its weight for the
revolutions that have failed to develop elsewhere. The Communist state becomes in a measure the substitute for the Communist revolution: such is the pattern of Communist evolution.

Communism remains its content, but it has absorbed also
the heavy weight of the state machine. "We go forward [from
Socialism] to Communism," declared Stalin at the party congress in 1939. "Will the state be retained by us also in the period of Communism? Yes, it will, if the capitalist encirclement
is not liquidated."

The state is the main instrument for liquidation of the capitalist encirclement: this is one of the most important lessons
drawn by Communism from its own experience.

Stalin and His Party in the War

DESPITE its perturbations and upheavals the war with
Germany has failed to alter either the principles of Soviet
foreign policy or the economic regime of the country. Moreover, long before the war the government had determined
upon a program for preserving inviolate the Soviet political
and economic system in the event of a conflict.

Two hours after the first German air raids on Russia, on the
night of June 22, 1941, the government ordered many arrests,
which were carried out in accordance with previously prepared lists. Among those seized were many suspect Communists who had been permitted to remain at liberty and many
nonpartisans who it was thought might become dangerous.

But the success of the German aggression in the first months
of the war could not but confuse and bewilder many minds.
It was asked: Had the policy of collaboration with Germany
of the past two years been really wise? Were not the Soviet de-
feats to be attributed to the incapacity of the party leadership?
All the springs of policy and ideology stood dangerously exposed.

This found particular expression in a decline in the prestige of the party, which appeared to have lost confidence in itself and in its philosophy. The doubts current abroad at that time concerning Russia's ability to resist were felt no less within the country itself. Stalin remained silent for almost two weeks after the German attack: This is the only instance in the annals of the second World War when the head of a government failed to address his people on the outbreak of hostilities. When he finally did venture to speak on July 3, 1941, it was an attempt to justify himself before the country, an effort to answer the doubters. "The enemy's best divisions and his best aviation contingents are already smashed," declared Stalin.

Concerning his 1939 pact with Hitler, he said:

"One may ask: How did it happen that the Soviet Government entered into a nonaggression pact with such treacherous persons and monsters like Hitler and Ribbentrop? . . . A nonaggression pact is a peace pact between two states. Could the Soviet Government have refused to accept the proposal?

"What did we gain by concluding a nonaggression pact with Germany? We secured for our country for a period of a year and a half an opportunity to prepare our forces."

This did not sound very convincing. Everybody knew that during that period Russia had lost an allied army in France, and everyone could observe how rapidly the German forces were advancing. To those who doubted Russia's capacity to resist, Stalin said: "The enemy is not as terrible as he is pictured by some frightened little intellectuals." But those involved were more than "little intellectuals." In the army itself there was lack of confidence, as Stalin had repeatedly admitted.

Only rarely and in passing did Stalin refer to his party in his first war speeches. It was impossible, in the atmosphere prevailing during those months, to take pride in its policy. The party's own lack of confidence and bewilderment found expression in the immediate disappearance from the press, from public addresses, and from propaganda of the words "Socialism" and "Communism," as well as all acclamation of Soviet industry, of the collectives, and of military preparations. The ideological content of the war was reduced to an extreme minimum, to unusually modest terms. The official *Bulletin of the Agitator* in July, 1941, published a program of lectures to be delivered throughout the country. This program was entirely without Socialist or Soviet content. The subjects covered were: War Against Fascism—A War for the Fatherland; Lenin and Stalin on National Defense; Fascism; The Front and the Rear; Care of Soviet Soldiers; The People's Heroism; The Defeat of the Germans in the Ukraine in 1918; The Partisans; The United Front of Peoples; The Occupied Regions, etc.

Lectures on such subjects could have been delivered under any Russian government and in any country. "The war," wrote this organ of the Central Committee of the Communist party, "is a war for the preservation of the peoples inhabiting the USSR; a war for life or death of the Soviet State; it is to determine whether the peoples of the Soviet land are to remain free or are to be enslaved once more."

All this was very elementary. There was no effort to present a philosophic synthesis. There was also little of those national emotions which gradually developed during the later stages of the war. At this period nationalism had not displaced Communism. There was merely a retreat along the entire ideological front.

Anti-Communist and anti-Soviet sentiment found expression in various forms in this early period of the war. Officially, all difficulties were attributed to the activities of the fifth column, for all oppositionists were proclaimed to be pro-Hitlerites. But at the very time when persons abroad were writing with enthusiasm that there was no opposition left in Russia after the purges, the Soviet press and radio were reporting a different story.

A man named Andronov was executed in Leningrad in August, 1941, for talk "calculated to undermine measures taken by the Soviet Government." A group of grinders engaged in "counterrevolutionary propaganda" was liquidated in Alma-Ata. On November 15, 1941, the Moscow Military Tribunal sentenced to death two engineers, two technicians, and an economist of a certain plant for "spreading appeals" among workers. This was reported by the Soviet radio. The "Bolshevik" told how a certain Sirotin had discovered a man "with leaflets"; how a certain Novikova had turned over to the militia "a counterrevolutionist who was spreading lies."

Although the press soon quit writing about opposition sentiments, there could be no doubt that these did not disappear.

Later came information dealing not with opposition but with a veritable fifth column eager to collaborate with Hitler Germany in the struggle against the Soviet regime. Many Orthodox priests in occupied regions of Russia entered into collaboration with the German authorities. This was significant because the priests would not have ventured to act contrary to the sentiments of their parishioners. Declarations in favor of Germany were published by high church dignitaries: Polikarp Sikorsky, Bishop of Vladimir in Volyn, who proclaimed himself head of the church in the Ukraine; the Archbishop of Mitava; the Archbishop of Narva; the Bishop of Kaunas; the Metropolitan of Latvia. In August, 1942, they met in Riga and sent a telegram to Hitler expressing "admiration of the heroic struggle" he was waging, and promising to "pray to the All-Highest to bless the Axis arms with speedy and complete victory."

Professor Okienko, former dean of Kharkov University, became archbishop of an "Independent Church."

These developments indicated the prevalence of many varied sentiments among the population.

Under the German occupation, especially in the beginning, dozens of Russian pro-Nazi newspapers were started, with their staffs of editors and correspondents. "On behalf of the intelligentsia" and "on behalf of the Russian people" the writers welcomed the "liberation from Bolshevism," often adding their joy of being freed from "Jewish rule." Names of well-known old Russian writers, such as Ivanov-Razumnik suddenly appeared in the collaborationist Russian press. Other pro-German personalities accepted positions as local mayors and in various departments of local government: in industry, transportation, health, and elsewhere.

The Soviet General Vlasov, who was taken prisoner in 1941, proclaimed himself an ally of Germany in 1943 and began to raise a "Russian Army of Liberation." He formulated his program as follows: England was and remains Russia's chief enemy; what is necessary, therefore, is a "frank, enduring friendship between the Russian and the German peoples." "After the war," he declared, "Russia must have a totalitarian system." He promised the Germans to create an army of 300,000 to 500,000 men from the population of occu-

pied Russian territories and from Russian war prisoners. He
was received twice by Hitler, who assured him (this was after
Stalingrad) that all he wanted was "to free Russia from Stalin."

Vlasov's army was first sent to Yugoslavia against the Partisans, where the troops distinguished themselves by their atrocities. Later they operated on the Baltic front, where a considerable portion deserted to the Soviet side. Vlasov himself
fell into disfavor for a time. He was still too "pro-Russian" for
Hitler. In December, 1943, he was arrested in Riga after a
propaganda tour, in the course of which he "talked too much
about Russia."

Later, however, Vlasov's men were again active in the war.
In 1944 they fought in the Savoy and Jura Departments of
France against French Forces of the Interior. The French
guerrillas were represented to Vlasov's men as Communists
and the war against them was pictured as a continuation of the
struggle against international Communism. In its issue of June
15, 1944, the Nazi-controlled *Paris-Soir* thanked Vlasov's
troops for their "defense of France." Finally, the "Eastern battalions of the German Army," as Vlasov's men were characterized by the Germans, took part in resisting the Allied invasion in Normandy. Thousands of these Russian troops, in German uniforms, and many Russian officers were captured by the
Allies and sent to war prisoner camps in England and America.

Hitler had made no provision for Russian Quislings in his
scheme, and the atrocities committed by the Germans in Russia constituted a potent argument against any notion of the
possibility of achieving the "emancipation of Russia," as conceived by Vlasov, through an alliance with the German army.
But Vlasov's experience, like that of other traitors, particularly
among priests, shows how erroneous is the belief that the Soviet
Government had succeeded by ruthless measures in eradicat-
ing in advance all opposition, all fifth columns, and all treachery.*

* It is important to recall that Vlasov had been an exemplary commander
while in the Soviet service, and that his devotion to Stalin had been beyond
doubt. Describing her visit to him on the central Russian front, Eve Curie characterizes him, in her *Journey Among Warriors*, as a great Soviet hero. He had
spent twenty-three years in the Red Army and had been devoted to his government and to the Communist party; he showed Mlle. Curie some German tro-
phies and spoke of Hitler with profound contempt. "He obviously considered
Stalin," wrote Mlle. Curie, "not only as the political leader of Russia, but also

Marxism-Leninism in the War

THE battle of Moscow in October–December, 1941, ended with the retreat of the German armies. The government, which had prepared to evacuate to the Urals, felt first relief and then a sense of stability.

There was a revival of self-confidence in the party and renewed faith in its ideology, starting with 1942 and growing stronger in 1943 and 1944. Party committees gradually began to function more regularly. Articles in the press began increasingly to praise the party's wisdom and services. Publication of the *Propagandist,* which sets the tone for propaganda throughout the country, was resumed in March, 1942, with an edition of 100,000 copies. Two channels of propaganda were indicated: emphasis on nationalism and stress on Communist ideology. Both were to be pursued simultaneously.

The development of nationalism was at first not so much a manifestation of a social movement as the result of a directive from above. National spirit and patriotism were necessary to overcome the initial "passivity and indifference" of the population and to strengthen discipline in the Red Army. A campaign against "indiscipline" and even desertions had to be waged until as late as the autumn of 1942. The press was filled with articles, reports, and stories exposing cowards and traitors at the front. Detailed accounts of German atrocities, public hangings, in the presence of tens of thousands, of Soviet citizens who collaborated with the Germans, extensive reports of the Krasnodar and Kharkov trials, were intended to serve the same purpose as the creation of the orders of Kutuzov and Suvorov. Only gradually was the sentiment of anti-German

as the Generalissimo of the troops." He said with pride: "Stalin's orders are not simply to push the Germans back but also to annihilate them." Taking leave of Mlle. Curie, Vlasov told her "with warm and direct sincerity, with his face and his voice very moving: 'My blood belongs to my Fatherland!'"

The value of constant pledging of allegiance to Stalin is another question. Walter Kerr in *The Russian Army,* for example, has an interesting description of a reception by General Rodion Malinovsky. At a breakfast attended by some American journalists many toasts were drunk to various Red Army heroes. But with each toast proposed by the Americans, General Malinovsky leaped to his feet and added: "Yes, and to Stalin, who organized the Red Army and is leading it to victory." For the rest of the afternoon "whenever one of us had sufficient courage to propose a toast, the General was up with an amendment that included Stalin's name. I do not think he ever missed. Eddy Gilmore whispered to me that this general would go far."

nationalism transformed from official propaganda into a popular movement.

But simultaneously with the growth of nationalism the traditional Communist party line gained in strength. This gain was all the more striking in the light of the party's loss of prestige in the first eight months of the war. In April, 1942, the *Propagandist* wrote: "Propaganda work has declined considerably during the war. The party organizations had failed to understand that not only must there be no let-up in propaganda activity in wartime but it must be given even wider scope.

"In the first year of the war," we are told from Gorky, "some party organizations paid less attention to problems of propaganda . . . The regional committee warned the party organizations of the need of stimulating attention to problems of party propaganda." Later, Emelian Yaroslavsky wrote that "many party organizations have failed to grasp the significance of mass party-political activity . . . What is needed is not a let-up but intensification of the work of lecturing."

In January, 1943, the Administration of Propaganda and Agitation attached to the Central Committee sent out a circular to party organizations dealing with "shortcomings in the work of party cabinets" (for consultations on Marxism-Leninism) which warned that there must be no weakening of "ideological-political training of cadres during the period of the war."

Increased activity of party-propaganda organs and thousands of lectures and articles have gradually restored the once shaken prestige of "Marxist-Leninist science." In March, 1943, Alexandrov, director of the Central Committee's division of propaganda, issued new instructions explaining why the "study of Marxist-Leninist science is necessary, obligatory for all." In support he cited Stalin, who had repeatedly stressed the universal obligation to study the "Marxist-Leninist science of society, the laws of social development, the laws of the development of the proletarian revolution, of the victory of Communism."

Participation in propaganda activity was now proclaimed to be the duty of every active Communist. Many Communists had dodged this work for various reasons, but now it was de-

clared that "the self-liquidation of many of our cadres in political work among the rural population cannot be tolerated." In
1943 it was declared menacingly that "some of our branches
have failed to appreciate the importance of propaganda of the
Marxist-Leninist theory in wartime, and have weakened in
leadership in propaganda work . . . In a number of regions
party and Soviet workers have ceased the study of Marxist-
Leninist theory . . . They have failed to fight against the
detrimental view that now is not the time to engage in political
self-education."

In Soviet terminology the return to Communist party ideology meant the revival of study of the book, *History of the Communist Party, Brief Course.* This book, published in 1938,
was written in part by Stalin and is based in part upon his
speeches and articles; it was subjected to close scrutiny before
publication. Within its three hundred pages it contains the
history of the Russian Communist party covering a period of
forty years. Written in orthodox Communist style, it presents
the official conception of Soviet Communism, its struggle
against other parties and Communist factions, the official history of industrialization, of the collectives, and of Soviet foreign relations. It has been translated into fifty-nine languages
and nineteen million copies have been distributed. All Communist education is now obliged to follow the line of this book.
Constituting an adaptation of "Marxist-Leninist science" to
Russian conditions, it is designed to serve as an antidote to the
dangerous tendencies inherent in daily nationalist agitation.
The introduction says: "The Communist party is guided by
the revolutionary teaching of Marxism-Leninism. Its leaders
have developed further the teaching of Marx and Engels under
conditions of imperialist wars and proletarian revolutions.
The study of the history of the Russian Communist party
strengthens confidence in the ultimate victory of the cause of
the Lenin-Stalin party, in the victory of Communism throughout the world."

The study of this book had almost entirely ceased at the beginning of the war. "The weakest spot," declared a report from
one of the provinces, "is the work of circles for study of the
history of the Russian Communist party. These circles embrace only eight hundred students. The majority of the circles

function badly. Attendance is low, the students work poorly."
A strong effort was launched in the spring of 1942 for revival of
this activity.

"The *Brief Course*," wrote the *Propagandist* in May, 1942,
"presents a general picture of the gigantic experiment of the
Bolshevik party. It presents the foundations of the Marxist-
Leninist theory. It shows the great power of this theory for the
solution of problems of practical activity. Historical events
have always developed as the classics of Marxism-Leninism had
predicted. Everything that Stalin has predicted, even before
the war and during the war, is now coming to pass with exacti-
tude." The importance of this bible of Stalinist Communism
may be gleaned, incidentally, from the fact that the fifth anniversary of its publication was widely hailed in the press.

In August, 1943, the magazine *Under the Banner of Marxism* gave directives as to how political economy was hereafter
to be taught in Soviet universities (this teaching had been interrupted for several years). It cited Lenin: "The proletariat will
be unable to make the social revolution if it is not prepared for
it by struggle for democracy." For this reason, wrote this influential journal, teachers of theoretical Marxist sociology "must
call attention in the classroom to the specific peculiarities of
the monopoly stage of capitalism, and indicate the place it
occupies in history as the prelude to the social revolution of
the proletariat."

Meanwhile victory followed upon victory at the front. The
Germans were retreating from the Ukraine and from Leningrad; the prestige of the Soviet Government rose to unprecedented heights throughout the world. Now the party began to
demand recognition of its services. Who organized the peoples
of the Soviet Union for struggle against the invaders? The
answer: the All-Russian Communist party. Victory over Germany, it was concluded, was, therefore, the victory of Russian
Communism. The newspapers broadcast the information that
half of those who had received the distinction of "Hero of the
Soviet Union" were Communists, that hundreds of thousands
of Communists had been awarded medals and decorations.
The party's prestige was rising.

Stalin has made three regular public appearances annually
during the war, no more and no less: on Red Army Day, Feb-

ruary 23, on May Day, and on the anniversary of the November revolution, November 7. But it was not until November, 1943, after two years of war, that he devoted part of his speech to the party. He could now speak of it with enthusiasm:

"The leading and guiding force of the Soviet people has been the party of Lenin, the party of the Bolsheviks . . . Under the leadership of the party of the Bolsheviks, the workers, peasants and intelligentsia of our country have won their freedom and built a socialist society. In this patriotic war the party stood before us as the inspirer and organizer of the nation-wide struggle against the fascist invaders. The organization of the party's work has united and directed toward a common goal all the efforts of the Soviet people, devoting all our forces and resources to the cause of the enemy's defeat. During the war the party has cemented still further its kinship with the people."

The theory of the dictatorship of the proletariat, on which silence had been maintained during the early period of the war, reappeared in the press. The Old Bolshevik Badayev recalled Stalin's words: "The Red Army is the army of the emancipated workers and peasants, the army of the November revolution, the army of the dictatorship of the proletariat." Gorkin tried to demonstrate in the *Bolshevik* that the "historical consequence of the realization of the policy of the party of Lenin and Stalin is the regime of victorious socialism. Its base is the dictatorship of the working class in alliance with the peasantry." The Soviet regime being a dictatorship of the proletariat, the workers were called upon to be the leader in their relations with the peasantry. For this reason "the guiding role of the party in Soviet organs having to do with the collectives becomes even greater under the conditions of war."

If Russia is victorious because of its Socialist order, it follows that this order would also be best for any other country. The objective of the war must be the establishment of such an order throughout the world, for it alone offers a guarantee against wars. But as it was forbidden to speak of this openly, the aforementioned Alexandrov wrote about it in veiled terms:

"One of the most serious, one of the most important aims of the present war must be the establishment of such a social order upon earth under which adventurists, provocateurs, and

imperialist parties would be deprived of the opportunity periodically to drag the majority of peoples and states into bloody
wars."

The overtones of Marxism-Leninism sounded at times
louder than the nationalist music. The one hundred twenty-
fifth anniversary of Marx's birth was marked in 1943 with
solemn articles; the twenty-fifth anniversary of the death of
George Plekhanov, founder of Russian Marxism, was likewise
celebrated with encomiums. The anniversary of Lenin's death
was marked annually with solemnity. Again and again press
and propaganda returned to the heroic period of Soviet wars
against Allied intervention and the world bourgeoisie.

Only one thing was now forbidden: to speak openly of social
revolution in other countries. Socialism, to be sure, is the guarantee of victory, but it is a purely Russian, Soviet matter. This
was offered occasionally in a rather comic, illogical, and mal-
adroit manner, as when, for example, Lenin was spoken of as
the creator of "Socialism in one country." In reality, "Socialism in one country" had already been abandoned in 1939.* But
now, for diplomatic considerations, it was found necessary to
emphasize this doctrine.

Two Dangers

THE foregoing picture of Russia at war is far removed from
the picture of a land of nationalist and religious traditions
so popular now. To be sure, there was much nationalism in
the artificially staged propaganda and in popular sentiment.
But even greater was the stream of traditional Communist
propaganda. The "Internationale" ("Arise, ye prisoners of
starvation") was abolished as the official anthem in favor of the
new neutral national hymn ("Great Russia has cemented forever the inviolate union of free republics . . . We will lead
the fatherland to glory"). But the old anthem was reserved *ex-
pressis verbis* for use by the party. Both anthems are used. One
contained the seeds of nationalism, the other the traditions of
Communism. Both anthems live peacefully side by side, but

* See Chapter V.

not without secret hostility. Both are preparing for the moment when they will enter into open conflict.

The balance was on the side of the party, of Communism. Stalin, who has always regarded his public speeches as presentations of a rounded teaching and not merely as diplomatic maneuvers, was very cautious. He personally paid little tribute to the new nationalist tendencies, leaving this function to his editors and propagandists. For example, he has never spoken in any of his speeches of the All-Slav movement or of the fraternity of Slav peoples. He has always kept in mind that all his speeches, his every word, would be commented upon abroad, but—and this he has considered more important—that they would also be discussed and analyzed in thousands of party study circles, in schools and universities; that he is destined to become part of a *Weltanschauung*. For this reason he has avoided the danger of having his loyalty to Marxism-Leninism questioned even for a moment for the sake of a transitory political success.

In November, 1943, the *Propagandist* openly demanded action against two dangers existing on the ideological front. The first was 'baseless cosmopolitanism,'' a synonym for Trotskyism. The other was "nationalistic prejudices and anachronisms." "We must not forget," wrote this official journal, "that efforts in these directions may bring us some injury!"

Rigid adherence to Communist ideology has been the antidote used against nationalistic deviations in recent years. This antidote has been accentuated to the degree of a mania—on orders from above, of course. "The entire people must remain loyal to the end to the Socialist ideas which have found expression in the life of Soviet society."

"The Soviet people defend their Socialist fatherland."

"Socialism contains within itself gigantic forces, and mankind has now entered a stage of development holding out the promise of brilliant possibilities." This old phrase of Lenin's was reprinted by the *Bolshevik* in 1943.

Has not the course of the war confirmed—all papers, magazines, lecturers now asked—the unprecedented importance of Socialism in Russia, has not Socialism saved itself from defeat? How could Russia have defended herself if, despite all difficulties, the program of lightning-like industrialization had not been put into effect? Could private industry have evacuated scores of plants to the east, for example? Would the villages have supplied the necessary foodstuffs if not for Stalin's reforms? "Without the collectives," wrote Professor Mitin in October, 1943, "we could not have provided food for the country and the Red Army, and raw materials for industry. The collectives system makes possible the solution of all difficulties that arise in connection with supplying the Red Army and the country with food and industry with raw materials." Even the patriotism of Soviet soldiers, it was now repeatedly asserted, is the conscious patriotism of men defending their Socialism.

Was not the *volte-face* in the direction of religion and national sentiment to be explained by the fact that the soldier was not at all convinced of the superiority of the new ideology and of the policy arising from it? To say that the millions of peasant-soldiers were marching to death to defend the collectives system against the Germans is to distort the facts. First, it must be remembered, the Germans did not destroy the collectives, and, second, not a single Russian peasant would offer to die for the collectives. The Russian soldier is defending something more elementary than any specific political order.

Both in Russia and abroad there is an inclination to exaggerate the "meaning of the war" in the psychology of the soldier mass. Are the millions of German soldiers really anxious to die for the ideas of National Socialism? Has it not been said often that the American soldiers fight magnificently without actually understanding the meaning of the war they wage? This is even more true in the history of Russia. The period of great military victories in Russian history was at the end of the eighteenth century: it was the period of Suvorov. This was precisely the worst period of the cruel serfdom, which reached its extremes under Catherine II. But those peasant serfs, humiliated and tortured at home, displayed marvels of heroism when mobilized into the army. There is no parallel between the state of the people's welfare and its heroism in war. It does not exist now as it did not exist in the past. Very important is the quality of military organization, the patriotism of the military intelligentsia, and the capacity and readiness of the Russian soldier to endure hardship and privation.

III

The Devil's Name Is Trotsky

STALIN fears popular movements in Europe. Stalin does not want revolutionary explosions. He has long since turned his back on world revolution." Dissident Communist factions of various hues and tendencies, and many noisy semi-Communist groups, have accused and continue to accuse the Russian party of treason to Communism—to world revolution. Among them Trotsky and his group have played the leading role. It was Trotsky who declared, beginning in 1924, that Stalin would betray the Communist cause and all the traditions of Leninism, that he would abandon internationalism for nationalism. Have not recent facts confirmed the treachery?

Similar sentiments are expressed by others, but with a positive estimate of Stalinism and its evolution. It is, indeed, fortunate, say these people, that Stalin has abandoned international Communism; to our great satisfaction he has quit fomenting revolutions in other countries. By confining himself to matters of internal Russian interests he has become a national Russian leader; and it is much easier to find a common language with nationalism than with revolutionary Leninism.

"It was but natural," declared Congressman Rankin in the House of Representatives on January 26, 1944, "that when Stalin came into power and got rid of the Trotsky crowd he should open the Churches and restore freedom of worship. Stalin is a gentile, and Trotsky was a Jew. When Stalin got into the war things began to change. He got rid of the commissars . . . he restored the insignia. Stalin not only did that but he changed some more of Trotsky's crazy stuff. Trotsky had organized the Comintern. Stalin broke up the Comintern. He said, 'We are no longer afraid of the rest of the world. We are convinced we can get fair treatment at the hands of our allies.' "

In Moscow, however, it is denied that either of these two views—Trotsky's or Rankin's—has any basis in fact. Moscow declares: "Stalin is the Lenin of today." Stalin is a true disciple of classical Communism, the perpetuator of its cause, the outstanding champion of world revolution today. The Communist opponents of Stalinism are themselves traitors and betrayers of high principles. Had their policy prevailed, defeat would have been certain. Stalin alone is leading the world Communist army to victory.

In this strange controversy the voice of official Moscow is closer to the truth. The policy of old Communism has assumed a new coloring under changed world conditions but it remains basically unaltered. Even more, Stalin's policy is the only possible Communist policy under the circumstances. Any other policy would have led to either an internal or an external defeat of Communism. The question is not whether this would have been good or bad. No other road was open to Communism.

The differences between Stalinism and Trotskyism are vastly exaggerated in the public mind. These differences do not arise from a conflict of Communism versus capitalism, or internationalism versus nationalism. The hostility between the two and the ruthless suppression of Trotskyism in Russia should not be taken as a measure of their differences. On the contrary, conflicts between two closely related tendencies, competing for influence over the same social elements, are frequently more bloody than any others.

The inspiration for many of the achievements of the Soviet Government in the past ten to fifteen years came from the arsenal of Trotskyism. A great deal of the activity of the Soviet Government has actually received the approval of the Trotskyist opposition, although this approval has frequently been veiled in polemical phrases. Stalin's program of rapid industrialization and collectivization, for instance, was taken from the "platform" of the Trotskyist opposition, but only after the suppression of the opposition at the end of the 'twenties. The authors of this policy were Trotsky, Zinoviev, and Preobrazhensky, who as early as 1923–24 maintained that the continued coexistence of private (peasant) economy and state economy was an impossibility and demanded that the Socialist economy of the state "devour" the private sector.

After he had exiled Trotsky and removed Zinoviev from his responsible post, Stalin explained before a party congress why Trotsky's program had been impossible of realization earlier.

"What would have happened," asked Stalin in June, 1930, "if we had listened to the 'leftists' of the Trotsky-Zinoviev group, and had opened the offensive [i.e., the campaign of collectivization] in 1926–27? We would have surely failed in this task."

Later, when the cruel and ruthless methods employed in "de-kulakization" became known, and especially with the onset of the terrible famine of 1932–33, the opposition assailed Stalin for the too rapid tempo of collectivization, contending that the operation should have been extended over a longer period. But this was only belated, irresponsible criticism from the sidelines.

An official declaration by five hundred members of the opposition in 1929 declared quite justly that "many of the ideas, slogans, formulations of our platform have become the official property of the party."

The destruction of the opposition, marked by exilings and executions, was denounced by the members of the opposition as a violation of their "elementary rights." It appeared that democracy had no more ardent supporters than the Communist opposition. Victims of ruthless suppression, they demanded liberty and accused the government of practicing "bloody violence," of promoting a "caricature of Socialism," of "degeneration." But the democracy they were demanding was only a replica of the existing system; all they really wanted was that the "ins" change places with the "outs."

"The opposition demands party, trade union, and Soviet democracy," wrote Trotsky. But the "freedom of organization" demanded was to be within the framework of dictatorship. Trotsky never explained how he proposed to square this circle. His own friends were then already demanding a purge. They demanded a breach with the "right Communists" and "acceleration of the tempo" of economic reconstruction. Had the opposition come to power it would have been compelled, though unwillingly, to apply the very same terroristic methods which it was then denouncing. Otherwise it would not have retained power.

Incidentally, the authorship of the institution of forced labor armies, this blackest phenomenon of contemporary Soviet reality, does not belong entirely to Stalin and his associates. It was Trotsky who in the early 'twenties proposed the creation of forced labor armies of millions to be utilized by the Soviet Government as it pleased. They could be moved from place to place and would serve as an important instrument of Socialist construction. To be sure, it had not occurred to him to make them a feature of the penal system. Trotsky was also the author of mass mobilization of peasant labor: "Our industrial life will acquire elements of militarism." And, indeed, after completing its maneuvers in 1920, the Third Army was sent to work in the Ural forests and on railway construction. The Fourth Army was assigned to harvest work in the Ukraine. It was decided also to create a new labor army in the Ukraine.

"When we start labor mobilization on a large scale," Trotsky wrote, "to draft hundreds of thousands and millions of peasants into production, we shall not be able to mobilize them with the help of trade unions; we can accomplish it only by military measures. They will be organized in companies, battalions, with strict discipline."

The Kronstadt uprising in March, 1921, put an end to these projects and compelled the introduction of the NEP. But ten years later these ideas, which had never disappeared from the thinking of Russian Communism, were again brought forward, strengthened by the experience gained in the Solovetsky and other concentration camps, and were made the basis of the system of mass forced labor.

On international problems Trotsky likewise shared the ideas common to all brands of Communism, including Stalin's. After Hitler's rise to power, when the contours of the coming war had become apparent, Trotsky was convinced, as were Stalin and the entire Comintern, that "in the event of victory France and England will do all they can to save Hitler and Mussolini." For fascism and Hitlerism were regarded by Trotsky, as they were by the official leaders in Moscow, as representing the last stage of capitalist development. All Communism has maintained (and continues to maintain) that there is a historical law according to which liberal and democratic capitalism becomes transformed, at a certain stage of its development, into a totalitarian capitalist regime, i.e., into fascism; and fascism can be transformed only into a Soviet regime. "Decayed democracy" and the old capitalism cannot replace fascism, for that would be as incongruous as the reverse transformation of the butterfly into a cocoon.

"How could the victory of the decaying democracies over Germany and Italy liquidate fascism?" asked Trotsky. "This would be contrary to socio-historical laws." This is precisely the theory held by official Moscow Communism.

Trotsky severely criticized the Moscow government when it signed the Soviet-German "treaty of friendship." What Trotsky criticized, however, was not the government's effort to preserve neutrality in the European war but only the treaty with Germany. What was necessary, Trotsky declared, was to remain neutral, without signing any treaty that would make Russia "Hitler's commissary." This was all very good, militant, but irresponsible criticism, for Stalin had no other choice. Germany did not and could not believe the Soviet Government's promises. To be sure of Russia Hitler needed a whole system of treaty guarantees, of economic obligations, territorial dispositions, and "spheres of influence." Without these neither side could feel secure. Not wishing to participate in the war on the side of France and England, Stalin had to sign a number of treaties with Hitler, thus becoming "Hitler's commissary." It was a case of "either or." Trotsky's criticism was unreal. *La critique est aisée, l'art est difficile.*

Trotsky leveled the same criticism against the Soviet attack on Finland at the end of 1939. While criticizing the war on Finland he maintained that "once having been begun it should have been carried to the end, that is, to the Sovietization of Finland. Stalin had promised this but failed to carry it out." That was what Trotsky wanted. At one time during the Finnish war Trotsky believed that the Red Army had succeeded in kindling a civil war in Finland, a belief based upon erroneous reports from Moscow. He declared with satisfaction: "The Red Army is expropriating the big landowners and is introducing workers' control, preparatory to expropriation of the capitalists." The above quotations demonstrate clearly how mistaken is the belief that Trotsky based his plans and hopes upon revolutionary movements in other countries, while Stalin was allegedly satisfied to operate only with the Red Army as a national Russian instrument. Trotsky welcomed the revolutionary role of the Red Army in Finland as he had welcomed, twenty years before, the Sovietization of Poland with Red bayonets. In the latter case he was in agreement with Lenin and Stalin.

There was no fundamental difference between Stalin and Trotsky as regards the "premature peace with Finland." It must be remembered that the Finnish campaign of 1939–40 had threatened to drag Stalin into a great international military conflict. On this point, too, the difference between the two men was not so much one of political principle as of the different circumstances in which they found themselves: the difference between a political leader and a brilliant but irresponsible critic.

On the basis of the historical record we can now strike a balance in the argument about "world revolution." In this argument Trotsky does not emerge the victor. He accused Stalin of strangling the revolution, of being narrowly nationalist, of lacking faith in the power of the movement, of corrupting "fraternal parties" into instruments of his own policy. He asserted that with a different policy in Moscow the world revolution would have greater chance of success. Today it is quite clear that the failure of world revolution to materialize in the period between the two World Wars was due to the absence of adequate revolutionary sentiment within the respective countries themselves. Wherever revolutions did occur in the period between 1918 and 1925 they petered out. The big Communist parties in Germany, France, Czechoslovakia had hundreds of thousands of members, but they were without adequate revolutionary fervor, these countries had not reached that hopelessness and despair which alone drive peoples to revolution.

It was possible to instigate revolutionary outbreaks, and this was done from Moscow in Germany in 1923, in Estonia in 1924. But these outbreaks were easily suppressed and left behind them only disillusionment. It was possible to bring in arms, money, instructors, ideas from the outside, but one thing it was impossible to import—a revolutionary sentiment. Without it the revolutionary drama becomes *opéra bouffe*. Neither Stalin nor anyone else had the power to conjure up the spirit of revolution from beneath the earth of Europe at that time while other quite different political ideas dominated the situation. Communist outbreaks could only provoke anti-Communist fury.* What they might have provoked was a European

* For years Trotsky had expected revolutionary outbreaks and he saw the signs of revolution in places where there was not the slightest justification for

alliance, headed by Germany, for possible war against Russia. But this would not have brought victory for world revolution, but the defeat of the Soviet Government. If all Communist groups, including the Trotskyists, regard the preservation of the Soviet regime in Russia as essential, as they profess to do, they owe its preservation to Stalin's policy of Soviet "national- ism."

Trotsky was right in one respect, however. The entire out- side world, and particularly the revolutionary elements, were frequently repelled by the reality of the Soviet system, which was so different from the promises of the early Soviet period. The wholesale violence and terrorism that prevailed cooled the sympathies of the outside world and crippled the activities of the Communists abroad. Supporters of the Soviet regime were able to accept these features during the stormy period of civil war in Russia, but the subsequent years of peaceful eco- nomic construction brought many protests. Repellent also was the profound poverty of the Russian people despite all the successes of industrialization, and, finally, the new class dis- tinctions that arose, provoking the perplexing, deadly ques- tion: Is it really worthwhile making new Soviet revolutions only to raise to power a new ruling caste? Trotsky was right when he pointed to Soviet reality as the most important anti- revolutionary factor.

But his criticism of the internal policy of the Soviet Govern- ment, so eagerly accepted by politicians and publicists of vari- ous schools, was very superficial. He blamed Stalin for the "absolutist bureaucracy" in power in Russia, for the develop- ment of an "unbridled oligarchy." He protested against the privileges enjoyed by the "higher-ups" and Stakhanovites. He perceived in the social structure of Soviet Russia a "monstrous perversion of the principles of the November revolution." For these reasons, beginning with 1933–34, he saw salvation only in

such hopes. This was quite in harmony with the spirit of official Communism. He merely compromised himself with his predictions. When a strike wave swept France in 1936 Trotsky wrote in the New York *Nation*, "The French revolution has begun . . . We must prepare ourselves. The industries and factories will elect their deputies . . . we must prepare for a victory. Soviets everywhere? Agreed. But it is time to pass from words to action."

The *Nation* illustrated Trotsky's article with a reproduction of Daumier's "Last Council of the Ex-Ministers." The ministers are shown terrified and run- ning away as the door opens and a goodnatured, fat figure of the Revolution in Phrygian cap enters.

a new revolution, which he termed (incorrectly) a political but not a social revolution: the overthrow of the "party bureaucracy" and a return to the creative mainsprings of Leninism.

But this Marxist, who had always denied the accidental in history and had always emphasized the primary rôle of historical laws, who attributed secondary importance to the role of the individual in the historical process, never answered the fatal question: Why did the Soviet revolution culminate in the rule of an "oligarchy," of a "bureaucracy"? He vented his wrath upon Stalin and upon the seizure of power by the "Stalinist clique." But this was not convincing: How did Stalin manage to fool all the forces of the proletarian party? Trotsky refused to see the natural, logical development from universal equalitarianism at the beginning to the "new oligarchy" at the end. For this reason he left everybody in a state of perplexity. Suppose it were possible to have a new revolution à la Trotsky, is there any guarantee that the new regime would not follow the very same course of development as Stalin's? Trotsky did venture to give a vague answer to this question when he said that unless the Russian revolution formed a link in a world revolutionary chain, it would "degenerate into Stalinism." But this, too, was unconvincing. It was a vicious circle. The "Soviet oligarchy" (a pseudonym for Stalin) killed the world revolution, but the same oligarchy was victorious because there was no world revolution. Only the figure of the evil genius, the conjurer and sneerer of history, Stalin, emerges from this ideological fog as the explanation of the great historical events.

Trotsky looked upon the emergence of class distinctions as a "degenerative" process, but it was the natural accompaniment of the economic restoration of Russia and, fundamentally, constituted progress. The somber aspects of that process, the blood spilled, the executions and concentration camps, were, of course, the product of the policy of a given government and would not necessarily inhere in a program of state and economic reconstruction under all conditions. But Trotsky's program to have the country return to the initial stage of a formless, classless Soviet society was essentially reactionary.

The "oligarchy" and the "bureaucracy" became for Trotsky the chief enemy. They embraced the entire new class of Soviet employees and the new intelligentsia. With a mechanical conception of history, he saw in the new high-salaried class a new *ruling* class. This was then and still remains quite untrue. What he did was to apply to Soviet society Lenin's division of all society into a "privileged top" and a "toiling population."

"Twelve to fifteen million privileged and 160,000,000 people who are profoundly dissatisfied."

In Trotsky's theory Stalin was the representative of the twelve to fifteen million privileged, and he, Trotsky, the ideologist of the toiling millions, or, at any rate, of the working class. He summoned the toilers to revolt against the privileged. Everything was turned upside down.

In reality Stalin's government was not and is not the government of the class of Soviet employees, but has lived in open or concealed hostility to that class. If that class were to come to power it would bring relief to the country, Trotsky's theories to the contrary notwithstanding. And the "uprising of the toilers," if it were victorious, would drag the new intelligentsia down once more to the lower level of the masses, and would lead in turn, through another painful process, to the formation of new higher classes.

The people's vague realization of the sterility of any new November revolution deprives Trotskyism of any chance of success. But Trotskyism might play a certain role if a revolutionary workers' movement were to develop in Russia. Trotskyism constitutes also the seed of future social movements, both in Russia and in Europe: of anarchic, primitive Communist movements arising from elementary protests against poverty, oppression, and disillusionment.

Under conditions of a new political high-flood in Russia, Trotskyism may become temporarily a "left wing" movement of the primitive anticapitalist, antimilitarist type, marked by political strikes and possibly local uprisings. It would have no chance of achieving political power, either in Russia or outside. But even after Trotsky's death it is not dead. On a world scale, Trotskyism would have a chance in the event of the collapse of official Communism. Its role might be to unify the fragments—the people weary of the cunning and mysterious diplomatic maneuvers, of the compromises with capitalism and collaboration with kings and emperors—strategies of Stalinist Communism that have repelled emotionally revolutionary elements.

BUT without losing sight of the distinctions between Stalinist
Communism and Trotskyism, it is important to remember that
Russia in Trotsky's time had in embryo all the elements of the
future Stalinist state. If after Lenin's death Trotsky had been
included in the "triumvirate" that succeeded Lenin, and if in
his conflict with Stalin he had managed to seize strategic positions and to achieve victory, it is almost certain that Trotsky
would have been compelled by circumstances to do everything
that Stalin has done in the past twenty years.

The program of industrialization was proposed by Trotsky
and his followers long before the Five-Year Plans, and the
tempo at which he would have carried out that program would
have been no different than Stalin's. With his distrust of the
peasantry it is natural to suppose that Trotsky would have
resorted to Stalin's collectivization program to solve the grain
problem. The ruthless methods used in the struggle against
the kulaks would not have repelled Trotsky; he had fully approved these methods during the period of the "Committees
of the Poor" in 1918. From the very beginning Trotsky had
rejected democracy for the non-Communist population. As
for the use of terroristic methods, he yielded nothing to either
Lenin or Stalin. The internal party struggle (against "Stalin's
faction"), becoming more acute from year to year, and marked
by purges and repressions, would have brought any leader of
the dictatorship to the point of general liquidation of political
opponents. Trotsky himself would not have been able to retain power without the use of these methods, if he wished to
avoid a return to "decaying democracy." And he was opposed
to any such return.

Trotsky's efforts to rebuild the Soviet economy and the Soviet State would of necessity have generated a new "bureaucracy" no less speedily than one developed under Stalin. No
other Soviet leader was as inclined by character and belief to
the system of hierarchical subordination as Trotsky when he
was at the height of his power. No one accorded such privileges to his bureaucratic associates as did Trotsky in the period
of the civil war and universal equalitarianism. It was Trotsky,
as already stated, who devised the classic program of militari-
zation of labor, and the idea of the state-apparatus, brought to
realization later by Stalin, was rooted entirely in Trotsky's
conceptions.

Trotsky, like most Russian Communists, was moved by deep

antagonism to Britain and by only slightly less antagonism to the United States. A firm and stable alliance with the democracies against Hitler would have been as impossible under Trotsky as it has been under Stalin before the Hitler attack. He, too, was opposed to participation in any great European war, and he, too, would have had to conclude an agreement with Germany in 1939.

To prepare the country for war Trotsky, like Stalin, would have embarked (though perhaps unwillingly) upon the restoration of "national-Russian traditions." Just as he was the true creator of the new Russian Army, Trotsky would have had to restore ranks and decorations in the army, and adopt many other features of the "Russian Thermidor" which he so bitterly denounced from his foreign exile.

Fata volentem ducunt, nolentem trahunt. The iron logic of facts is stronger than the strongest of men. It was this logic that transformed "the greatest enemy of Soviet Russia," Winston Churchill, into an ally and collaborator; the antimilitarist Stalin into the builder of Russia's greatest army; passionate patriots of old Russia into a group of Russian traitors in Berlin. Cruel facts would have compelled Trotsky, had he been in power, to adopt the policy which he assailed.

Of course, outwardly the policy would have been given a different coloration. There would have been other phrases, other slogans, a different terminology. Trotsky would have known how to paint his policy in bright hues, he would have been more generous in the number of public appearances, and would have lent much brilliance to his political actions. But the substance would have been the same.

Communism in power can be only Stalinism; nothing else is possible. The Moscow formula, "Stalin is the Lenin of today," is quite correct. Discontented opposition elements may build all sorts of theories. But they need only come to power to return to the path of Stalinism.

OCCASIONALLY, when he was not embroiled in his conflict with Stalinism, Trotsky was able to manifest a farsightedness and a gift of prophecy which place him in the first rank of the political figures of the period between the two wars.

In 1938 Trotsky wrote that "the social bases of the Soviet regime [planned economy and state ownership] would resist the test of war," although in the event of war he expected

great political changes in Russia. In the spring of 1939, when
the entire world waited from week to week for the signing of
an Anglo-Soviet treaty against Germany, Trotsky wrote that
"an agreement with Hitler would signify security of frontiers"
for Stalin, and that by signing such an agreement Russia "could
systematically supply Germany with almost all raw materials
and foodstuffs she lacks."

Even more remarkable were Trotsky's predictions concerning the course of the present war, expressed in those early
months when France appeared powerful and Russia and the
United States barricaded themselves behind the walls of neutrality. Trotsky did not believe in the power of France, or in
the weakness of Germany. Nor did he foresee a German victory.

"The international propaganda which hastens to picture
Hitler as a cornered maniac is very stupid," he wrote. "The
situation is still very far from that.

"The Polish Government and the Czechoslovak Government are now in France. Who knows whether the French Government, together with the Belgian, Dutch, Polish and Czechoslovak may not be compelled to seek refuge in Great Britain?

"I do not believe for a moment in the realization of Hitler's
plans for a Pax Germanica and world domination. New nations, and not only European, will come forward to bar his
road . . . But before his hour strikes much and many will be
wiped out in Europe. Stalin does not want to be among them."

Trotsky declared prophetically: "Only a new world coalition will be able to break the German Army through a war of
unprecedented proportions."

Trotsky combined a capacity for objective evaluation of historical events with utopian "Trotskyist" conceptions and un-
realizable prognoses of world revolution. Toward the end of
his life, however, doubts had begun to penetrate his soul. As
though arguing with himself, he wrote sadly in October, 1939:

"If the November revolution does not find its continuation
in the course of this war or immediately thereafter in any of
the advanced countries . . . we shall undoubtedly have to
raise the question of reëxamination of our concept of the present epoch and its moving forces.

"Have we really entered an epoch of social revolutions?"

IV

The New Religious Policy

WHEN the Calvinist King of France, Henry IV, found himself hard pressed in his conflict with the French Catholics and it appeared difficult to take Paris, Henry, that prototype of political "realists," declared that *"Paris vaut bien une messe"* ("Paris is worth a mass"): he embraced Catholicism and the capital opened its gates to him. Was it worth sacrificing ponderable interests for the sake of vague ideology? asked the realistic king.

There are many people who imagine that something similar is now happening in Russia in the field of religion. They read of brilliant church services in Moscow, of the reopening of closed churches, of the election of a patriarch, of the government agreeing to the restoration of churches wrecked at the front, of the solidarity of the Orthodox clergy with the government in all questions concerning the war—and they imagine that "the great realist in the Kremlin" is emulating the policy of his French prototype, and that before long Russia will have either complete freedom of religion or that the Orthodox Church will be restored to the position it occupied before the revolution in 1917.

Moscow, on the other hand, does all it possibly can to strengthen the impression that there is a genuine restoration of religious freedom. In conceding an inch to the church Moscow seeks to make the world believe that it is granting a mile. Nothing pleases Moscow more than the belief cultivated by the foreign press that Russia is returning to her traditional roads:

"Bright with candlelight and the splendor of clerical garb, the church presented a magnificent spectacle, perhaps as magnificent as it has ever witnessed. It was like a page from ancient Russia . . ."

A page from ancient Russia! As though by accident the

author of this report from Moscow, Maurice Hindus, uses a phrase which Moscow was eager to have used. It wants to spread the belief among all inside and outside the country who prefer the old Russia to the new that "a page of ancient Russia" has turned up again amid the Soviet metamorphoses, that Russia has turned her back on her Communist ways, substituted bishops for Marxists, conservatives for revolutionists, and transformed her government from an instrument of world revolution to a bulwark of world stability.

The history of the religious policy of the Soviet Government exposes the error of this conception, so widely current because human beings are so prone to forget the recent past. The true meaning and character of the evolution Russia has undergone on this question may be clearly discerned in the tortuous history of Soviet religious policy.

Russia has experienced no less than three violent outbursts of the antireligious movement, of persecutions and the closing of churches, in the twenty-seven years of the Soviet regime. And three times, after each outburst, came periods of relief, of moderation, of compromise.

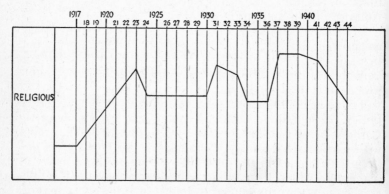

The first big wave of antireligious persecutions, which had already begun during the civil war, struck the church in the period of the NEP, 1921–23. While some concessions were being made to private economy and many observers had imagined that a return to "ancient Russia" was impending, the "revolutionary offensive" continued in the sphere of religion. Arrests and executions of priests assumed a mass character.

"Freedom of conscience" as guaranteed by the Soviet constitution had no real significance beyond propaganda aims. Paragraph 13 of the first Soviet constitution provided:

"The church is separated from the state, and freedom of religious and of antireligious propaganda is recognized for all citizens."

"All citizens" (not only the workers) were accorded the right of religious propaganda. Yet the years following adoption of the constitution were a period of ruthless persecution of religion. Religious propaganda was rigorously suppressed.

The constitution, adopted in 1924, and drafted with great care on the basis of previous experience (Stalin participated actively in the drafting), separated the school from the church but reaffirmed the phrase concerning the rights of citizens to religious propaganda. Paragraph 4 declared:

"To assure the workers of true freedom of conscience the church is separated from the state, and the school from the church, and freedom of religious and antireligious propaganda is recognized for all citizens."

In explanation of the Soviet Government's policy on questions of religion, Stalin declared in his interview with an American labor delegation in 1927:

"The party cannot be neutral in respect to religion, it wages an antireligious propaganda against all religious prejudices because it stands for science . . . There are cases of party members interfering with the full development of antireligious propaganda. It is good that such members are expelled."

The persecutions in the first period of Soviet antireligious policy reached their zenith in 1923. The execution of the Catholic priest Budkiewicz provoked an international conflict, with particularly serious consequences to Soviet Russia's relations with England. The Soviet Government found it wise to make concessions. Its religious policy experienced a shift. The persecutions were moderated and the remaining open churches were permitted to function.

The antireligious movement was halted in part. The Union of Militant Godless, founded in that period, continued to function, supported by the Komsomol, and the distribution of antireligious literature continued, but the persecution of priests was considerably alleviated.

By that time the basic feature of the subsequent antireli-

gious movements—from the end of the 'twenties to the war—
had become crystallized. These movements ceased to be as
popular and spontaneous as in the first ten years of the revolution, and assumed in all their alternating outbursts and reces-
sions an artificial character. The population, especially the
youth, continued to display a lively interest in religious and
antireligious problems; supporters of religion declined in
number. But the original fervor ("we will climb up to heaven
and disperse all the gods") had abated, the sensational digging
up of relics of saints was over. The international effect of Soviet religious policy moved the government, for its part, to put
on the brakes on antireligious stunts.

The principal center of the antireligious movement was in
the GPU, which had a special division concerned with religious problems whose task it was to accelerate or moderate the
pressure, as need required. In more recent years the Union of
the Godless worked in close contact with and under the direction of the GPU.*

The moderation of religious persecutions in the middle and
late 'twenties gave rise to the same kind of discussions and
hopes that now prevail. The Metropolitan Sergius, the acting
patriarch (later chosen patriarch), who died in 1944, addressed
the following manifesto to believers in July, 1927:

"We inform you that in May of this year, upon my instructions and with permission of the authorities, a Patriarchal
Synod has been established by the administration of the Patriarch's Office.

"We hope that this legalization will gradually be expanded
to the lower church administration.

"The joys and successes of the Soviet Union are also ours."

But in 1929–30 came collectivization, and the attitude of
the government toward the church experienced a radical
change. The local church constituted an important element in
village life, and the attitude of the clergy toward the collectivization was known to be hostile. The entire course of internal
policy swung to the left, and many promises previously given
were wiped out in a moment. Mass closings of churches were

---

* The official book on *The Komsomol and Antireligious Propaganda* contains many observations like the following: "Cells of the Union of the Godless
frequently confine their activity to distributing membership cards in the Union
of the Godless.

"Godless members of the Komsomol have become too tame."

resumed, many priests were exiled, wholesale arrests were under way everywhere. The persecutions were soon extended to the cities; in 1932 priests were exiled from the cities in batches as "nonworking elements." The severe repressions continued for several years. The aforementioned Paragraph 4 was revised as follows by the Congress of Soviets of the RSFSR in 1929:

"In order to assure the workers of true freedom of conscience, the church is separated from the state and the school from the church, and freedom of religious worship and of antireligious propaganda is recognized for all citizens."

From now on there was to be freedom only for antireligious propaganda but not for religious propaganda. Believers were accorded only "freedom of religious worship," which meant the right of priests to perform services but no more.

In July, 1930, the Communist Party Congress decided to intensify the antireligious propaganda.

How difficult was the position of the representatives of the church, and how great were the concessions they were obliged to make for their self-preservation may be seen from the interview given by the Metropolitan Sergius in February, 1930, and published by the entire press under the signatures of two metropolitans, two bishops, and two other prelates:

"QUESTION: Is there persecution of religion in Russia?

"ANSWER: There never were persecutions of religion in Russia . . . True, some churches were closed, but this is not done on the initiative of the government but by will of the population, in some instances even by decision of the believers themselves.

"QUESTION: Is religious propaganda permitted in the USSR?

"ANSWER: Religious services and sermons are not forbidden. The teaching of religion is permitted."

The next question concerned repressions and cruelties practiced against priests.

"ANSWER: All this is pure invention, slander. We have had no limitations placed upon the administrations of our church organs to date."*

Only in 1934–35, after collectivization had been completed

---

* The details of this interview, historic in its way (published in *Izvestiya*, February 16, 1930), are told in William Henry Chamberlin's *Russia's Iron Age*, Chapter XXI.

and the international situation required that the Soviet Government embrace the policy of collective security and support of the League of Nations, did the government again moderate its church policy. Mass persecutions ceased. Antireligious processions were forbidden. It was permitted to light Christmas trees, to manufacture wedding rings, etc.

Once more official pronouncements declared: "We do not persecute religion by any means. We demand from church parishioners that they refrain from interfering in politics. The old clergy, bound to the old regime, would not abandon its struggle against the Soviet power, and it was necessary for us to resort to repressions. But now they have apparently turned their faces in our direction—and the church is free." This was almost literally a repetition of the arguments used in the 'twenties, which had been followed by new outbursts of repressions.

Meanwhile, the new constitution, drafted in 1936, in this period of religious liberalism, did not signify a return to Lenin's formulas. It again excluded religious propaganda: "Freedom of religious worship and freedom of antireligious propaganda is recognized for all citizens."

On the other hand the new constitution abolished the civil disabilities imposed upon "nonworkers," which had applied also to priests. The right of franchise in elections to the Soviets (even the right, on paper, of being elected) was accorded also to priests. However, the significance of these constitutional reforms was negligible.

At the end of 1937 came a new wave—the third—of persecution of religion. This was the period of the great purge. More than ten thousand religious parishes were closed according to Professor N. S. Timasheff.* Severe repressions descended upon priests, with arrests, exile, imprisonment in concentration camps, and even executions. The old trite accusations of espionage, industrial sabotage, and all the other crimes attributed at that time by the NKVD to many others were directed also against priests.

In 1939, with the conclusion of the purge, the repressions against priests ceased. Another period of tolerance ensued. It continued until the outbreak of the war with Germany.

In 1940 the observance of Sunday was restored with the reestablishment of the seven-day work week. While there were

---

* *Religion in Soviet Russia.*

some repressions of priests in the new regions annexed to Russia, the general policy was a cautious one.* To avoid misunderstanding, the Central Committee of the Communist Party was now moved to remind its members that they were forbidden to practice religion.

AND so the history of the period of 1918–41 follows a tortuous line. Periods of severe repression alternated with spans of relative tolerance. For the religious policy was only part of the general internal policy with its ups and downs. But with the end of each span of repression, the surviving representatives of the church would begin to console themselves with the hope that a profound evolution had taken place in the ideology of the government, and that the new rights accorded to the church would remain inviolate.

The chart on page 56 records the changes of Soviet policy on religion. The line indicates the years and the measure in which the government altered its policy. It is to be observed that at no time did a turn favorable to religion win all the ground lost by the church through previous repressions. Only a few of the closed churches were permitted to reopen and exiled priests were not given their liberty. A new generation of priests was not permitted to develop, and in many instances laymen, and occasionally women, served as substitutes for the clergy. The right to publish the Bible was not restored, nor was it permitted to import it from abroad, even if it was sent free.

At the time of Hitler's invasion of Russia, after twenty-four years of the Soviet regime, Russia had:

28 bishops—a decrease of 75 per cent since 1917.
5,665 priests—a decrease of 90 per cent since 1917.
3,100 deacons—against 15,210 in 1917.
4,225 churches—against 46,457 in 1917.
37 monasteries—against 1,026 in 1917.

Regarding the attitude of the population toward religion, Soviet sources noted before the war that about two thirds of the village population and approximately one third of the city population, i.e., about half of the population, considered them-

* The Swiss press reported that in Bessarabia priests were ordered in December, 1940, to move into the interior of Russia. In Riga churches were closed at Christmas, 1940.

selves as adhering to various churches. These figures are from a census taken in 1937. Because they showed a surprisingly persistent devotion to religion, they served as the motive for a new antireligious campaign, begun in 1937 and halted at the beginning of 1939.*

The war brought great relief for religion and the church.

The principal reason for the new reforms lay in the religious sentiments preserved by the population, particularly in the villages. It was possible to ignore them when the government had to do with collectives and purges, but when the peasants were mobilized for a life and death struggle it was necessary to take a "step backward" and to adapt the policy to the needs of "backward elements." The present situation, involving as it does great popular activity, particularly in matters concerning the war, has compelled a retreat from the straight Communist line on the ideological front. The concessions granted during the war were specifically a compromise with the Russian peasantry. This was the first and most important motive of the reforms.

The first but not the only one.

Much of what has taken place in the relations between the government and the church in the period from 1941 to 1944 has become known abroad; what remains unknown is the actual character of these relations, which have developed on the principle of *do ut des*. The government made one concession after another to the church. But for every concession received the church was obliged to pay immediately with political moves favorable to the government; at times this assumed a quite overt character.

For a number of years Hitler's government had encouraged the activities of Orthodox prelates and priests resident in Germany and consisting almost exclusively of émigrés from Rus-

* Because many feared to answer the question "believer" or "nonbeliever" in the census, little value must be attached to the final figures. The Soviet press has contended that believers had little genuine faith. The *Komsomolskaya Pravda* received the following letter in 1937 from a person who had taken the entire course of antireligious propaganda:

"We repudiate the writings about God and we assert that there was not and there is not any such person. This fact has been established on the basis of scientific data concerning the origin of man as well as the origin of the universe. But what interests me is another thing: Do sorcerers and conjurers really exist and what is the power they possess by which they corrupt people and transform them into swine, dogs, etc.? You may, perhaps, deny this, but these are facts."

sia. Hitler appropriated money for the construction of an Orthodox cathedral in Berlin; nineteen Orthodox churches received government appropriations for repairs. All this was by way of preparation for the great political campaign which developed immediately after the invasion of Russia by German troops.

In the occupied regions a number of Orthodox priests declared their support of Germany and prayed for the success of the German arms. Some high dignitaries of the church went over to the German side. Attention has already been called to the Riga conference of church leaders in occupied territories and the blessing they conferred upon the German army.

The Germans paid particular attention to the church in the Ukraine. By conferring favors upon it they sought to wean it away from Moscow, and in this respect they had some success. Their second aim was to obtain support of the church against the Vatican; in this respect they were not so successful. Not until the end of 1942 did the Germans become rather cool toward matters concerning the Orthodox and Ukrainian churches.

The pro-Hitlerite policy of the Orthodox clergy in the occupied regions of Russia was an important factor in determining the policy on religion pursued by the Soviet Government during the war. It was wise to come to the "defense of religion" in the struggle with heathen Hitlerism. German propaganda sought to create a great European bloc against "Godless Bolshevism," and Moscow replied with a counterblow: defense of religion against the heathen, revival of the patriarchate, and restoration of churches destroyed by the Germans.

One of the motives for a change in Soviet religious policy was the effect which the antireligious policy as pursued over a long period had created in neighboring allied and enemy countries. The religious beliefs of the populations constituted an obstacle to the policies recommended by Moscow for the various national movements (in which Communists were to play the directing part). In Yugoslavia members of the Orthodox Church constituted half the population (more than half among the Serbs); in Bulgaria they were two thirds; in Rumania, two thirds; in Greece, 99 per cent. The "All-Slav Meetings" in Moscow were appealing to the national sentiments of the Slav peoples; Orthodox religious leaders were in a position to appeal also to non-Slav peoples, such as the Rumanians and Greeks. It was natural, therefore, to combine the All-Slav propaganda with Orthodox propaganda. In June, 1943, a group of six bishops, headed by the Metropolitan Nikolai, made their appearance at a solemn meeting of the All-Slav Committee in Moscow.

Moreover, there were a number of political problems presenting a source of disagreement between Russia and her allies on which an authoritative nongovernment voice, the voice of public opinion, expressing itself in support of Russia would be more effective than the Kremlin's. On the question of the second front, for example, the Orthodox Church spoke out with determination in support of the government's position. Many other such questions may arise in the future.

IMMEDIATELY after the beginning of the Soviet-German war the highest church authority in Russia, the Metropolitan Sergius, declared his support of the war in the name of the church. At a solemn service in Moscow, on June 29, 1941, he prayed for success of the Russian arms.

In September of the same year the *Godless* and the *Antireligionist* ceased publication. In America and other countries this was interpreted by some as the consequence of intervention by President Roosevelt through Averell Harriman, who at that time had made his first visit to Moscow as an official representative. Harriman did talk about the matter to Stalin. But as indicated above, there were many other extremely important reasons for a change in Soviet religious policy.

On the anniversary day of the November revolution the Metropolitan Sergius hailed Stalin as "the divinely appointed leader of our armed and cultural forces leading us to victory." Metropolitan Nikolai of Kiev wired Stalin wishing him a long life. A week later came the sensation of his appointment as a member of the Commission of Inquiry into German Atrocities. The churches participated in war-fund drives.

Very soon, in February, 1942, the Metropolitan Sergius, who had been evacuated from Moscow to Ulianovsk (the former Simbirsk) issued a manifesto against the Orthodox priests who had gone over to Hitler and were forming an "independent" church in the Ukraine. He pointed out that the leader of this movement, Bishop Polikarp Sikorsky, had previously pledged allegiance to the Soviet Government. The Metropolitan Sergius threatened the renegades with excommunication and called upon the Orthodox faithful to repudiate them.

Then followed another sensation. The church leaders—for the first time since the revolution—published a book in Russian on religion entitled *The Truth About Religion in Russia*. Expensively printed, despite the difficulties experienced by the printing industry in wartime, and richly illustrated, this book sought to prove that religion was free and that, in general, there had never been any persecution of religion in Russia on the part of the government. Any unpleasant developments that had occurred had been due to the activities of the Union of the Godless and not of the government! (As already indicated, this loyal interpretation had been used as a defense mechanism by the clergy since 1930.) Despite its loyalty and patriotism, however, this book was not distributed through book stores. It was circulated only among Soviet grandees and institutions abroad. It is worth noting that it was printed in the printing shop which used to print the *Godless*. Apparently the NKVD division which had previously directed the antireligious propaganda was now directing the proreligious activity behind the scenes. No doubt the very same persons did both jobs.

On Good Friday, 1943, the Metropolitan Sergius read over the radio an address to the Orthodox population of all countries, but directed particularly to the Serbs, Czechs, and Greeks. Naturally, it had previously been approved by the government.

The biggest moment in the history of the Orthodox Church came in September, 1943. The government permitted the election of a Patriarch. On September 4, 1943, Stalin, in the presence of Molotov, received the 76-year-old Metropolitan Sergius, who was accompanied by two other metropolitans. This was followed immediately by announcement of the restoration of the Synod, composed of six men, and of the election of Sergius as Patriarch. The day after his reception by Stalin the new Patriarch demanded a second front, addressing the following sharp remark to Russia's allies:

"We Russians are the world's most patient people, but the cup of our patience is overflowing."

At the same time a conclave of nineteen metropolitans, arch-bishops, and bishops made public a manifesto declaring:

"There are individuals found among the clergy and laymen who, forgetting the fear of God, have dared to build their own welfare upon the misfortune of all. They meet the Germans as welcome guests, enter their service and sometimes go so far as direct treachery, betraying their brethren to the enemy, as, for example, guerrillas and others who are sacrificing their lives for the country.

"Everyone guilty of treachery to the common cause of the church and desertion to the side of fascism as an enemy of God's crucifix will be deemed excommunicated; and if he be bishop or priest he will be unfrocked. Amen."

The Patriarch was given the use of one of the finest houses in Moscow, formerly occupied by an official German delega-tion. Churches began to be restored, particularly in territories cleared of the Germans. Churches previously reopened under the Germans continued to function. The Alexander-Nevsky Monastery was restored; Troitsko-Sergiev partly so. The for-mer, where Suvorov was buried, experienced a flow of visitors, and military men were ordered to kneel before his grave.

At the beginning of 1944 training of new priests was per-mitted. Establishment of the Orthodox Theological Institute was authorized, as were also various theological courses. Con-trary to the new practice in universities, tuition is free, but students must not be below eighteen years of age.

Finally, in order not to compromise the church with a con-nection with the NKVD, a separate government Committee on Affairs of the Orthodox Church was set up to act as liaison between the church and the government. In June, 1944, the Soviet Government decided to create an official committee dealing with the affairs of all churches.

SUPPORT of the clergy became necessary also in the struggle with the Vatican, which continued to play a very important role in the European war.

The Vatican's moral influence was thrown entirely on the anti-Hitler side of the scales, particularly after 1939, when Catholic France, Poland, and Czechoslovakia fell under Ger-man domination. But, unlike other anti-Hitlerite powers—Britain and the United States—the Vatican, as a spiritual power, could not think of collaboration with the Soviet Government without a radical change in Soviet religious policy. The Vatican could not simply forget, as did the temporal powers, the activities of Communism in all countries, the religious persecutions which had held sway in Russia only five years before, the fate that had been inflicted upon Catholic priests in Spain, and similar events.

For this reason the Vatican remained not only an anti-Hitlerite but also an anti-Communist power. It could afford the luxury of such consistency because it had no armies and navies of its own, did not concern itself with strategy, and was not trying to solve problems of first and second fronts. Foreseeing the defeat of Germany, the Vatican feared the spread of Communist, antireligious movements in Europe, and adopted, therefore, a very cautious attitude on the question of collaboration between non-Communists and Communists in liberated territories. The Vatican had thus become a great anti-Soviet force during the war, during the very period when the Soviet Government had hoped to expand its political and intellectual influence in Europe.

To stand in its old position of unstable legalistic "freedom of conscience" was not wise for the Soviet Government. It was necessary to bring into action another religious power against the Vatican, a power that would wield greater influence in the Christian world in matters of religion than could the Soviet Government. The Orthodox Church, and particularly the figure of the Patriarch, stood out as the proper authority for this purpose.

With improvement of relations between Soviet Russia and her allies (after the Moscow and Teheran conferences) at the end of 1943, the Vatican appeared as Moscow's sole serious opponent in the anti-Hitlerite camp.

On February 1, 1944, *Izvestiya* again assailed the Vatican. "The Vatican's foreign policy—wrote the official organ—has earned the hatred and contempt of the Italian masses for supporting fascism. The disgraceful role the Vatican played in Hitler's and Mussolini's Spanish adventure is widely known. The Vatican emerged in the role of a supporter of armed intervention."

The foreign policy of the Soviet Government was thinly veiled behind an apparently theological dispute which other-

wise would seem quite incomprehensible in wartime. Patriarch Sergius attacked the very principles of the Papacy, in
April, 1944. "The uninterrupted presence of Christ in the
church," the Patriarch wrote in his *Journal of Moscow Patriarchate,* "and the spiritual marriage between Christ and the
church make inconceivable the concept of an intermediary
between the two such as a vicar on earth." He concluded with a
hint of a political nature: "I could conceive of a union of
churches around some chief who could not be a vicar of Christ
but a bishop of some world capital."

In 1944 a new feature appeared, however, in the attitude of
the Soviet Government to the Catholic world. The territories
with a prevailing Orthodox population were reoccupied by the
Red Army in the first months of that year, and the Soviet troops
stood at the gates of Catholic countries: Lithuania, Poland,
Czechoslovakia. In the Balkans and in Austria the influence of
the Catholic church is strong, too. Achievement of the war
aims of a zone of Soviet influence in eastern Europe, and especially a favorable solution of the Polish problem, required
collaboration, at least at the beginning, with the Catholic
forces in these countries.

Therefore the attacks on the Vatican were supplemented
now by conciliatory political moves. On the invitation of
Stalin, Father Orlemanski of Springfield, Massachusetts, made
his trip to Moscow; the Italian Communist leader Ercoli went
to a mass in a Catholic church, and other similar maneuvers
were to be expected in the near future. A kind of agreement, at
least a wartime truce, with the Vatican was becoming necessary, and Moscow would be ready to make certain concessions
to achieve it.

SOVIET church reforms followed in quick succession. Solemn
services attended by thousands, and numerous declarations by
church leaders, created the impression that the Soviet Government had entered upon the road of complete religious liberty,
even of encouragement of religion. But this was far removed
from the facts.

When the Archbishop of York, known for his liberal views,
visited Moscow in October, 1943, he attended a solemn service
and spoke at length with the Patriarch and his associates. Upon
his return to London he declared: "The Russian Patriarch and

his colleagues were most anxious to make it plain that they had complete freedom of worship within their churches."

"Within their churches" meant that the priests and parishioners were not disturbed by the police or by Godless agitators during services. This and this alone constituted their freedom. But, added the Archbishop of York, "very many churches are still closed or secularized."

As if to emphasize Communist principle and devotion to old positions, President Kalinin wrote in June, 1943, that the government continued as before, to regard religion as "a misguiding institution."

This statement is confirmed by the following figures on the number of churches in Moscow, where the church enjoys greater freedom than in the provinces: in 1900 there were 351 churches in Moscow; in 1934 there were 40 churches functioning; in 1938, 25; in 1939, 15. In the spring of 1943 this number rose to 30, and at the end of the year there were about 50. Thus three times as many churches were open as on the eve of the war, but the number was many times less than before the revolution.

The situation in the provinces was even more difficult. Every local church parish, however small, provokes fear and distrust on the part of the authorities. Every parish lives its own life and must, perforce, exhibit differences of opinion on various questions. It is not so much the sermons that can be dangerous for the regime as the conversations of parishioners among themselves and their collective life. A police government is bound to fear that a church parish may be transformed into a cell of discontent and opposition. Its autonomy is a dangerous thing, however efficient may be the system of espionage operating within.*

For this reason, and not only because of the shortage of priests, the number of open churches remains small. The free-

* In an interview with a representative of the Religious News Service (August 11, 1944), Georgi Karpov, head of the Soviet Committee on Orthodox Affairs, declared that there were "no barriers to church expansion" any more. He did not, however, give the number of newly opened churches, after a year of his Committee's activity. He mentioned the following legal reasons for rejecting petitions for the opening of new churches: first, where there is no church building available (private houses have been used for church services in the last decades in Russia); second, "when people in a small hamlet already having two or three churches want another." This alleged abundance of churches and unreasonableness of the believers seem curious.

dom of religion granted during this war may not last long. It is but another move in the tortuous history of Soviet religious policy.

It has also become clear that separation of church and state has no basis in fact under a political regime such as exists in Russia. Under Soviet conditions, the church cannot develop its activities if the state does not assist it: under such circumstances the restoration of churches without the help of the state's economic organs is impossible. It is impossible to obtain the ornaments and habiliments necessary for services without the coöperation of government agencies. The printing of books and magazines in Russia requires not only money but also the active collaboration of various government agencies. The Synod, the Patriarch, the Theological Institute, and the rest can be housed only with the assistance and at the will of the government.

For this reason the church is not actually separated from the state in Soviet Russia. Living by the grace of the government, the church faces the risk of losing its new privileges at any moment; hence it is compelled to coöperate fully with the government politically, and at times church leaders find themselves in an undignified position. The church leaders, who also are "realists," accept many compromises in order that the churches may be permitted to function. But at the same time they are forced to swallow many bitter pills.

The church does not play a great role in the social life of Russia today. But the history of religion and of religious policy illustrates glaringly the nature of the political system and the conditional character of the political shifts.

V

The Soviet Concept of Foreign Policy

Words must have no relation to actions—otherwise what kind of diplomacy is it? Words are one thing, actions another. Good words are a mask for concealment of bad deeds. Sincere diplomacy is no more possible than dry water or wooden iron. JOSEPH STALIN.

STALIN thus expressed his conception of diplomacy in 1913. Of course, he added the adjective "bourgeois" to qualify the substantive "diplomacy." His idea of international politics concurred with that of Charles Talleyrand, who had said, a century earlier, that "language has been given to man to conceal his thoughts."

No government or political party has ever offered the world as many precise theses, platforms, manifestoes, and programs as did the Soviet Government and its party. From this wealth of material the deep roots of Soviet policy can be discerned and its growth traced. But in the late 'thirties this frankness was abandoned for its opposite, and Talleyrand's concept became the basis of political strategy. There was nothing enigmatic about the philosophy, plans, and program of Lenin and Trotsky, or of Stalin in earlier years. But now silence is golden and the schemes are the carefully guarded secrets of an intimate circle.

CERTAIN basic conceptions persist in Moscow's ideology. Nothing has altered in Stalin's attitude toward capitalism—he remains convinced that it is dying. As official Moscow sees it, the coalition of the Soviet Union with capitalist states during this war does not constitute evidence of the stability of capitalism; on the contrary, the war demonstrates the truth of the old Bolshevik axiom that "the long-drawn-out crisis of world capitalism" must assume the form of universal catastrophe. Millions of lives must be sacrificed because capitalist society can find no way out of "the inherent contradictions" arising from private ownership of the means of production, no solution to the "clash of imperialist powers" struggling for world domination. The enormous sacrifices the USSR has been compelled to make and the war itself are due to the fact that the Socialist fatherland is encircled by capitalist powers—all potential enemies—according to the ideology which still prevails in the Kremlin.

The main features of all of Stalin's theories were inherited from Lenin, including the concept of declining capitalism and the inevitability of imperialist conflicts in this era; the Russian revolution of 1917 marked the beginning of the crisis of world capitalism:

The first period of this crisis lasted about six years. In Europe, and especially in central and eastern Europe, it was a time of storm and stress, of direct Communist struggle for power. It ended with the victory of Socialism in one country and retreat of revolutionary forces everywhere else.

The second period, from 1923 to 1928, was one of apparent convalescence for capitalism; according to Stalin, this represented the relative stabilization of bourgeois society in the economic and political fields. However, this period differed from previous periods of capitalist stability and expansion; it was brief and insecure and culminated in the worst crisis ever known. The depression of 1929–33 gave new proof of the inability of decaying capitalism to solve any of its fundamental problems.

The third period, from 1929 to 1937, was characterized by mass unemployment, bankruptcy, declining production, economic and political instability. Capitalism was in its death throes, Stalin reiterated in speech after speech.

The widely publicized and systematic analysis of "the general crisis of capitalism" ended at this point. Between 1917 and 1937 Moscow had sought the widest possible distribution of its many publications giving in endless theses and programmatic manifestoes a full explanation of Communist concepts and Soviet policies. The second half of the 'thirties constituted the period of Soviet efforts at collaboration with the democratic capitalist countries through the League of Nations, and pacts with France and other powers. Silence became necessary now. "Words are one thing, action another. Good words are a mask."

It is not difficult, however, to find in fragmentary speeches

and ideas expressed by the Soviet leader and his closest col-
laborators the links between the ideology of all the preceding
"periods" and that of the ensuing fourth period. Moscow interpreted world developments as follows:

Between 1937 and 1941 the capitalist countries, having
failed to overcome their internal crises and increasing antago-
nisms in international relations, were being swept inexorably
toward a world war. According to Stalin, the first skirmishes of
this second World War began in 1937–38. German troops occupied Austria in 1938; they took possession of the Sudetenland,
then the rest of Czechoslovakia, and, finally, of Poland. In Asia
the war began in 1937 with Japan's attack on China.

Communists everywhere followed Stalin's lead in charac-
terizing this phase of the war, and the next phase during which
Germany occupied most of western Europe, as a strictly imperialist conflict. It was presented as a new attempt of Germany and Italy to force a redivision of the world's colonies,
markets, sources of raw materials, spheres of influence. Both
groups of imperialist powers sought world domination. "The
progressive elements of mankind" could not sympathize with
either of the contending power groups. Hence the Soviet
Union was justified in her neutrality.

The fifth period began at the moment Germany violated
the pact and invaded Russia, on June 22, 1941. An entirely
different and nonimperialist force was then drawn into the
war, which altered everything. The war assumed a dual character on June 22. The imperialist struggle for world hegemony
continued; the entry of Japan and the United States only made
it global. But the belligerency of the Soviet Union added to
this imperialist rivalry the struggle for the preservation of the
Socialist fatherland against fascism and imperialism. This dual
character of the war led to the coalition of the Big Three; the
USSR entered into this alliance to protect Socialism; Britain
and the United States entered it because they were unable to
crush German imperialism alone. The capitalist countries seek
to utilize Russian military forces for their own national self-
interest, but they hoped that German and Soviet armies would
mutually exterminate each other so that neither would again
become decisive factors in European affairs. The Kremlin remains as suspicious of Anglo-American motives as it ever was.

The fifth period is a part of the general crisis of capitalism.

AT the very moment that the Soviet policy of "Socialism in one country," with its emphasis on Russian nationalism, its praise of tsarist heroes, its seeming abandonment of the hope of world revolution, has won laudatory comment from high places abroad, this policy has been replaced by a new one.

For, as Moscow sees it, the policy of "Socialism in one country" was correct during periods of revolutionary defeat, of relative stability of capitalism. But this policy "which brought incalculable advantages" to the cause of Communism, in Stalin's phrase, came to a natural termination in 1939 when the world was plunged into a new holocaust and a new dynamic period of history began.

September, 1939, clearly set the demarcation line; for the first time in nineteen years Soviet troops crossed the European frontier into foreign territory. In the course of the next year, a series of countries—Estonia, Latvia, Lithuania, eastern Poland, northern Bukovina, and Bessarabia—were "liberated, with the aid of the Red Army, from the yoke of their fascist regimes." Soviet regimes were established, with nationalization of the local economy. Socialism was now triumphant in more than one country.

This expansion of the sphere of Socialism, which continued for about a year, reached its culmination in July, 1940. Russia's western neighbors—Hungary, Rumania, Bulgaria, and Finland—reacted to it first by moving closer to Germany, then by an outright alliance with her, and, finally, by joining with Germany in an attack on Russia. From that moment on, it became necessary for the Soviets to devise a new strategy, both in the military and in the political domain.

FROM the moment when the Soviet Union found itself involved in the war, the defense of the USSR became the sole principle guiding the activities of world Communism.

According to Moscow the greatest event of the twentieth century has been the rise of the first socialist society and the consequent prospect of extending this revolutionary change to other lands. Everything would be lost if the Soviet Union were to be defeated. World capitalism would dismember the Soviet Union; by exploiting Soviet territories and peoples capitalism would find an escape from its impasse and thus over

come its crisis, at least temporarily. This would retard for a
long time the development of Socialism in the world. Untold
new sacrifices would then be required to bring about a victorious revolution in any country.

But if the Soviet Union emerges victorious from this war,
this will transcend in significance an ordinary military triumph. Victory will not mean merely the victory of Russia over
Germany, but the victory of Socialism over fascism—which is
"the final phase of capitalism."

What is National Socialism? To this seemingly academic
question Moscow gives an answer that all its supporters everywhere must accept; an answer that involves extremely important political conclusions: Hitlerism represents the power of
the capitalist oligarchy, of finance capital, which in the past
had governed through the institutions of Weimar democracy,
but which, hard pressed by a growing revolutionary movement, was compelled to shed its democratic disguise and to
enter upon the road of ruthless capitalist dictatorship.

It is hardly necessary to say that this theory has no basis in
fact, that Hitler's power was founded upon the support of
other elements; that only a minority of big business magnates
came to his aid; the majority—former conservatives and liberals—remained cool to his appeals until after his access to power.
By simplifying events and interpreting them to suit its theoretical and political scheme, Moscow identifies "German fascism" with German capitalism. From this it draws the conclusion that the defeat of Hitler will be the final defeat of German
capitalism.* Moscow does not envisage a return to the status
quo ante bellum for Germany, a new Weimar Republic, but
rather a Germany with close military, political, and economic
ties with Russia.†

---

* "Six million votes were received by the German Communist Party at the
elections. The German bourgeoisie perceived that the retention of bourgeois
democratic liberties might play a nasty trick on it, that the working class might
utilize these liberties for the development of a revolutionary movement. For
this reason it decided that there was but one way to retain the power of the
bourgeoisie in Germany—to destroy all bourgeois liberties, to reduce parliament
to zero and to establish a terroristic bourgeois-nationalist dictatorship." (*Short
Course in the History of the Russian Communist Party* [1938], p. 208. Prepared
with the direct collaboration of Stalin.)

† This does not exclude, of course, so far as Moscow and the German Communists are concerned, any tactical alliances with some German "bourgeois
parties" against others. There must be an interim period during which Com-

Moscow regards Russia's alliance with England and the United States as necessary for three reasons: First, as a means of supplying Russia with arms and food; second, as a direct military instrument against Germany; and, third, as a weapon against a Japanese attack on Russia. It is necessary to preserve the alliance, even at the cost of temporary compromise and acceptance of political obligations which seem to repudiate the basic principles of Bolshevism.

Moscow believes that after Hitlerism has been weakened, fear of the growing power of the Soviet Union may move England and the United States to adopt an anti-Soviet policy, thus bringing to an end the present alliance. International combinations inimical to the Soviet Union may become the order of the day. To delay that moment and to avert the break before the Soviet Union's aims are attained, the policy of the Soviet Government and of all Communist parties must be to make concessions which Moscow justifies by references to the classic example of Lenin's strategy and tactics in 1917, under the Kerensky regime, against which the Bolshevik party had been preparing an uprising. In August of that year, General Kornilov had assembled a military force and moved it against Kerensky with the avowed aim of suppressing the Bolshevik movement and establishing a "bourgeois-military dictatorship," as Lenin termed it. Lenin rallied all his supporters to the defense of the Kerensky Government and moved its Red Guards against Kornilov. When Kornilov's forces had been smashed, the Bolshevik party resumed its struggle against Kerensky and two months later overthrew his government in the November revolution.

The Anglo-American-Russian coalition must be maintained for a certain time. To make this coöperation possible it is necessary to eliminate from statements of policy, from the press, and from propaganda, everything that might interfere with it. Furthermore, the struggle against German occupation has intensified in the peoples of Europe the urge for national independence, created suspicion in small states of the great powers, and made the sovereignty of one's own country a matter of primary concern in the eyes of the people.

munists will work within a People's Front or the equivalent with any groups which will support their program for the gradual transformation of the country. Thus Italian Communists are for the moment collaborating with monarchists in Italy.

For these reasons social revolution must not be the slogan for any popular movement in Europe at the present time. The aim in wartime is restoration of democracy outside of Russia; it is necessary to afford full equality for the Communist parties and to give them the opportunity to strengthen and expand their organizations. In this lies the principal value of democracy.*

The task of bringing about a close political alliance of various countries with Russia (particularly adjacent countries like Poland, Czechoslovakia, as well as Yugoslavia, Bulgaria, Hungary, Rumania, and Finland) must be separated from the problem of their internal social transformation. The present period makes possible political alliances as well as the establishment of preponderant Soviet influence on the foreign and military policies of these countries, but excludes any profound social transformations. Contrary to previous concepts (1918–24) a Soviet-Socialist upheaval does not now constitute the prerequisite of an integral political alliance with the Soviet Union; on the contrary, such political alliances must precede the future liquidation of capitalism in these countries.

The Soviet Government, to avoid offending the painfully tense national feelings of countries oppressed by Germany, has already recognized the national rights, not only of the component national elements within the USSR, but also of the future members of the Soviet Union by expanding formally the autonomy of the various Soviet republics. Each component republic has been assured, on paper at least, of the right to have its own armies and to conduct its own foreign affairs. While preserving the principle of a centralized leadership, the Soviet Government may be expected to grant technically even wider formal rights to other peoples who may later join the Soviet Union.

* While thus retreating to the position of "bourgeois democracy," Communism interprets democracy in its own way, however. According to this interpretation, democracy and fascism have one distinction. Democracy is a political system under which Communist parties can operate freely. Fascism is a system which compels Communism to go underground. Democracy is not synonymous, however, with political liberty. It is also compatible with mass repressions, such as those which took place in the Baltic States in 1940–41, in Spain during the period of Soviet intervention on the Loyalist side, etc. Thus the concept of democracy and abandonment of the slogan of social revolution do not exclude profound social transformations; however, the latter must be rationalized, with national, "antifascist" arguments, not with revolutionary propaganda.

IN some countries Moscow expects Communism to attain full power, in others only limited influence. In countries where the Communists may come to power (Yugoslavia may become the first example) they must aim for the time being at a "bourgeois-democratic," not a Communist, transformation. While abolishing "the remains of feudalism" the Communist party and its government must not immediately proceed to expropriate all capitalists; and the Communists must be particularly careful in their treatment of the peasantry—agrarian reform, not collectivization, must be the immediate program.

However, in most countries liberated from German occupation (Italy, France, for example) the influence of Communist parties emerging from underground will often be insufficient to attain complete control of the government. Hence, Moscow considers it necessary, contrary to all previous policy, for these Communist parties to seek participation in coalition governments. The old Leninist axiom that Communists everywhere must assume power only as the dominating force in a great popular revolutionary movement has been abandoned. This constitutes one of the most important *tactical* distinctions between Stalinism and Leninism. Today Stalin demands participation of Communists in coalition governments, and for these reasons:

1. They must be in a position to exercise control over the activities of "semi-fascist or wavering elements" which may act contrary to the interests of the Soviet Union.

2. It is necessary for them to counteract anti-Communist influences emanating from America or England.

3. It is necessary to be prepared for sharp conflicts between the Soviet Union and its present allies: Moscow must not permit nations freed from the domination of Hitlerism to become bases of support for Anglo-American imperialism in a struggle against the Soviet Union.

4. The Central Committees of the respective Communist parties or its "front" organizations must carefully control the activities of their representatives in the governments, removing all those who fail even in small matters to obey the instructions of their party, derived from Moscow. For purposes of political strategy, requiring due recognition of the nationalist tendencies in various countries, it is recommended for the present that the names of some Communist parties be changed, if necessary even dropping the word "Communist," in line with the formal dissolution of the Comintern.

5. To the extent to which Communist parties in countries freed of the German occupation acquire influence and strengthen their positions, they must seek to increase the number of their representatives in coalition governments and to obtain strategically important posts, such as the ministries of the interior, and of propaganda, without, however, upsetting the framework of the "anti-fascist coalition."

6. Any social transformations taking place must proceed under national slogans, especially under the guise of repressions directed against Vichyites, Quislings, fascists, who have collaborated with the Germans during the occupation; this would apply to virtually all of Europe. As punishment for collaboration, big industrialists and bankers may be expropriated. In addition, economic enterprises and real estate acquired by the Germans during the war must remain state-owned or controlled as a socialist fund in the hands of the governments controlled by or under the influence of Communists.

7. Social changes in countries adjacent to Russia must help to create an economic bloc: the powerful heavy industry of Czechoslovakia, for example, may be linked to Russian industry; the coal, oil, and other industries of Poland and Rumania may be combined with Russian economy. This pro-Soviet bloc is to serve as the basis of close political collaboration and alliance.

In accordance with this strategy the Communist parties in neutral countries must refrain for the present from raising slogans of social revolution and anticapitalist propaganda, limiting their aims to demands for national unity, friendship for Soviet Russia, and more complete democracy.

In England the Communists have eliminated from their present slogans all ideas likely to diminish England's aid to the Soviet Union, particularly the demand for immediate independence of India. World Communism considers the salvation and strengthening of the first Socialist state more important than the independence of India; from the Indian Communist party it demands postponement of its independence program until the end of the war in which the Soviet Union is involved.* For the same reasons the British Communist party is obliged to oppose strikes in war industries likely to reduce

* After being suppressed by the Indian Government for eight years the Indian Communist party was again permitted to function and two hundred Communist leaders were released from jail when Gandhi and other nationalist leaders were arrested (1942–43).

the measure of military aid to Russia. This policy of "civil truce" or "class collaboration" is also designed to silence anti-Soviet agitation in England.

In the United States, Moscow is relying upon the reëlection of President Roosevelt and the liberals of the Democratic party. Moscow considers the Republican party its chief enemy. A political victory for the latter is regarded as dangerous, particularly because it might lead to a reduction in aid to Russia and conceivably even to cessation of military collaboration with the Soviet Union. Under the conditions of the present war the Soviet Government and World Communism are interested in the retention of power by the Democratic party as long as the Communist party has no hope of obtaining power. For this reason the Communist party of the United States is supposed to pursue a particularly flexible policy, the main features of which are:

a. Abandonment of independent activity as a party in electoral contests.

b. Abandonment of propaganda for a Communist revolution and acceptance of "free enterprise."

c. Opposition to strikes.

d. Abandonment of any public characterization of the war in the Pacific as an imperialist war. On the contrary, the Communist party must support its government in this war, for it is only because of this war that Russia is made secure against an attack from Japan. But secondary attention has to be paid to the war in the Pacific, in which Russia is not participating.

e. The Communist party must give the appearance of a national American party, independent of any international Communist center. Only when the last shot is fired on the eastern European front will the American Communist party be permitted to consider radically changing its present position.

CURRENT declarations and programs of conservatives and liberals in England and America urge the speediest possible restoration of "stable conditions" in Europe and stress the need of preventing "chaos" after the war. In Moscow these programs are regarded as false and hypocritical, designed to conceal the fear of popular movements and uprisings in postwar Europe and Asia.

The Kremlin publicly accused England and the United

States of seeking to restore the prewar political and social rule of the most archaic elements. Moscow pointed to the desire of England and America to restore the Yugoslav, Greek, and Italian monarchies, to avert a revolutionary upheaval in Germany, to their ambiguous position in relation to de Gaulle, to their intention of restoring most of the old frontiers without change. For, according to Moscow, political activity in a liberated Europe leads inevitably to "chaos"; it gives life to movements which cannot escape the leadership of revolutionary parties.

This viewpoint did not, however, preclude Moscow's making agreements with monarchies; or establishing committees of German officers; or altering its relations with de Gaulle in accordance with his readiness at any given moment to collaborate with the French Communists. In all such instances Moscow justified its actions by the immediate military exigencies of the Soviet Union.

On the other hand, while grossly exaggerating the military importance of guerrilla warfare, Moscow supported and encouraged its own underground in the occupied countries. It failed to admit that the big role played by Communists in these underground movements did not correspond to their strength in the general mass of the population. Actually, as long as the underground organizations remained the sole politically active force, they could not reflect accurately the political sentiments of their countries. Moscow exaggerated the importance of the Communists in the underground and expected the underground organizations ultimately to expand into central governmental organs. Under this concept these organizations did actually appear before their peoples as future governments. However, in view of the exigencies of the war situation, they were instructed to stress their national liberating character, and to maintain unity with other parties and political groups. Enjoying the diplomatic and military aid of the Soviet Government to a greater degree than aid from other countries, they in turn fervently supported the Soviet Union in all questions concerning the war and the postwar period.

NOT only does Moscow regard as real the danger of a great international anti-Soviet coalition, but it believes this danger to be increasing in proportion with the growth of Soviet Russia's prestige. The Kremlin particularly fears that postwar Germany might become a weapon of "world imperialism" against the Soviet Union.

This belief is related to the basic theory that neither the defeat of Germany nor the collapse of Japan will cure the fatal illnesses of capitalism, and that capitalism will again be plunged into crises unless the peoples of Europe find sufficient strength to liquidate the system. These crises will find expression in unemployment, hunger riots, uprisings, fascist revolts, localized wars. The unstable structure of new and old states will be the consequence of the instability of capitalism itself. In its search for escape from this hopeless situation "world imperialism" may again turn against the Soviet Union.

In Moscow's view there is danger that the United States may become the "spearhead of world capitalist reaction." By alliance or compelling England's support by economic, financial, diplomatic, or military means, the capitalist forces of America (or of an Anglo-American bloc) will strive to achieve world hegemony after the defeat of Germany and Japan.

The Soviet Union, together with its future neighbors and allies, must mark the frontiers at which the world domination of the Anglo-American forces is to be halted: their domination will eventually embrace the entire world, with the exception of the Soviet sphere. This situation will entail the danger of new wars for Russia, which must be prepared for new great conflicts, and must, therefore, preserve its military might. The struggle with "the hypocritical, rapacious American democracy," as Lenin put it, as the "bulwark of dying capitalism," will require the use by the Soviet Government of ideological weapons entirely different from those now employed against Nazism and fascism.

According to this concept, the Soviet Union will continue to face the serious threat of war until all or at least the majority of the nations of Europe and the Far East abandon the economy of capitalism, or at least until they enter into a close alliance with the USSR. The only supernational organization that can preserve peace is a Union of Soviet Republics expanded to maximum proportions and embracing within its confines "countries which have abandoned capitalism," as Stalin has expressed it.

THE crux of the problem of postwar reconstruction is Germany. Moscow expects that the slogan of the "German bourgeoisie" will be independence from Soviet Russia, while the "progressive forces of Germany" will put forward a counterprogram of close alliance with the Soviet Union.

While western and southern Germany will probably be occupied by British and American troops, the Red Army will occupy the eastern portion. Part of East Prussia will be incorporated into the Soviet Union as a GSSR (German Socialist Soviet Republic); Pomerania, part of Silesia, western Prussia (with Danzig) will be annexed to Poland; a new Polish Government will have a close alliance with the Soviet Government. Austria will be detached from Germany and may possibly enter, with its neighbors, Czechoslovakia and Yugoslavia, into a firm alliance with Russia. Finally, a certain part of Germany, annexed neither by Poland nor by Russia, will be temporarily occupied by the Red Army. These German territories, with a population of about fifteen to twenty million, having been freed from Hitler rule, will of course have the right to follow a pro-Soviet orientation. This will enable German Communism, long the jewel of World Communism, to rebuild its shattered forces and gain power.

At the same time, the alliance of part of Germany, and later of all Germany, with the Soviet Union, or Germany's direct affiliation with the USSR, will afford the latter a measure of security against military attack which it could not possibly enjoy under conditions of capitalist encirclement. The combined military forces of Soviet Russia and the new Germany will easily be able to repel any attack. Together they will exercise a decisive influence upon the immediate future of all European countries.

AT the beginning of the Russo-German war, Moscow was convinced that its goal would soon be attained by the German people itself. It was a remnant of the old illusion that any army attempting to wage war against the land of the Soviets was bound to disintegrate, and that in any country responsible for such a war a revolution was certain to flare up. It was believed that a revolution in Germany would annihilate the economic power of the social classes that constitute the basis of Hitler's regime.

The war against Russia, Stalin said in 1934, one year after Hitler's rise to power, "will be certain to unleash the revolution." He repeated it again and again. "It is scarcely possible to doubt that a war against the Soviet Union will lead to a revolution." The mutinies that took place in the British and French armies in Russia in 1918–19 were fresh in Soviet memory.

When the war started in 1941, Stalin was convinced that Russia would number among her "true allies" the German people, "enslaved by the Hitlerite bosses." "Germany," Stalin declared in November, 1941, "is a volcano ready to erupt." In July, 1941, his lieutenant Lozovsky, the Deputy-Commissar for Foreign Affairs, indulging in wishful thinking, wrote: "The idea that the salvation of Germany and of her people consists in the destruction of the Hitlerites is making headway. More and more often one reads on walls in Germany the words, 'Heil Moscow!' "

The job of overthrowing Hitler's government and destroying the social roots of "German fascism," it was felt, could be left to the German people. "It is probable," said Stalin, "that this war will bring about the end of Hitler's clique," but "it is not our aim to destroy Germany," because "the German people must not be identified with the Hitler clique."

These hopes were soon shattered. The war dragged on, but no revolts took place in Germany. Will they occur as the war nears its end? Will they be of a radical nature?

If the Germans are too oppressed and too weak to achieve their liberation by themselves, if the volcano does not erupt, drastic measures will be needed in Germany; this is the conclusion that the course of the war has forced upon the Communist mind. What the German people cannot achieve must be done from the outside.

When it was first announced, the Soviet idea of using German labor for the rehabilitation of Russia caused a sensation. However, the real meaning of this proposal can be understood only in relation to the problem of uprooting "German fascism." The hundreds of thousands, perhaps millions, of workers to be sent to Russia for forced labor are to be recruited not only from the army but also from among the propertied class of Germany. They are responsible for the war from Moscow's point of view, and their elimination is just as necessary as the restoration of Russia with the help of German labor.

Writing on "Complicity in International Offenses," the official publication, *War and the Working Class,* enumerated the different groups of war criminals. "The big financial and business magnates" are a "party to the Hitlerite crimes," for "with their funds, factories, and guns they support and maintain the system of government banditry"; likewise, all "individuals exploiting forced labor" and "owners of industrial equipment that had been removed from the occupied territories."

"Stern punishment must be meted out to all the culprits."

According to these principles, punishment is foreseen for every German who has actively supported the German policy in wartime or benefited by it. Thus the ring of criminals will be very wide. It will include not only active party members but politicians in general, people connected with different parties and of various shades of political opinion, a large section of the middle class, farmers, state officials, and many others.

The elimination of "socially dangerous" elements was the constant policy of the Soviet authorities even in countries that had not waged war on Russia. In eastern Poland, the Baltic countries, and Bessarabia, as soon as those territories were occupied by Soviet forces in 1939–40, from 10 to 12 per cent of the population belonging to the upper strata of society and including political intellectuals of all parties (except one, of course) were labeled "socially dangerous," sent off to the east, and organized into labor battalions. The social and political Soviet transformation of the lands named went on more easily after they had been "freed" from those at the top. The remaining population did not dare to develop any opposition; and the reserves of labor essential to the Soviet economy were supplied by the newcomers.

To a still greater degree the same pattern applies to Germany. It kills four birds with one stone:

From a purely nationalistic point of view, it is the Great Revenge—revenge for the horrors of war, for the millions of dead and wounded, for the devastation of a great country, for innumerable crimes and atrocities. "It will be remembered by the German people, and a future would-be Hitler will have to ponder well before he starts an aggression."

From the point of view of international security, it will deprive Germany of the classes that, according to Moscow, are the instigators of wars. Whether the Allies will continue to work with the Soviet Government is uncertain; but, in any case, Germany will cease to be a European danger, says Moscow, after her upper strata have been liquidated.

For the inner development of Germany, this measure is intended to release kindred political forces, as soon as other classes and parties have been eliminated. These forces, and especially the Communists, have been weak for the last twelve years; but everything is being done in Russia to increase their influence, especially through the German war prisoners, or a part of them, who will return from Russia; future German governments will at least be strongly influenced by them, if the Moscow program is realized.

Finally, Russian manpower, which has suffered enormously from the war, will be partly restored. The Russian economy will be the gainer when a large labor army consisting of hundreds of thousands of upper-class Germans has to take orders from the Central Economic Departments.

Moscow does not consider it probable (and herein consists its great mistake) that this policy will alienate the whole German people—and not only its capitalist classes—from Russia for generations; that the danger of war may arise not only from the German bourgeoisie but from the other classes as well; it does not perceive the enormous hazards involved in such a punishment. Will the Allies agree to it? If not, they must be denounced as the savior of fascism at the eleventh hour and as enemies of Russian security. In this event the Soviet Government will have to proceed on its own initiative in the German territories occupied by its army.

VI

The New Social Structure

THE differentiation of the new Soviet society into classes, contrary to the principles of a classless society, is often regarded as a denial of Communism and as a betrayal of principles.

No greater mistake could possibly be made in any evaluation of Soviet policy than to accept this view. To be sure, this Soviet policy is characterized by flexibility, and realism in the choice of methods for attainment of its aims; it frequently chooses to follow roundabout paths leading to these aims; it is quite ready to destroy old formulas, institutions, and former leaders—if the aims require such action. But certain of its aims remain unaltered, and some of its principles remain unshakable. Not to perceive these principles behind the tactics is to fail to see the woods for the trees.

Somewhat tired of the compliments from abroad, the Moscow *Bolshevik* wrote in January, 1944: "Abroad they often say that the Bolsheviks are unsurpassed realists. Yes, but Bolsheviks are realists with principles. Their realism is a realism coupled with a great historical outlook."

The principle of state economy was and remains the highest principle of Soviet policy; it continues to determine not only its economic policy but its policy in all other spheres. Individual economy continues to be regarded as an evil, even when it does not involve employment of hired labor and its limits are reduced to a minimum. Private enterprise employing hired labor is considered a crime with which there can be no compromise; this has been particularly true since the great economic upheaval of 1929–34. The second inviolate principle of Soviet policy is the preservation of all power in the hands of the political group which is determined to protect the country from any restoration of individual economy; the preservation of that power by any and all means of internal policy, however ruthless; and the pursuit of a foreign policy which would facilitate the development and expansion of the system of integral state economy.

A great deal has changed in Russia during the past quarter of a century. But the government has never abandoned the two basic principles: state economy and the strong totalitarian political regime. We may say that Russia's misfortune consists in the firmness with which these two principles have been retained, in the lack of realism and refusal to compromise in this respect.

It is not the realism of Soviet policy but its narrow application which constitutes the main evil. This becomes clear if we grasp the political motives which have guided the policy of gigantic industrial expansion, a process which has transformed Russia into one of the great industrial countries, and the collectivization of agriculture.

More Inequality!

ONE day in 1919 the head of a Red Guard detachment in the city of Voronezh confiscated Professor Dukelsky's second bed. "He demands," wrote Professor Dukelsky to Lenin, "that I sleep with my wife in one bed." To this Lenin replied to Dukelsky that the Red Guard chief was quite right. "Of course," wrote Lenin, "the desire of intellectuals to have two beds, one for the husband and another for the wife, is quite legitimate," but "the average Russian citizen has never had as much as one bed."

That was the period of the religion of equality, of equality of human beings practiced to its uttermost limits. It was not an intellectual concept, a theory, a scheme—it was the reflection of a most elemental emotion emanating from a tremendous moral urge. It was the embodiment of the idea of Supreme Justice, which was to be attained with the complete destruction of the shameful foundations of the old regime. The people were to govern themselves and to establish justice upon earth: the Great Darkness was at an end, the Millennium had begun. In like manner did the Levelers and Diggers of the English revolution believe that the Kingdom of God was at hand. In like manner, also, did the mighty voices of equalitarianism resound in the French revolution, with their program of "the agrarian law" and of equality "worthy of the natural condition of man."

Everything that stood in the way of equality was to be abolished, at once, completely: that was the spiritual crux of the November revolution and of the ideology of the early period of the Soviet regime. Equality in consumption and strict rationing were to eliminate inequality in the distribution of food supplies. The floor space of houses and apartments was carefully measured and the available space equally distributed among the population. The peasants divided landlords' estates, the workers seized the factories and drove the old owners into the street. Expeditions from the cities requisitioned grain supplies from the villages for the hungry cities. Soldiers tore shoulder straps from officers' uniforms. All ranks were abolished to make sure that not a vestige of the old inequality would be left. Instead of the aristocracy the workers and peasants were to rule the country, and "every housemaid must learn how to govern the state," for all were now to be equal. Political democracy, in its accepted sense, was found to be inadequate because it did not guarantee social equality. Lenin hailed the Paris Commune because it had equalized the pay of state employees and workers, and he promised for Russia "the reduction of the pay of all, without excepting government leaders, to the regular wage scales of the worker." How distant all this now seems . . .

No less ghostly is the sound now of the decrees and manifestoes of those early years; thousands of human beings died for those ideas and thousands of enemies of them were maimed, tortured, and killed.

"Henceforward the Army of the Russian Republic consists of free and *equal* citizens bearing the honorable calling of Soldier of the Revolutionary Army," and, therefore, "all privileges associated with former ranks and ratings, as well as all insignia of rank (epaulettes), are abolished. All titles are eliminated. All decorations, etc., are eliminated. All separate officers' organizations are dissolved."

A decree promulgated a month or two later declared, "All titles and ranks of civil officials are abolished." All were to be equal.

Every army is held together as a cohesive whole either by a great cause or by rigid discipline. The discipline of the Red

Army in its early years was not very considerable, despite the strict regime; but it was strengthened by one of those simple, naïvely elementary ideas which alone are responsible for great upheavals. This idea was not scientific Socialism, or Marxism; no theory at all guided the development. It was indeed simple, like the Cross of the Crusades, like the abolition of slavery in the American Civil War. The reign of equality, of justice, and happiness for all had arrived. The selfishness of the landlords and capitalists stood in the way of the coming of the millennium. It was necessary, therefore, to destroy them, and no sacrifices were too great. Every sacrifice was considered justified, and every cruelty, however great, was believed endowed with high human purpose. In this idea lay the germ of the future ruthless terror.

Besides, grim reality compelled the realization of general equality as speedily as possible, independent of all theory. The economic catastrophe of the first years of the Soviet regime, 1918–22, had reduced living standards, even without benefit of ideology, to the lowest possible level of subsistence, and, at some moments, even below that. Money lost almost all value, rations were more or less equal. The bourgeois and landlords went to work as employees of state institutions, while state employees lived no better than the workers. In April, 1922, investigation disclosed that the workers were earning 5.71 "commodity rubles" per month, and government employees, 5.74. Equality was attained—on the basis of the lowest minimum subsistence.

The same degree of puritan frugality applied to the ruling party. Party officials did, to be sure, enjoy greater material opportunities than common citizens. The party leaders enjoyed privileges and, never subjected to the *uravnilovka* ("the application of general equality"), they believed that the interests of the Communist cause gave them the right to a certain measure of comfort, "essential to work." However, this was done quietly, shamefacedly, for it involved a breach with popular sentiments. The young Molotov was among those who insisted upon the need of limiting the wages and salaries of Communists, especially those Communist employees who were in the higher income brackets. On his initiative, a party conference in 1922 decided—that, too, was a sign of the times—that "Communist employees whose monthly earnings are above the scales set for the 17th category, must contribute from one quar-

ter to one half of the surplus to a relief fund. Communists receiving above set scales are obliged to contribute to the fund
the entire amount above the set scale." Molotov would have
been incredulous if he had been shown a picture of himself
as he was destined to appear in 1944—in a gold-trimmed diplomatic uniform, as prescribed by a recent decree.

BUT the enthusiasm of equalitarianism soon ebbed. Equality
in material conditions may be good if it is achieved on a high
level, but equality in hunger led to disappointment. When the
process of economic reconstruction began in the 'twenties, the
Soviet Government found that it could not take a single step
forward without breaching the surface cover of equalitarianism in a thousand places. Otherwise economic progress in
Russia would have been impossible. When the peasants were
given the right to sell their products in the free market, the
inevitable consequence was a considerable differentiation in
earnings. Distinctions developed between workers and state
employees. Finally, the new wage scales introduced for the
workers created marked differences between the higher and
lower brackets.

The reaction against the *uravnilovka* was in swing. At first
this reaction was confined to narrow economic spheres, but it
soon spread beyond these limits. In contemporary phraseology
this was a manifestation of "realism," but a realism limited by
principles and habits of thought.

Lenin, Trotsky, and Stalin ventured to adopt the NEP in
1921, admitting it to be a retreat from the Communist achievements of the earlier Soviet period. But a year later, in March,
1922, Lenin proclaimed "the end of the retreat." A little later
Bukharin addressed the peasants with the slogan, "Enrich
yourselves"; but he came to regret these words, which continued to plague him to the very day of his execution. Inequality inevitably proved victorious in practice, while equality was remembered only as a synonym for misery. *But it was
very difficult to incorporate the idea of inequality into the
framework of Communist ideology.*

The new period began with the second Soviet revolution—
the sweeping industrialization and collectivization. The instructions given from above were, "Down with equalitarianism!" Those who attempted to resist were ruthlessly eliminated. In his conflict with the "left-wing factions," Stalin fre-

quently denounced in sharp terms the "nonsense that money was unnecessary" and "trade was a dead letter." He assailed the demand for social equality by dubbing it ironically the *uravnilovka*—contemptuous Russian slang for equalitarianism.

"These people think that Socialism requires equality, equality in the needs and personal life of the members of society," Stalin declared in January, 1934. "These are petty bourgeois views of our left-wing scatterbrains. We know how greatly our industry has been injured by the infantile exercises of our left-wing scatterbrains. The left-wingers do not understand that money and moneyed economy will remain with us for a long time."

Michael Tomsky, leader of the Soviet trade unions, objected to any further differentiation in wage scales, to any additional distinctions of wages between higher and lower paid workers. He was removed and his place taken by the more subservient Shvernik; Tomsky ultimately committed suicide.

"More inequality!" was now also the cry in the army; officer ranks were restored, fraternizing between higher and lower ranks was forbidden, and the authority of officers over privates was extended. The idea was adopted of "Distinguished Men in the Soviet Land," that is, persons who had distinguished themselves in one way or another, and had thus won the right to a higher standard of living. This new aristocracy *in spe* won its rights by labor and sacrifice; it was more reminiscent of those ancient conquerors from whom, through storm and stress, stemmed the future lords, junkers, and noblemen, than of the modern men of property. But the new Soviet aristocracy no longer engaged in the coquetry of unselfishness and equality with the "common man." It demanded earthly compensation, at once and as much as possible. Let each be paid for his deeds, and in accordance with the deeds.

A new class society was in the process of development.

"Socialism Is Inequality"

IT became Stalin's task to bring this chaos of ideas into some sort of unity, to reconcile the new system of inequality with Communism, and to combine the new concepts with the traditions of Lenin's epoch. This task appeared all the more difficult because it was no longer possible to blame the ugly reality, the great poverty of the overwhelming majority, upon the avarice of capitalism, or to charge that this reality was the legacy of capitalism. The inequality now in force was a *new* inequality.

Stalin's concept was based on a distinction between Socialism and Communism.

When the Communist League was founded a hundred years ago, and Marx and Engels proclaimed their "Communist Manifesto," the term "Communism" was used in reference to the future classless society. Later, for various reasons, the term "Socialism" came to mean the same thing. Particularly in Russia, since the beginning of this century, the term "Socialism" alone was used to express the ideal of a harmonious, happy, just social order—an order without poverty, war, and violence.

To be sure, there have been many efforts, in political literature, to distinguish between Communism and Socialism. Marx and Engels themselves (and later, Lenin) spoke, in passing, of the "lower" and "higher" stages of Communism. But Lenin, too, and his entire party regarded Communism as a matter of the near future, the realization of which required only the attainment of a certain technological level. "Communism," he said, "is the Soviet power plus electrification," i.e., a matter of a few years as far as its realization was concerned.

It became Stalin's task, proceeding from the ideas expounded by Lenin, to develop the theory of Socialism as a specific social order, distinct from both capitalism and Communism. According to Stalin's theory, the order now existing in Russia represents complete Socialism. In such an order there is no private economy, there are no persons who live without working, but social equality does not exist. People are paid not "according to need" but "according to deed." In November, 1935, Stalin declared in an address that "the distinction between intellectual and manual labor continues to exist," and that "the productivity of labor is not yet so high as to insure an abundance of consumer goods."

Communism will represent a higher stage of development, he said: "Communism means that in a Communist society everyone works according to his abilities and receives consumer goods not in accordance with what he produces but in accordance with his needs as a culturally developed human being." He assailed those who thought of "material equality on the basis of poverty."

According to Stalin, the transition from Socialism to Communism would be a "painless" process, i.e., without revolution and without a change in government, for the Soviet Government (unlike the preceding Russian governments) was not an obstacle to the realization of complete Communism (contrary to the allegations of the Trotskyites). It is the best possible government for its realization. According to Stalin, it was quite possible to build Socialism in one country alone, and the transition from Socialism to Communism, he maintained, was likewise possible, theoretically, in one country (theoretically—because a military conflict might interfere with the development into Communism). Stalin would not recognize any internal economic impossibility of attaining complete, ideal Communism in one country.

Speaking at the party congress of 1939, Stalin clearly indicated this possibility: "We are moving forward, to Communism," he declared; nor did he regard the "capitalist encirclement" of Russia as an obstacle. Communism, like Socialism, could exist in one area. This pronouncement was immediately taken up by Professor Mitin, the principal commentator on Communist sociology, who developed and emphasized Stalin's new idea. "In his address before the 18th Congress," said Mitin, "Stalin demonstrated the possibility of the transition from Socialism to Communism in one country."

Neither Stalin nor his professors dwelt on these questions more concretely. Their idea, never clearly developed, was to raise production to levels which would bring abundance and surpluses in all spheres; distribution would then become possible not by means of exchange of commodities or through money, but without limitation, just as water is delivered to everyone in unlimited quantity. Such a path to Communism would not impinge upon the welfare of "Distinguished Persons"; for this would not be equalization downward but the elevation of the lower spheres from existing levels. Only a detail was missing—the necessary gigantic production, such as has not been even remotely attained by any country in the world. As regards Russia, she was, on the eve of the war, endlessly

removed from any such possibilities. Stalin's scheme bore no
relation to the facts. Its important element was that the existing poverty and social injustice were attributed to Socialism,
as, in the past, they had been ascribed to capitalism. Socialism
as an imperfect system was now juxtaposed to the mysterious,
nebulous ideal of a perfect Communism, which, to be attained,
required only the loyalty of the citizens of Russia to their government.

The Melting Pot and the New Social Classes

THE conflict between equality and inequality under the
Soviet regime proceeded under an ideological cover
which concealed important social processes.

The period of equalization, embracing the first three to four
years, marked the melting into one mass of all classes and
groups of the old society. All classes were thrown like so much
scrap into a melting pot beneath which burned the fires of the
revolution dissolving all the old identities. Countesses in dirty
aprons served tea to workers and employees in Soviet institutions, court ladies cleaned the streets of snow, steel barons func-
tioned as members of house committees and together with por-
ters and shoemakers solved questions of keeping toilets clean
and obtaining firewood. Workers moved to the villages and
became peasants, while peasants migrated to the cities to try
their luck. Poor people were moved into mansions, while professors and generals had to find room in modest quarters.
Medals, epaulettes, ranks, fortunes disappeared, and new ones
had not yet been created. Everything was topsy-turvy.

But gradually new shapes began to emerge from this socially
amorphous mass. There was a differentiation within the new
mass, and new classes began to appear in the historical arena.

It was a painful process, at times encouraged, at other times
delayed by directives from above; complicated, at some moments, by monstrous repressions, or supported, as it suited the
will of the powers-that-be; progressing silently at some points
or giving rise to bitter factional conflict. There was, for example, a weak effort to facilitate the rise of the class of "nepmen"
—private traders and small industrialists; later they were liqui-

dated. At one time well-to-do peasants were promised certain rights; subsequently these rights were abrogated. At one point foreign concessionaires were invited into the country, with offices, staffs of employees, bank accounts; later they were expelled and lost their money. Each of these classes, as it appeared, provided itself with clients, quarters, comforts; money was utilized on occasion in an effort to establish contacts with government institutions, and to create a favorable social atmosphere. Later all such people, their entourage, and the *décor* they had managed to create around them were hurled back into the melting pot, and the new class, before reaching maturity, disappeared in a flash. Most of these embryos of privileged elements perished in 1929–31 in the new outburst of the revolutionary flame.

They perished, but there was no turning back any longer to any primitive equalitarianism; the process of differentiation proceeded hesitatingly along a new line of development.

This differentiation continued in the 'thirties, with the development of industry and the collectives. The process had not yet been concluded by the end of the 'thirties, but it was not interrupted by the war.

The new social organism has not yet fully crystallized. It faces many crises and metamorphoses, which will inevitably be reflected in crises of a political character.

Soviet society as it appeared at the beginning of the 'forties consisted of four principal classes:

The highest class was that of state employees. It comprised at the beginning of the war from ten to eleven million people, about 14 per cent of the active population.

Workers, rural and urban, comprised from eighteen to twenty million people. Industrial workers, the basic element of this class, numbered about eight million.

Peasants, nearly all collectivized, totaled about forty million, i.e., about half of the working population.

The forced labor class, the exact extent of which is not known, and the number of which has fluctuated at frequent intervals, may be estimated at from seven to twelve million.

These are the four principal elements of the new Soviet society.* In addition, there are the armed forces, pensioners,

* See second footnote on page 98.

etc., whose significance is of secondary importance in the social structure. A comparison of the social pyramids of 1914 and 1940 would appear as follows:

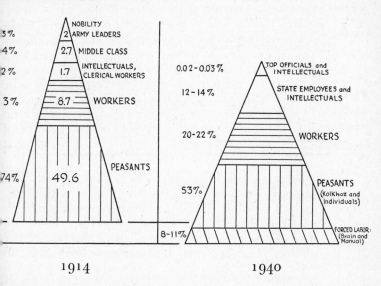

1914   1940

The distinction between the social structure of 1914 and 1940 may be reduced to the following points:

First, the Soviet pyramid is lower, never having attained the upper limits of the social structure of old Russia. There are no millionaires of the old type, there is no court, there are no magnates of the old industry, and even the highest elements of Soviet society enjoy a standard of living lower than that of former capitalists of the middle category.

Second, the Soviet pyramid begins at a lower social point. Its lowest class—forced labor—lives on a very much lower level than did the least secure elements of the old order.

Third, the upper classes of the Soviet pyramid are greater numerically than all the higher classes of old Russia put together. The Soviet Union has more government employees than the entire number of nobles, capitalists, state employees, and intellectual workers of old Russia.

But the picture of the social structure of Soviet Russia viewed with regard to national income is quite different.

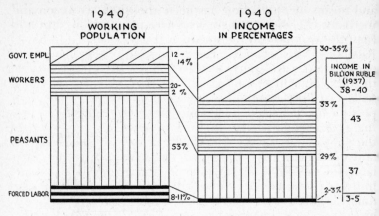

The highest class, comprising from 12 to 14 per cent* of the
population, receives from 31 to 35 per cent of the national income (that is of products distributed and not retained for the
state's various needs). The share of the workers is about the
same despite the fact that they number almost one quarter of
the population. The peasants, who comprise over half the
population, receive a share less than that allotted to the employee class. The least secure, of course, is the class of forced
labor, whose share in the national income is insignificant, although its place in the national economy is extremely important.†

The proud assertion then of Paragraph 4 of the Soviet Constitution that "exploitation of man by man has been wiped out
in the USSR, because private ownership of the instruments

* See second footnote on page 126.
† The above figures, as well as the diagrams, are based on the available material and are drawn with all possible objectivity; however, they must be regarded
as rough estimates. Although Russia has an income tax and account is taken
annually of the income of the various classes, the results are kept a strict state
secret. Information divulged by official sources concerning the class structure
of the country likewise leaves many questions unanswered. In 1937, for example,
official sources reported that the peasantry comprised 61 per cent of the population; in 1939 these sources placed the figure at 46 per cent. The official source
failed to explain the discrepancy.
   Official statistics do not of course mention the category of forced labor. The
workers of this category sometimes appear in the column "Workers," and thus
add to the numerical strength of free labor, or they do not appear at all. For
these reasons the actual numerical strength of the different social classes as
given above does not necessarily coincide with the figures of the official statistical tables.

and means of production has been abolished" is unconvincing indeed. To be sure there is no private ownership; but how can it be asserted that the system as it has developed in Soviet Russia, with its social extremes, is devoid of the elements of exploitation, particularly in the Communist-Marxist sense of the term? The huge interest paid on government loans represents a striking example of "unearned increment," making it possible for the beneficiaries to live without the need of working, or at least to live by the work of others. The guaranty of the right of inheritance is another example. The most important example of all is the large compensation paid for their labor to "the highest ten thousand," and the incomes of many individuals estimated in hundreds of thousands of rubles annually. "Payment according to the quality of labor" is the formula adopted by the Soviet Government to justify in Marxian terms its new concept of exploitation.

The methods of "exploitation" used are as old as the world, and the Soviet system has added nothing new to hoary experience. These methods are: first, wage labor; second, an unfree peasantry; third, slave labor. What *is* new in the Soviet system, distinguishing it from capitalism, is the universal application of these methods by the state. There are no slave owners, industrial magnates, feudal landlords in Russia. But the state is the employer of the free workers, as well as the slave owner and feudal lord. Only the state has the right to use all the historical methods of exploitation, while distributing the product as it sees fit.

This system differs radically from capitalism, and Soviet economists are unquestionably right when they emphasize this distinction. Whether it is a better system for the people is another question.

Industrial Expansion on Communist Lines

EVERY new plant," said Stalin in inaugurating the program of industrial expansion, "represents another fortress of the working class, which strengthens its positions in the struggle with capitalist elements." Every new plant increases the number of workers in the country and decreases the number of individual artisans and peasants; the establishment of a new plant increases the number of that portion of the population which the government regards as most devoted to it, or, at any rate, most obedient. The political objective of expanding the numerical weight of the workers was the main motive behind this policy of rapid industrialization. Military considerations were added later, and have always occupied second place.

In every country industrial development is based on well-calculated business considerations. A new plant must produce more cheaply than other plants, or, at any rate, its operating cost must not exceed those of other plants—otherwise it cannot function. This is a simple fact of progressive industrial development.

But there are occasions, especially in time of war, when problems of accounting and price are forced back to secondary consideration by political necessity. Bombers must be produced at any cost, even in plants which produce at greater cost than is necessary; military railways must be built even though they may have no economic justification for the future. The deficit is borne by the state, that is, by the people, whenever political considerations require new industrial construction.

Soviet industrial development in peacetime offered a model of the *political* development of an economy. It is guided by political principle, not by the calculation of surpluses, cost, and price; although every new plant must, of course, take into consideration the factors of cost of construction and production, these calculations do not have any great significance. Only rarely has the cost of construction been kept down to the figure originally set for the erection of new or expansion of old industrial units, involving the expenditure of hundreds of millions of rubles. In nearly all instances huge additional appropriations were required, and this was considered a matter of course. The problem of the cost and selling price of the product was regarded as secondary—for did not the state have the right to fix prices arbitrarily, and were not the deficits covered from its resources?

Political considerations demanded the development of industry—that was enough. The village shoemaker was able at times to produce shoes from local raw materials more cheaply than were huge shoe factories, but this convincing economic consideration had to give way before political principle. The

mall storekeeper could sell his wares cheaper than the Commissariat of Internal Trade; but freedom of individual econ-
my was contrary to principle. Small private shops may pro-
uce radios, while big plants are unable to meet the demand;
he same is true of many other commodities. But this was
trictly forbidden. Everywhere realism had to give way to prin-
iple.

Some Soviet "industrial giants," representing the achievements of the most modern techniques, are located in the most
distant regions. During the war they have unquestionably
roved useful, but they had been built and had operated for a
ong time for the purposes of a peacetime economy. In the
pinion of many experts, some of the big plants in the Urals,
n Siberia, and other distant places are not economical in the
ustomary sense of the term because of natural circumstances
—distances, inaccessibility, and so on. Their construction and
peration were due not so much to reasons of military pre-
aredness as to political considerations of a general Soviet
haracter.

Before the first World War, for instance, at a time of high
rotectionist tariffs the industry of Leningrad operated with
English coal. Its delivery by sea made it cheaper than Ukrain-
an coal. The Soviet Government, however, in order to stimu-
ate the development of the Russian coal industry, refused to
buy coal abroad. For this reason, coal from the Don Basin de-
ivered over a long distance to Leningrad proved more expen-
ive, not in money (for prices were arbitrarily fixed) but in the
mount of labor power expended, railway cars employed, and
eadjustments necessitated by the needs of production and
ransport. The result was an additional expense covered by the
tate. But the resources of the state, in the final analysis, come
rom the people—from taxes, prices, wages. Once more realism
gave way to principle.

Another instance was the mechanization of Russian agricul-
ure. Nowhere in western Europe or America was agriculture
o backward technically as in prerevolutionary Russia. But
nowhere in the world on the eve of the second World War was
here such an abundance of agricultural machinery, including
he most complex appliances, as in Soviet Russia. This great
ransformation, most of which took place during the 'thirties,
was carried out rather for political than for economic consid-

erations. In the United States only 21 per cent of agricultura
units used tractors, in Russia 93 per cent; in the United State
there were 75,000 combines, in Russia 154,000; in France then
were only 100, in Germany 15!

The organization of the peasantry into collectives in 1929
34 could not have lasted had the old agricultural system r
mained unchanged. Only after the horse had been to a grea
extent supplanted by the tractor, and the tractor had becom
the property not of the peasants or the collective but of th
nearby state tractor station, did the newly established eco
nomic system in the villages begin to correspond to the polit
cal purposes set by the government. The disappearance o
individual economy, the transformation of Russia into a lan
of large-scale agriculture, once it was accomplished, const
tuted a finished, rounded system. But did this represent a sav
ing of labor power, or, on the contrary, an increased expend
ture of labor power for the production of wheat, meat, and s
on? Was the transformation rational in the most realistic sens
of the word, i.e., as measured in terms of prices? These que
tions were relegated to the background. Even if it had bee
demonstrated that the new economy was not rational, politica
considerations would have demanded it imperatively.

Yet, the question of the collectives remains one of the mo
important in Russia, where half the population still works o
the land. In prerevolutionary times the peasant spent only
few rubles annually for the purchase of tools and implement
he was unable to buy even the most necessary, the cheapes
tools. His product was almost wholly the result of his ow
labor. The new system presents an entirely different, extremel
complex picture.

To gather the grain in the fields under the new system it i
necessary that many thousands of workers first obtain th
necessary metal in the mines of the Ukraine or the Ural
Others must dig coal. Still others carry the coal and iron or
on the railroads to huge plants. In these plants thousands c
workers make steel and iron. Then other trains carry the meta
to plants manufacturing agricultural implements, where add
tional thousands of workers and engineers manufacture th
machines, machine parts, and repair material. These ma
chines are distributed by rail, water, and trucks across th
country, into all corners where there are machine-tractor sta

tions. At the same time masses of workers employed in the oil wells of Baku or Grozny dispatch the oil to refineries. The oil is then transformed into gasoline and sent all over Russia by means of various types of transport. At machine-tractor stations and on Soviet state farms millions of people are occupied in the operation and maintenance of the machines.

Everywhere, in all these mines and plants, a large personnel of technicians, bookkeepers, overseers, watchmen, directors is required, in addition to the thousands of workers directly employed in production for the needs of agriculture. Other requirements include the operation of stores, with their managers and salesmen; houses or barracks for handy men and repair men, carpenters, furniture makers; technical schools for training of workers, with their own teachers, directors, guards, and so on.

This colossal apparatus turns out no greater volume of production than the peasants formerly produced almost entirely with their own labor: in general, grain crops, which had continuously increased before the revolution, have not shown a substantial increase in the past twenty years.*

Under the new system agricultural production proceeds on two levels: the first is operated by that portion of industry, from the mine to the machine-tractor station, necessary to keep agriculture going; only the second level is operated by the collectivized peasants. Quite naturally, their share of work is smaller than before and for this reason the population of the villages has decreased without injury to agricultural output. Millions of people, transferred to industry, continue, however, to work for the needs of agriculture: they constitute the human material required by industry to make possible the operation of agriculture. Their remuneration and their living in the cities is more costly than before. This constitutes precisely the effect of the social revolution called the collectivization: the diminution of the peasant class, unreliable politically and, therefore, dangerous for the regime, and an increase in the number of city workers.

Is the new economic system more profitable, that is, have the

* Grain crops in the 'thirties equaled approximately the prewar figures, being sometimes a bit lower and at other times a little higher. Only in 1937, a particularly good year, did they show an important increase over 1913. The crops in 1935-39 were not higher than before the collectivization and mechanization in 1925-29, according to research by Dr. N. M. Jasny.

commodities produced become cheaper (in terms of gold or hours of labor)? Research to date has failed to provide an answer. But there is reason to believe that the answer is in the negative. The sweeping mechanization was carried out not because of economic necessity but because of political considerations.

Between 1928 and 1941 Russia was not only industrialized but superindustrialized. Her agricultural economy was not only mechanized but supermechanized. She was protected from outside competition by a system of superprotectionism. For this reason her population was compelled to make sacrifices which were not merely temporary. Despite the great investments, the people did not improve their standard of living. If ever realism in the national economy gains the upper hand over "principle," that is if the needs of the "common man" begin to dictate policy—and that is extremely likely after the war—Russia will inevitably be compelled to reëxamine the economic validity of many industrial plants, to curtail the mechanization of agriculture, to reduce production costs and the utilization of excessive machinery, to increase the agricultural population, and, in this manner, to expand the amount of commodities available for popular consumption.

The Population Problem

THE population problem in Russia is more political in character than in any other country. Biological phenomena, the normal rate of births and deaths, have less influence upon the evolution of the population than anywhere else. Wars and internal social and political upheavals play a far greater role. The growth of population in the face of an almost stationary population in western Europe has political and military implications. The Soviet Government itself has made the task of facilitating population increase an important feature of its political program.

How strongly political factors determine population growth in Russia may be seen from a few figures. In 1914 Russia had a population of about 170,000,000 (with Finland, Bukhara, and Khiva); a quarter of a century later, after suffering territorial losses, after an alternating decrease and increase in population the figure remained at 170,000,000. Had Russia experienced a normal development under conditions of peace after 1914, had the rate of population increase continued on the level preceding the first World War, Russia's population would have been between 280,000,000 and 290,000,000 today. At the present time, however, it is certainly below 160,000,000.

Two hundred eighty million in theory and 160,000,000 in reality! Of this deficiency of 120,000,000, Russia lost 28,000,-000 in the territories lost after the first World War (the Baltic States, Poland, and others); but not less than 75,000,000 of the shortage (due, in part, to a deficit of births) represents the difference between the aforementioned larger theoretical figure and the actual situation. Political phenomena responsible for this enormous deficiency include:

1. Losses in the first World War.
2. Epidemics and an accelerated death rate in the period from 1914 to 1920.
3. Civil war, 1918–20.
4. Famine, 1921–22.
5. High mortality among deported elements of the population, 1929–34.
6. Famine, 1932–33.
7. Second World War, direct losses.
8. Mortality among war prisoners and excess civilian deaths.
9. Deficit of births because of war conditions.

Population losses due to the first World War and civil war (including the deficit of births), as estimated for 1925, amounted to 1,800,000 in England and 5,600,000 in Germany; the losses suffered by Russia totaled 28,000,000.* The effect of political developments is clearly visible from these figures. After 1925 political factors continued to dominate the population problem in Russia. Even the famines of recent decades were due to political causes rather than natural catastrophes. Walter Duranty has termed them "man-made famines."

It seems as though every nation develops some kind of in-

* According to Frank Lorimer, whose unpublished manuscript on Russian population is quoted in the publication of the League of Nations, *Future Population of Europe,* of the total of twenty-eight millions, two millions are attributed to emigration, less than ten millions to birth deficits, and more than sixteen millions to military and civilian deaths. One third of the losses occurred during the first World War, two thirds during the revolution.

stinct guiding policy in matters affecting population. France, for instance, with her declining birth rate, placed Maurice Gamelin at the head of her armies; his policy in 1939–40 was "to spare the blood" of French troops. In practice this meant capitulation rather than fighting bloody battles and incurring the consequent losses. Russia, at the other extreme, with her enormous birth rate, has produced war leaders who despise economy in the expenditure of lives and are prepared to offer gigantic sacrifices.

In 1944 the League of Nations made public a serious scientific study on *Future Population of Europe and the Soviet Union*. The authors of this objective analysis did an immense amount of work before reaching their very interesting conclusions. For Russia they foresee a population of 250,000,000 by 1970.

There is a fatal flaw in their assumptions, however, for they do not take into consideration the losses suffered by Russia in the current war. They knew, of course, at the time of the publication of their work that Russia had already lost many millions and would lose millions more, but it is impossible to work scientifically with uncertain figures such as those covering Russian war losses now, and in the future. Therefore, the authors eliminated them. Their conclusions are mathematically correct but they have no relation to the facts. How much of their data will be discounted by subsequent history nobody knows, but it seems likely that a very large percentage of the Russian citizens foreseen by the authors will be eliminated by the actual development.

Other authors, not so conscientious, predict a population of 400,000,000 for Russia in the near future. A book published recently by a German writer in this country predicted that Russia would have a population of 550,000,000 by the year 2000!

SOVIET theory holds to the idea that the more favorable the material circumstances of life the more the population multiplies, and that for this reason the growth of population in the land of Socialism should, and indeed does, proceed at rapid pace. According to this theory cessation or retardation of population growth is a sign of decay, i.e., it is a product of capitalism. This is what ails Europe. In Russia the "might and power of Socialism finds clear expression in the unprecedented rapid

empo of population increase"—15.0 per cent in twelve years.*
During the same period, according to *Pravda*, the population
f Italy increased only 9 per cent, of Germany 7 per cent, and
ven of the United States only 11 per cent.

For this reason, "in order to liquidate radically the crisis of
population," in other nations, "it is necessary to liquidate
apitalism and to establish a Soviet regime."

The first drafts of the Five-Year Plan envisaged a rapid
growth of the Soviet population. It was assumed that the annual increase would be 3,000,000 to 3,500,000, and that the
otal by 1930 would be 160,000,000; in 1933 Stalin proudly
sserted that the figure was already 168,000,000, and in 1937,
ccording to him, it was to be 180,000,000 for "the death rate
has declined, the birth rate has risen, and the net growth is
mmeasurably greater . . . we now have an annual increase of
population of 3,000,000." If this development had proceeded
ininterruptedly Russia would have had a population of more
han 192,000,000 in 1941; together with the new regions (the
Baltic States, Bessarabia, etc.) it would have exceeded 215,000,-
00—and this would indeed have been a fabulous growth. The
econd Five-Year Plan anticipated a population of 180,700,000
or January, 1938. Actually it amounted to approximately
68,000,000.

But in 1937 a census was taken in Russia and it showed such
deficiency compared with Stalin's predictions and the as-
umptions of the Five-Year Plans that the directors of the
Census Bureau were executed. The results of the census were
not made public, and a new census was ordered for 1939. But
he new census also showed a deficiency of 10,000,000 to 12,-
00,000. The government had to recognize it as official. Its
esults have been erroneously interpreted both in Russia and
broad.

Erroneous, first of all, is the theory that cultural and mate-
ial improvement necessarily leads to rapid growth of popu-
ation. On the contrary, the most rapid increase of population
s observed frequently among the most backward peoples who
have many families of eight to ten persons. On the other hand,
ultural development usually leads to a decline in the birth
ate. The most rapid population growth ever experienced by
Russia, greater than in the Soviet period, was not in the cities

* *Pravda* on the 1939 Census.

but in the villages in the nineteenth and early twentieth cen
turies, before the first World War. It may safely be assumed
that there will be a decline in the Russian birth rate if and
when living conditions for the general population improve.

Erroneous, too, is the widely held idea concerning the char
acter of population growth from 1917 to the present.

At the end of the eighteenth century the population of
European Russia amounted to 25 per cent of that of the whole
of Europe. It has remained approximately at that level until
today; namely, 26 per cent in 1880, 28 per cent in 1900, 24 per
cent in 1930, 25 per cent in 1940. (It was 29 per cent in 1940
along with the new territories acquired by Russia.) Those in
clined to belief in mystical forces may draw relief and support
from this amazing constancy. For a period of 150 years Europe
had experienced many bloody wars with different population
losses for individual nations; there was an enormous decline in
the birth rate in the West and Russia's frontiers have changed
several times during this period. West and East traveled their
separate courses of development, but Russia's proportion re
mained almost constant.

In order to evaluate correctly the future political-military
power of Russia two important factors must be taken into con
sideration.

Since the end of the nineteenth century Japan's growth ha
added a new potential front for Russia and has increasingly
absorbed her forces. Like the United States, which has been
compelled to build a two-ocean navy instead of the one which
had guarded her "Atlantic Front" of the nineteenth century
Russia moved into the difficult position of a nation with two
fronts, a position analogous to Germany's. Before that Russian
manpower and industry had been concentrated almost en
tirely on the European side of the international balance of
power. Since 1890 or 1900 she has been able to use only part
of her economic resources and manpower in the task of coun
terbalancing other European forces.

Asiatic Russia has grown with astonishing rapidity. At the
end of the eighteenth century the population of Siberia and
Russian Central Asia amounted to 1,000,000; in 1914 it was
21,000,000, and in 1939 it had risen to 33,000,000.* Today it i

* Bukhara and Khiva are included in 1914 as well as in 1939.

probably 38,000,000, the increase being due primarily to the evacuations of population from western Russia. The population of the whole of Asiatic Russia, including the Transcaucasus, was about 41,000,000 in 1939.

But European Russia, as distinct from all other regions of the vast country, has always been and will remain for a long time the soul of the nation. The entire population of European Russia (within her 1921–39 frontiers) was about 112,000,-000 in 1914; twenty-two years later it numbered 129,500,000.

The weight of a nation in international affairs depends first and foremost on her adult male population. The male population of Russia in Europe (within the frontiers of 1921–39) has grown less rapidly: it was about 54,000,000 at the time of the revolution, about 55,000,000 nine years later, and about 60,-000,000 in 1939. (Although in possession of all the exact data, the government has refrained from making public many features of the census which would have helped clarify this question in details.)

Even before the first World War, Russia, like most other countries, had more women than men—the women predominating by less than one per cent. Naturally, more men than women died during the war period. But in all belligerent countries the considerable predominance of women over men at the end of the first World War had gradually declined as the older generation disappeared and the new came into being.

But Russia presents an astonishing exception. In 1914 there were 67,700,000 men and 67,900,000 women in Russia (the future Soviet territories of European and Asiatic Russia). The difference was insignificant. In 1926 there were 71,000,000 men and 76,000,000 women—a difference of 5,000,000; in part this was explained by the effects of the war and civil war. The most significant feature of the situation, however, was that subsequently, from 1926 to 1939, a period of peace when a gradual normalization was to have been expected, the actual development was in reverse. In 1939 there were 81,600,000 men and 88,800,000 women in the territory of European and Asiatic Russia, a difference of 7,200,000. The excess of women over men had increased tremendously. It was a development unprecedented for any country.

This excess of women over men was even greater when considered from the viewpoint of European Russia alone. For

Asiatic, and particularly non-Slavic peoples, have always had more men than women. In European Russia the excess of women over men was probably 9,000,000 in 1939. (No official figures are available and one must fall back upon indirect deductions.)

Adult men die off more rapidly in Russia than women, a fact constituting the most serious population problem for the Soviet Union. The economically active sex lives under much greater dangers to life and health in Russia than anywhere else, for in addition to occupational hazards there are also political hazards, such as the deportation of millions of kulaks in 1930–34, which affected for the most part the male population of the villages. Their deportation to the east and north resulted in a rapid death rate among the males. (According to available information women constitute only about 10 per cent of inmates in labor camps.) The expansion of the deportation system contributed to the population increase of many regions in Siberia, but this also explained the decrease of the male population in European Russia and the increased death rate of males.

In the new world war Russian losses at the front, consisting almost exclusively of males, may well reach figures utterly unprecedented in Russian and world history. To these losses must be added:

The tremendous death rate of Russian war prisoners held by Germany and her satellites.

The high death rate of the civil population of Russia, particularly in the occupied regions, the transportation of several million people for forced labor to Germany and the death of a considerable portion of them.

The evacuation of at least 12,000,000 to the east under extremely difficult conditions.

It may be considered certain that Russia will emerge from this war greatly weakened in population, particularly in the number of males able to work. European Russia, the heart and brain of the country, will probably decline to the population status of 1914, while the number of males will fall even below that.

But after the war, too, political factors will continue to play the decisive part. The biological capacity for increase is great and is enhanced by public health improvements and the development of medical science; on the other hand the rate of population increase is retarded by the general expansion of culture and civilization. But much stronger in Russia is the effect of political factors, which, beginning with 1914, have enormously reduced the natural growth of population.

Hitler has said, "Let us not forget that the Slav East is more fertile than all the rest of Europe." Napoleon said, "In a century Europe will become Cossack." But the fact is that until now wars and the domestic policies of Russian governments have belied these predictions.

VII

The New Upper Classes, I. Their Rise

WHILE the old classes were making their last efforts to resist the new regime in Russia, a new class of government employees was taking shape—a class without precedent in any other country either in point of numbers or in significance. In the cities, where political life was concentrated, there remained, apart from the silent workers, only the employee-intellectuals. Nowhere and at no time had such a phenomenon been known before. All those who had previously performed the functions of tradesmen, salesmen, agents, middlemen, journalists, doctors, lawyers, actors, artists, manufacturers, engineers and parliamentarians now entered into the composition of the new class. In the villages, too, administrative and economic functions now began to be taken over by the growing cadres of the new employees. A new social class, remotely resembling the old Russian intelligentsia, was coming into being.

This new intelligentsia, made up of state employees or state officialdom, constitutes the highest class of Soviet society.* It governs the state, administers the economy, conducts the schools, directs the army, takes care of the sick, creates literature, runs the press, and concerns itself with science. The differences that exist between the various sectors of this new great social class—income, ideological, and political differences—do not disturb the internal harmony of this unique class of intellectual workers. Its growth under the Soviet regime, its influence, its relation to the government, and its political orientation become increasingly significant year by year.

Those who would foresee the future of Russia must first make a careful study of the new intelligentsia. In postrevolutionary periods in all countries, when popular movements sub-

* Before the revolution the term "intelligentsia" was rather vague; it meant chiefly members of the liberal professions. In the Soviet period it is being applied to all white-collar workers, thus embracing not less than 80 per cent of employees in the government's offices. The terms "intelligentsia" and "government employees" became almost identical and are so used in this book.

side and political struggles become restricted to the activities of limited social circles, it has always been the intelligentsia that came forward as the fountainhead of new ideas and creative instrument of public opinion. The "middle estate" had more leisure and wealth than the lower classes, i.e., those engaged in manual labor; and the intelligentsia had more knowledge. The "middle estate" and the intelligentsia were the decisive elements of public opinion in western Europe in the nineteenth century, and their conservative or oppositionist tendencies have frequently determined the course of political development. Later, with the growth of industry, the old middle propertied classes of the cities ("the petty economy") diminished in size, but there was no polarization of the population. Between the "highest 50,000" and the lower millions there always evolved a "new middle estate," possessing, to be sure, neither capital nor its own economy, but continuing, in many other respects, the political functions of the urban amalgam composed of artisans, storekeepers, poets, scientists, and orators. Like its predecessor, the old middle estate, it enjoyed a standard of living higher than that of manual workers. Its position in society, in the national economy, and in the state, its intellectual life and interests often made it one of the decisive elements in politics.

In no country, however, is the role of this class so great as in present-day Russia, and for the following reasons: first, in Russia, as distinguished from other countries, it is not only the middle estate in the accepted sense of the term, but also the highest class, for above it there is no landed aristocracy, nor are there any financial or industrial magnates; second, the lower elements in Russia are inarticulate; and third, as regards its numbers, the new middle estate has assumed unprecedented proportions.

Communism and the Intelligentsia

THE deep ideological and political antagonism which, in the early period of the Soviet regime, divided Bolshevism and all the propertied and middle classes of old Russia applied particularly to the intelligentsia, upon whose members Communism wielded little influence. From the ranks of this old intelligentsia came the more capable and skilful leaders of all the anti-Communist movements, political, religious, and philosophical. There were in its midst few supporters of the old prerevolutionary Russia; its tendencies found expression in ideas ranging from moderate-liberal to left-wing Socialist. This old intelligentsia resisted the new regime before submitting; and even in submitting, after a struggle of three or four years, it remained a source of protest and discontent.

At the same time the dissolution of the old social order was proceeding rapidly. The higher classes disappeared one after another, and by the end of 1920 there were no more landlords, industrialists, private bankers, or big businessmen in Russia. After another ten or fifteen years most of the small traders and individual peasants had likewise disappeared. The intelligentsia alone survived, despite its antagonism to the regime in the early period of the new order. It proved impossible to wipe out the intelligentsia, even though the government had the power to do so. The intelligentsia was needed more than ever—in wrecked industry, in the medical profession struggling desperately against disease and epidemics, in the field of education, in the new military academies, and in the army. All government institutions were being filled with new people, and many posts, except the very highest, had to be entrusted to the oppositionist intelligentsia. It constituted the government machine and —such was the paradox during those early years—it sent anti-Communists to the Soviets at every opportunity that offered. The fact is that the Soviet regime was governing through an anti-Communist administrative apparatus.

"The bourgeois intelligentsia," said Lenin, "does not represent an independent economic class and therefore does not constitute an independent political force." His theory was that the intelligentsia would remain the enemy of Communism as long as there were higher classes to utilize its services, but that it would veer to the support of Communism after capitalism had been abolished. According to Lenin, the intelligentsia constituted a transitory, not a permanent, independent class, and had no place of its own in the great battle of history. It was entirely possible to move it to the side of Communism, but in any case it was "necessary to learn from it without making, however, the slightest political concessions to these people."

In those days promises of material advantage alternated with threats. Despite the fever of equalitarianism raging at that time, Lenin promised privileges to scientists, engineers, and the "bourgeois intelligentsia" in general. He offered "these people" inducements to build great new laboratories, to expand the universities, and to create working conditions for scientists superior to those of any other country. But he frequently added that the resistance of the intelligentsia must be ruthlessly broken.

He carefully followed the fluctuations in the sentiments of the intelligentsia and looked forward to the time when it would be possible to bring it wholeheartedly to his support. More than once he declared prematurely that the change had come in the sentiments of the intelligentsia, when, as a matter of fact, the evolution had barely begun. "Tens and tens of thousands [of intellectuals] have served us faithfully because they were moved to our side," said Lenin. "They came to us from the other camp, having been transformed into our conscious supporters."*

In reality, without consciously joining the ranks of Communism, the intelligentsia gradually withdrew between 1918 and 1920 from active participation in politics; it seemed hopeless to fight, and, besides, there was inner disillusionment combined with loss of faith in former political ideas. What came to dominate the intelligentsia was not so much a Communist orientation as a general disorientation.

The political vacillations of the regime with respect to the intelligentsia continued with remarkable regularity, but the basic attitude was one of distrust. Neither the restoration of industry in the 'twenties, accomplished with the aid of the technological intelligentsia, nor the expansion of scientific institutes and other institutions, nor the great expansion of the state apparatus, providing a place for everybody, including even the least capable of the intellectuals, their wives, mothers, and children—nothing could convert the intelligentsia to active support of Communism. Some intellectuals to be sure eventually found their way into the Communist party, but this fact only increased the regime's distrust of the rest.

Periods of moderation were regularly succeeded by periods of ruthless repression. In 1928 came the great Shakhta trial, which ended in the conviction of forty-nine "Wreckers"—engineers and technicians—five of whom were shot. They were accused of having deliberately disorganized and wrecked the

* Address, December 5, 1920.

coal industry, of having been in contact with foreign governments and émigré counterrevolutionists, of having flooded the
mines, and, in general, of having committed sabotage with the
object of turning the workers against the Soviet regime. The
trial had all the earmarks of a political demonstration, and was
viewed as a signal for a new attack upon the intelligentsia. Far-
reaching conclusions were drawn from it. "The bourgeois intelligentsia," declared Stalin, "is infected with the disease of
wrecking . . . The malicious wrecking on the part of the top
elements of the bourgeois intelligentsia constitutes the chief
form of resistance by the moribund classes of our country."
Another trial staged by the government concerned sections of
the food industry. It was not held in public, but forty-eight
food specialists were shot.

Those were the years of collectivization, of the first Five-
Year Plan, of mass exile. Several thousand engineers and intellectuals were arrested, and from these prisoners were created
the cadres of engineers and directors employed on the great
public works built by the labor of inmates of forced-labor
camps. Two years after the Shakhta trial there took place the
similar trial of the so-called Industrial party, in which another
group of influential intellectuals was accused of wrecking.

The case of the "Academicians" occupied public attention
from 1929 to 1931. This involved more than 150 scientists and
professors, who were scattered through various prisons, the
case being concluded, without a public trial, only in the summer of 1931. Many were executed and others sentenced to various terms of exile. Thus it was a very difficult period for the
terrorized, utterly helpless mass of the intelligentsia.

But the fear that dominated the intelligentsia, together with
its uncertainty as to its status and rights, reacted unfavorably
upon the progress of economic construction. The situation,
however, soon took a new turn.

Fluctuations in Policy

A NEW crop of intellectuals made its appearance. Young
people of the Soviet generation were being graduated
from secondary and higher educational institutions. They were
carefully sifted before being admitted to study courses, and

most of them were members of the Communist Youth League
who had no recollection or knowledge either of the old regime
or of democracy. Ignorant of the traditions of the old intelligentsia, but familiar with the required Soviet political terminology, these people at first evoked no suspicion or fears on
the part of the regime. On the contrary, the road to the solution of the accursed problem of the intelligentsia now appeared
to have been opened through the succession of generations,
and through selection and training. Among the new elements
there were many children of workers, and this served as an
added guaranty of "loyalty." Many of the new young intelligentsia joined the party, increasing the percentage of Communist engineers, lawyers, doctors, and so on.

Six months after the trial of the Industrial party, the regime's anti-intelligentsia attitude was succeeded by another
policy: the government seemed to turn its face toward the
intelligentsia. In June, 1931, Stalin declared that whereas,
only two years before, the intelligentsia "had been infected
with the wrecking disease," leaving the government no re-
course but ruthlessness, "new sentiments among the old technological intelligentsia" had now taken shape. "Even the confirmed wreckers of yesterday are beginning to coöperate with
the working class," said Stalin. "The attitude of the old technological intelligentsia has already begun to change."

For this reason Stalin now promised a new policy. "Our policy now," he said, "must be to attract the intelligentsia and
show concern for it." "We must alter our attitude toward the
technological intelligentsia of the old school." This was an
attempt at *rapprochement* with the old as well as the new
intelligentsia, for it was the period of feverish industrial construction and collectivization.

Half a year later, however, Stalin again thundered public
threats against wreckers and saboteurs, including those "professors who in their wrecking go to the length of infecting
cattle in collectives and on Soviet farms with plague germs and
the Siberian anthrax, spreading meningitis among horses, and
so on." He accused them of "organizing mass looting and theft
of state property and of the property of coöperatives and collectives." "Theft and plunder in plants, warehouses, and commercial enterprises—these are the main activities of these
people," he charged. Addressing his associates, Stalin accused

them angrily of "gazing indifferently upon such manifestations." This time the accusations and repressions fell upon
both the old and new intelligentsia.

Soon after came another change. From 1934 to 1936 arrests
among the intelligentsia diminished and working conditions
improved. The general policy was directed toward the promo-
tion of national unity and class collaboration; the lack of legal
status of various Soviet social groups, as reflected in the former
constitutions, gave way to nominal equality before the law. For
the intelligentsia, this appeared to indicate a readiness on the
part of the regime to overlook past sins: the sins of bourgeois
origin, of earlier sympathy with oppositionist parties and
groups, past offenses that had led to arrests, and other dark
spots in biographies. Indeed, in his address dealing with the
new constitution (November, 1936), after speaking of the
status of the workers and peasants, Stalin declared: "The intelligentsia has suffered many changes . . . It is now united in
its roots with the working class and peasantry . . . The intelligentsia is now a full-fledged member of Soviet society, and participates together with the workers and peasants in the building of the new classless society."

Nevertheless Stalin retained his doubts. The intelligentsia
had by now developed into a potentially powerful force; even
numerically it had become larger than the industrial working
class, while its social significance was out of proportion to its
numbers. During the discussions of the new constitution
(1935–36), a proposal was brought forward—with the apparent
purpose of emphasizing the final *rapprochement* between the
regime and the intelligentsia—to add to the first article of the
Soviet Constitution (the one stating that the Soviet Union "is
a state of workers and peasants") the words "and of the toiling
intelligentsia."*

But Stalin opposed this. "The intelligentsia," he said, "has
always been, and remains, but a layer between two classes, a
prosloika. Previously it was recruited from the nobility, the
bourgeoisie, and, in part, from the peasants and workers. In
our time the intelligentsia is recruited primarily from the
workers and peasants. But it remains a layer between two

* This proposal was offered very cautiously, for the word "toiling" left room
for future persecution of "capitalist restorationists," i.e., of any group of the
intelligentsia.

classes, not a class." The proposal to mention the intelligentsia
in the constitution was rejected.

Lenin's concept of the intelligentsia as an intermediate layer
might have been justified at a time when it was numerically a
handful. But at the end of the 'thirties this argument, coming
from Stalin, was an anachronism, and served only to accentu-
ate the continued distrust of the intelligentsia, even of its loyal
portion, including that belonging to the Communist party.

Indeed, at the very moment that the new constitution went
into effect (1936), the regime launched the operation which,
generally known as "the great purge," was in reality a great war
against the new intelligentsia. The purge affected intellectual
circles almost exclusively; it struck primarily the Communist
portion of the intelligentsia, but also nonparty circles. At the
end of the purge, Stalin declared that 500,000 new employees
had been added to the government apparatus during that period; most of these replaced those who had been purged. The
mass character of the purge, the severity of the punishments
inflicted, the senselessness of the arrests, and the unbridled
power of the NKVD served to determine for a time the relations between the regime and the intelligentsia.

Theories hostile to the intelligentsia, especially to the party
intelligentsia, again prevailed in party circles. Only those can
be considered true champions of Communism, it was said once
more, who live by manual labor, in mines, plants, and fields;
but when they "break away from their class" and move up to
nonmanual occupations, when they attend universities and
technical schools, they begin to think and feel differently: they
become unreliable from the Communist point of view.

The great purge ended at the beginning of 1939, and was
followed by a new swerve in the direction of the intelligentsia.
At a party conference in March, 1939, Stalin said:

"There are widespread views in our party hostile to the
Soviet intelligentsia . . . There is a careless, contemptuous
attitude toward the Soviet intelligentsia, which is treated as a
stranger, even as an element hostile to the working class and
the peasantry. The intelligentsia has experienced a radical
change . . . These comrades continue to regard the intelligentsia and to treat it in a manner that was justified in the past,
when the intelligentsia served the landlords and capitalists."

Interpreting in his own way the history of the dissolution and death of the former intelligentsia, Stalin concluded: "Hand in hand with the process of differentiation and break-up of the old intelligentsia went the stormy process of formation, mobilization, and gathering of forces of the new intelligentsia. Hundreds of thousands of young people, children of the working class and peasantry, went into the schools and technological institutes. A new Soviet intelligentsia, closely bound to the people, was thus created. But there are those in our party who assert that workers and peasants cease to be human beings, or become human beings of an inferior kind, when they pass through educational institutions."

Then came the second World War and, nine months later, the fall of France. A military-industrial fever seized Moscow, the general situation again grew tense, and new blows began to descend upon the intelligentsia, directed this time particularly against their numbers in industry. The decrees of the second half of 1940 placed upon the directors of plants, engineers, and technicians responsibility for bottlenecks and failures for which the persons in question, directors of enterprises or their branches, could not possibly have been responsible. The penalties imposed were very severe. A series of trials resulted in jail sentences of from five to eight years. They were demonstration trials designed not so much to punish the accused as to put fear in the hearts of others.

The wartime policy with respect to the intelligentsia ever since the middle of 1941 has again been a dual one. The war, on the one hand, has facilitated collaboration among all elements and classes of the population; officially the bourgeois origin of some, and even the anti-Communist record of others, have been forgotten. The new intelligentsia has been encouraged, advanced to prominent positions, acclaimed: those who have been thus favored include writers like Ehrenburg, Tolstoy, and Sholokhov; generals and marshals like Zhukov, Vatutin, Vasilevsky, Malinovsky, and Rokosovsky; metropolitans, patriarchs, inventors, and professors. At the same time, the new intelligentsia has been kept under rigid control. The close watch maintained over the military intelligentsia is only one aspect of the general system.

Thus, after twenty-seven years, the problem of the intelligentsia remains unsolved. It is perhaps the greatest problem confronting Russian Communism.

A Strange Amalgam

IF we may judge the political physiognomy of the new intelligentsia by its origins, it appears to be a curious conglomerate of all classes of old and new Russia, with a strong admixture of the old elements.

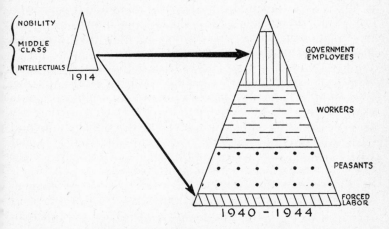

Only an insignificant percentage of the propertied classes of old Russia transferred to manual labor after the revolution, that is, became workers or peasants. Among the latter there are no former nobles, big businessmen, or intellectuals. On the contrary, these elements of the population went into the government service, for the most part in accordance with their special capacities. Moreover, in consequence of economic necessity, the members of their families, including their wives and mothers, who had not had to work, also became Soviet employees, though only rarely workers. In this manner the former propertied classes joined the ranks of the new intelligentsia, whose composition is as follows:

1. *Prerevolutionary Government and Communal Employees.*

Before the first World War these numbered between 600,000 and 700,000. The number increased in the first half of the first World War; if we include communal and other public service employees, the total before the revolution was about 1,000,-

ooo. After the revolution some of these remained in the Baltic States, eastern Poland, and Bessarabia after those regions had been lost by Russia, while others, particularly higher-ranking employees, emigrated to other countries. We have no figures showing the effects of these changes, but it is probable that more than 500,000 former government employees remained in the Soviet Union.

The Soviet revolution destroyed the old government machine, but the former state employees remained part of the new higher class.* As their numbers were diminished by death, their children gradually filtered into economic and administrative life as Soviet employees. Many had abandoned their old traditions, while some had been sincerely converted to Communism. On the whole, however, these elements retain strong recollections of the old regime, of old Russia, of the security of their families under the old order, of the old religion, and the old army. This group includes a particularly high percentage of former nobles.

2. The Former Nobility.

With the exception of those who were exterminated or who managed to emigrate, the members of this group and their families have become government employees. Personal friendship and intellectual affinity bound them to the first group—the old government employees. In old Russia they were represented politically by the small but powerful Nationalist party that dominated the government. Time has altered this group, too, but if there still remain in Russia any persons who dream of a restoration, they are probably part of this element.

Before the first revolution, there were 114,000 persons with estates of more than 100 *desiatins* (270 acres); they and their families totaled about 400,000.

The old Russian nobility, which included practically all the great landowners and many government employees, represented about 1½ per cent of the population, i.e., about 2,500,-

---

* For example, Kaganovich created something of a sensation when he reported at the 16th Party Congress, thirteen years after the November revolution, that there were 251 former nobles, businessmen, theologians, and former employees of the ministry of finance employed in the Commissariat of Finance, comprising no less than 41 per cent of the higher staff. He disclosed also that there were 39 "strangers," including 15 nobles, landlords, priests, etc., employed in an important division of the Central Committee of Trade Unions.

ooo persons of all ages at the time of the revolution. If we exclude from this number minors, émigrés, and those who perished in the civil war or later, there remain no fewer than 1,000,000 former nobles or their descendants, who have been incorporated in the Soviet administrative apparatus. It is paradoxical but true that the number of state employees originating from the old nobility is greater under the Soviet regime than it was before the revolution.

3. Prerevolutionary Military Elements, Mainly Officers.

At the time of the revolution there were about 300,000 army officers. Many of these joined the White armies, and later emigrated. A great many were killed in the civil war. On the other hand, the Soviet Government, as is well known, tried hard to enrol former officers in its military service, and many old generals received important posts in the Red Army. Their children also belong to the apparatus of Soviet officialdom, partly military but for the most part civil (except during the war period). They probably total between 100,000 and 150,000 persons, who still wield considerable influence despite their limited numbers.

4. Former Priests and Their Children.

At the time of the revolution Christian priests and their families numbered between 500,000 and 600,000. The ministers of non-Christian religions numbered 50,000. Very few remained in their profession. A great many were either exiled or executed. Probably about 200,000 or 300,000 are now Soviet state employees.

The four groups just discussed were the pillars of old Russia. Between 1,500,000 and 2,000,000 persons originating from those groups are now part of the Soviet administration.

5. Commercial and Industrial Elements of Old Russia.

This was a class made up of various elements, from small traders to bankers and industrial magnates. They numbered together with their families between 5,500,000 and 6,000,000 persons. Few of them emigrated; some remained in regions that Russia had lost.

These former large and small capitalists who remained in

Russia tried for some years to continue their independent economy, and felt rather hopeful during the period of the NEP. But every year, in increasing numbers, they joined the army of Soviet state employees, and their children made no effort to follow the bourgeois line. Within ten years all opportunities for private industrial and commercial enterprise had disappeared.

A very small percentage of this class became workers or peasants; a great number went into the government service. No fewer than 2,000,000 or 3,000,000 persons of "bourgeois origin" are now in the state apparatus. Some fill minor positions as salesmen, stenographers, etc., but the majority are brain workers, i.e., they belong to the intelligentsia.

6. *The Old Intelligentsia.*

Before the revolution this term was applied to all educated persons and to those of intellectual interests. These included students, who played an important political role in old Russia, and various grades of state employees; the educated elements of the higher classes were frequently thought of as members of the intelligentsia. But for the sake of clarity and precision, we define the intelligentsia as persons engaged in intellectual pursuits; except for the aforementioned state employees, the intelligentsia included doctors, lawyers, journalists, actors, teachers, artists, engineers, and a great many others engaged in a variety of occupations.

The transformation of these social groups into Soviet state employees was easier and more rapid than in the case of other classes. Those formerly employed in private enterprises adjusted themselves automatically to the government service with the transfer of industry and trade to the state. Engineers remained at their old posts and became Soviet employees. Opportunities for private practice were gradually reduced also for doctors, lawyers, and writers, and all of them eventually found themselves incorporated in the Soviet administrative machine.

These groups totaled between 1,000,000 and 1,300,000 at the time of the revolution, or, together with their families, from 3,000,000 to 4,000,000 people. The fifth and sixth groups constituted in old Russia the bulwark of the liberal but not of the revolutionary opposition. For years after the revolution, the majority of Soviet employees were recruited from the two last-named groups.

7. *Workers.*

After the November revolution, many workers went into the government service. The first to do so were members of the Communist party who, in many instances, now received important jobs; then came nonpartisan workers and, last, workers belonging to other parties. They received posts in the offices of newly formed organizations—trade-unions, plant committees, coöperatives, and various commercial and industrial institutions. For workers transfer to the government service meant great social advancement. This was even truer of their children, who now began to prepare themselves for intellectual occupations offering greater opportunities.

The number of workers and persons of proletarian origin in the government service continued to grow in the 'twenties and 'thirties. In the 'thirties even those workers who had migrated from the villages in the Soviet period and had received some training in the cities and risen to higher levels got government jobs. They were of mixed worker and peasant origin. Many workers, however, received posts not in the economic but in administrative and other government bureaus. The special confidence accorded by the government to persons of proletarian origin facilitated their administrative careers. The number of workers who became government employees amounted to scores of thousands; no exact figures have ever been published. But their entry into the government service involved a loss to industry of the more intelligent and better qualified elements. Only in 1940, almost on the eve of the war, did the Soviet Government begin to take measures to stop this depletion of industry.

8. *Peasants.*

Soviet employees of peasant origin are to be found in considerable numbers among the lower grades of the government apparatus, particularly in the field of agriculture. Many peasant youths who went to the cities managed to get through various schools and even higher educational institutions. Many of them took their places in the ranks of the Soviet intelligentsia as agronomists, veterinarians, teachers, etc. Official statistics afford an interesting contrast between the prerevolutionary period and that preceding the present war. Before the revolution peasants made up from 14 to 20 per cent of the students in colleges and universities; the children of workers were almost entirely absent. In 1938, on the other hand, the children of peasants and workers totaled between 50 and 53 per cent of all such students.

Rapid Increase

TO understand the fantastic growth of the new higher class, we must bear in mind that the total number of government employees, about 1,000,000 at the time of the revolution, had reached 2,767,000 by 1924. Ten years after the Soviet revolution, when industry had barely been restored to prewar levels, although Russia meanwhile had lost 20 per cent of her population by being deprived of the territories previously mentioned, the number of government employees had reached 4,000,000. Neither the workers nor the peasants had increased in number during that ten-year period; only the total number of government employees had increased fourfold. It was strange to see the army of intellectual workers overtaking all others numerically. Two years later their number rose to 4,600,000.

But then came the years of "the great upheaval," 1929–30, the period of industrialization and collectivization. The number of industrial workers began to grow rapidly, but the hosts of government employees remained far in advance. By 1933 they had reached the gigantic total of 8,011,000, and by 1935, 8,780,000.*

The 1937 census disclosed the fact that the intelligentsia had reached a total of 9,591,000, or between 13 and 14 per cent of the population. Its numbers continued to rise, reaching more than 10,000,000 by June, 1941.†

* These figures are actually underestimates, for they do not include the figures covering the following state agencies: NKVD; the apparatus of the Communist party and the Komsomol; the Commissariat of Defense. These three groups added several hundred thousand to the army of government employees. The exact figures are a state secret.

† There are an additional 2,000,000 employees, or 3 per cent of the popula-

To understand the significance of these figures, we must remember that all the higher classes of prerevolutionary Russia, including the government apparatus and private industry, totaled about 7 per cent of the population. If we add to this the prerevolutionary intelligentsia and the office workers, the total came to 8 or 9 per cent. These were the organizers of the national economy and the administrators of the old empire.

The present situation indicates that the state and economic apparatus, organizing and directing the physical labor of the masses, has more than doubled. To support the apex of the social pyramid was a great burden before the revolution, when it was necessary to maintain from 10,000,000 to 12,000,000 members of the propertied and middle classes. But far greater is the burden of maintaining 24,000,000 to 28,000,000 government employees (these figures include their families) simultaneously with intensified investment in industry.

What is the explanation of this phenomenon? Is it the fact that the government is now spending more money and using more people in education, science, medicine, and sanitation? The number of teachers has reached 970,000; the number of doctors, 130,000, and so on. But all these changes in policy, education, and public health do not begin to solve the riddle of the many millions of government employees.

What is more, despite their constant increase, their numbers were never sufficient; new cadres were being sought uninterruptedly. Even during the period of great industrial unemployment in the 'twenties, government employees were never discharged. "We have no people!" is the cry heard from the provinces whenever instructions covering new tasks and new plans arrive "from the center." The shortage of manpower for the Soviet machine was the subject of discussion in the Soviets and at party meetings. Young people graduated from secondary and higher schools were snapped up without delay; tens of thousands were thus poured annually straight from the schools into the administrative and economic machine. But it was like drinking salt water; the greater the amount swallowed, the greater grew the thirst, and again and again rose the cry

tion, who cannot be included either in the intelligentsia or in the ranks of manual labor; these are minor employees. The total number of government employees on the eve of the war was therefore between 12,000,000 and 13,000,000, or 17.5 per cent of the population.

to Moscow: "We have no people." Moscow replied angrily: "You must find them! Seek and ye shall find!" And once more the search was resumed.

Efforts were also made to reduce the dimensions of the monstrously swollen machine, for it constituted an intolerable burden on the state budget. Although the matter was not discussed publicly, the higher circles understood perfectly that the millions of government employees weighed very heavily upon the national economy, for 12 or 14 per cent of the population consumed as much as 30 or 35 per cent of the national income. "Reduction of the apparatus" was constantly discussed by the central and provincial authorities. Periodically draconic measures were resorted to with a view to achieving this purpose, when by a stroke of the pen chiefs were ordered to cut their staffs 10 to 20 per cent. There were scores of such orders. But, contrary to many other decrees of the Soviet Government, these failed to produce results. At first the orders were obeyed, but the work began to suffer and then, gradually, almost imperceptibly, new cadres of employees were engaged, and frequently the new total exceeded the old in many a Soviet institution. The central authorities, their attention being engaged in other drives, could only shrug their shoulders.

For example, there was a big leap forward during the first Five-Year Plan, when the total number of government employees increased from 4,000,000 to 8,000,000. The plan had modestly envisaged that the "number of government employees will increase by 6 to 10 per cent during the five-year period"; in reality, the increase was unprecedented. The second Five-Year Plan provided for a reduction of 600,000 in the number of government employees. Instead of the prescribed decrease, there was a marked increase.

This applied not only to government institutions but to all other organizations, such as the trade unions.* When he ap-

---

* The range of the trade unions' activities is very large, particularly since the liquidation of the Narkomtrud (Labor Department) in 1933. Its functions, among them Social Security, have been transferred to the trade unions. Sport, recreation of workers and employees, rest homes, a system of schools, and lectures are in the province of the trade unions. The "shop committees" and "plant committees" with their thousands of members, technically elected by the workers, and their thousands of office employees are a component of the Soviet trade-union system. Finally, in every political campaign special duties and functions fall to the trade-union apparatus: they recruit workers from among the peasantry; they help advance Stakhanovism; they participate in state and communal

peared before the Central Committee of Trade Unions in December, 1934, Shvernik, the head of the trade unions, spoke with horror of the "inflated apparatus of the trade unions in industrial plants": 117 paid employees in the plant committee of a rubber factory in Leningrad, 87 in the Frunze plant, 77 in the Gorkunov plant, 74 in the Petrovsky jute plant, and 84 in the Tsuriupa club. Moscow demanded that the trade unions cut their staffs. But two years later it was disclosed that "the trade unions have 76,500 paid employees, in addition to cultural workers." Expenditures for maintenance of the apparatus amounted to three quarters of the paid-up dues. Because of this, it was ordered in 1937, though not for the first time, that "expenditures for maintenance of the apparatus must not exceed, depending upon the union, 25 to 50 per cent of the paid-up dues." But in August, 1940, the Central Committee of Trade Unions again decreed: "Cut the apparatus in half or down to a third, and also stop paying trade-union officials out of plant funds." This order contained certain figures illustrating the general problem presented by Soviet employees:

The Moscow automobile plant had 931 paid trade-union employees; the Gorky automobile plant, 648; the Kolomensky plant, 183; and the Moscow Hammer and Sickle plant, 203. In 1938 the Union of Employees in the Commissariat of Trade had 2,807 paid employees; after its division into six independent unions, the number of paid trade-union officials increased to 3,546. The Union of Coal Miners had 444 paid employees in 1938 and 742 in 1940. Additional trade-union employees were paid by the plants; for example, 103 trade-union employees were on the payroll of the Moscow automobile plant.

The Leviathan

THE unprecedented expansion of employees in the government service is rooted in the insolubility of the basic problem—the impossibility of controlling from a single center the administration of the whole economic, political, cultural

projects, such as building homes, observing "weeks of cleanliness," accelerating industrial production, fulfilling the five-year plans, getting food, distributing allotments of garden land; they do everything, in fact, except perhaps exert real influence on wage policy and working hours.

and scientific, material and intellectual, urban and rural life of a great country. The more the functions of the state expand, the more difficult becomes their performance. When they become all-embracing, the Soviet State makes gigantic efforts to cope with them. The growing pressure finds expression in the recruiting of new cadres of employees and directors. The greater the burden upon the state, the more numerous the bottlenecks and the more frequently does it seek extraneous remedies.

The frequently unsatisfactory performance of the state machine has given rise to chronic shake-ups and readjustments, transfers and regroupings. There have been a great many of these in the history of the Soviet government apparatus, but they have never produced adequate results. For this reason another measure resorted to has been the establishment of new divisions, sectors, institutes, and commissariats, whose task it has been to correct mistakes. These new institutions soon developed their own shortcomings and they, in turn, were subdivided, expanded, or multiplied, adding new masses to the army of government employees.

Taken by itself, every state function seemed logical and normal. If all private stores, for example, are closed, the Commissariat of Trade must substitute its own outlets. But private trade, particularly in Russia, consisted mainly of thousands of small stores, in the cities and villages, with their own small "capital" of microscopic dimensions, each with its single owner, who was also his own bookkeeper, salesman, economist, and statistician. Only in the cities did some stores employ salesmen. When the state took over all private trade, it appointed an employee for each store; in some cases the appointee was the former owner. But it was necessary to control the employee, to keep a record of goods bought and sold. Furthermore it was necessary to supply the thousands of stores, to check the quality of the goods, to systematize prices, and to perform scores of other functions. For these purposes there was born at the top the grandiose brain of the Commissariat of Trade. And as the task of distributing the goods in a country of 160 to 170 millions is an unusually difficult and thankless one, the Commissariat of Trade was constantly being subdivided and expanded.

The Commissariat of Domestic Trade was created in 1924. Within a year, quite logically, it embraced foreign trade also, and became the Commissariat of Trade. At the end of the 'twenties came the liquidation of the NEP, with the abolition of private trade of every description. The Commissariat of Trade was thereupon divided into two departments, domestic trade being placed under the jurisdiction of the new Commissariat of Supply. The latter set up a number of vast subdivisions having to do with retail trade, produce, industrial commodities, consumer goods, the maintenance and operation of stores and local trade networks, the supplying of health resorts, hospitals, hotels, the regulation of prices, and a great many other duties. A year and a half later this tower of Babel was condemned. A new organization was created, with another expansion of the apparatus. Soon each of the sixteen republics of the Soviet Union had its own Commissariat of Trade, operating under the direction of the All-Union Commissariat of Trade in Moscow. The number of employees in this vast apparatus of trade has never been published, but it far exceeds the number of former storekeepers, salesmen, and delivery men.

No one in particular bears the responsibility for the development of this monstrous machine. On the contrary, most of those directing it are reasonable people, able, devoted to their work, unsparing in their efforts, even to the extent of not sparing their health. Every step they take is carefully thought out, including the unification or division of bureaus, the formation of new commissariats, and the enlistment of scores of thousands of employees. If, in spite of everything, this incongruous system has been built up, the fault is not that of individuals or their motives. The underlying trouble is the insolubility of the basic problem—centralized organization and control by the state of all Russian business and of the country's economic and social life as a whole.

Many more illustrations could be cited to emphasize this situation. Even in large-scale industry, more amenable to state control than small business, one sees the same phenomena. The number of engineers and technicians has naturally increased under the Soviet regime, keeping pace with the great industrial expansion. They totaled 1,400,000 on the eve of the

Russo-German war. But there are many more of them than would be the case in private industry under analogous conditions.

The Soviet economic journal *Problems of Economy* gives a comparison between two electric stations, one in the United States, at South Amboy, New Jersey; the other in the Soviet Union, at Kemerovo. Each produces the same amount of electricity. The American station employs 51 persons, 17 of them office workers. The Soviet station employs 480 persons, of whom 91 are office workers, 106 are in the "division of fuel and transport," 98 in the "boiler room," etc. In Russia, 11 men are required to produce 1,000 kilowatts of electricity; in the United States, 1.3.

The same Soviet journal presents a comparison of two mines, one of the Pittsburgh Coal Company; the other, bearing the name of Lenin, in the Urals. "The American mine employs 8 persons in the office, the Russian 67. The production of the Pittsburgh mine is three times as great as that of the Soviet mine, which employs 48 engineers and technicians, 6 of whom direct operations, 8 are employed above ground and 29 in various sectors; in addition there are 22 foremen (one for every 10 miners), who supervise but do not participate in production. The mine bearing the name of Lenin employs eleven times as many technicians as the American mine."

The number of workers in Soviet industry increased 17 per cent from 1932 to 1936, but during the same period the number of government employees increased 25 per cent. In the Soviet machine industry the number of workers decreased 5 per cent between 1937 and 1939, while the number of employees increased 13 per cent.

A Soviet industrial official, the same journal reports, visited an electric station in Switzerland. On one of the doors he saw a sign "Director." He found the director sitting behind his desk. The following conversation took place:

"Where is your chief engineer?"

"I am the chief engineer."

"Where is your secretary?"

"I have no secretary."

"But who receives daily reports, etc.?"

Instead of replying, the director opened a cabinet, explaining that those in charge submitted all material to him.

"But who conducts your correspondence?"

"I have very few letters to write."

"But what do you do when you have to write a letter?"

"When I do have to write occasionally, I do the writing"—and the director opened a drawer in his desk and pointed to a typewriter.

In view of all this, one can readily understand some of the reasons for the unprecedented expansion of the employee class in Russia. If we look more closely, we see the basic groups that make up the intelligentsia. Engineers and technicians, for example, numbered 207,000 in 1926 and 1,400,000 in 1941. But those who benefited most by this policy were the bookkeepers and their next of kin, the statisticians and economists: in 1926 they constituted a very large group numbering about 1,000,-000; but thirteen years later this typical category of the secondary bureaucracy had expanded to 2,000,000, running far ahead numerically of all other elements of the intelligentsia. The bookkeepers alone numbered 1,700,000! No country has such a large army of bookkeepers and statisticians as Soviet Russia. Together with their families, they constitute a population equal to that of Texas or Sweden, and twice that of Ireland. The bookkeepers are divided into ranks, like army men: there are chief bookkeepers, senior bookkeepers, just plain bookkeepers, and keepers of accounts. The statisticians, too, comprise several divisions.

The last effort to cut down the number of government employees was made in the spring of 1941, when Voznesensky declared at the party conference: "The number of employees in industry is considerably higher than in 1937. We can and must reduce the ratio of all employees, at least to the level of 1937."

VIII

The New Upper Classes, II. Their Future

Rigid Hierarchy

THE new Soviet intelligentsia is destined to play a decisive role in the internal changes confronting Russia. Its experience has made it the only great social force capable of initiative and activity. It is already the dominant element in the social life of the country, though not in political leadership. Future developments, despite the fact that they may involve a series of crises, are bound to bring it to the fore in politics also.

In Russian literature, art, and science the intelligentsia has always been the creator, critic, and observer. Russian novels are now being written by intellectuals, for intellectuals, on themes dealing mainly with the life of the intelligentsia. Shakespeare's principal characters were lords, counts, gentlemen, and merchants; Tolstoy's and Pushkin's were princes, counts, nobles, and officers. Today the Soviet reader wants to see himself, the Soviet intellectual, in literature; and the writer, his confrère, willingly satisfies this demand. Some writing is still being done, by order of the government, about peasants, soldiers, and, rarely, workers. But for the past ten years these heroes have surrendered first place in interest to the intelligentsia. The magazines take their themes principally from the life of Soviet employees; the best satires reflect the life of the Soviet state apparatus. The theaters rarely produce plays about workers or peasants. Even the great political newspapers, so dull to the average reader, with their endless articles on purely economic themes both in peacetime and in wartime, become understandable when we remember that they are written with a view to instructing Soviet employees in their activities.

The Soviet employee has come into literature not only as a reader but as an active force. Though he has broken through the barbed-wire barriers, he has not yet broken through the

censorship. Literature and the theater, in his eyes, suffer from
the fact that they are required to please the party authorities.
For the censorship is one of the party's weapons in its struggle
against the rise of the intelligentsia.

Not everything is aboveboard in the personal and social conduct of the component elements of this new great class. It
should not be idealized. Many of these people have reached
their present status after suffering great privations and by ruthlessly overrunning their associates. In the long years of the
Soviet regime, many saved their own skins by betraying their
closest friends. All of them grew up in an evil, nerve-racking,
dangerous period, when men stopped at nothing in order to
survive.

Because of all this there is a great deal of toughness and cru-
dity in the upper circles and much meanness below. The cru-
dity at the top is frequently accompanied by humiliating ser-
vility below. Higherups are addressed as "you," and the reply
is frequently "thou." This appears to be in the order of things,
one of those old, persistent traditions which return by themselves, without resort to artificial means.

In history a quarter of a century may be but a moment, a
mere transition period. But in the everyday life of the people
it is the history of a whole generation, a complex of new habits,
conceptions, terms, interests, tastes—in short, a new way of
life. Even periodical disturbances of the way of life become
part of it. This established existence is felt to be all the more
unshakable because no revolutionary disturbances appear to
be in the offing, and every citizen is apparently fated to live
out his life in these apparently unalterable circumstances.

Government employees feel they must remain employees
but at the same time must try to live better. To establish oneself, to learn the entrances and exits, to master the formulas,
to obtain contacts—in short, to find one's place and to hold it is
the course to be pursued, for upon this depends life itself, one's
own and one's family's. Under such circumstances all those
questions which formerly occupied first place in the life of
Russian government employees and which have always concerned officialdom in all countries assume primary significance: salary, expenses, per-diem compensation, allowances
for quarters, extra allowances, and so on; added to these, in
Soviet Russia are extra payments in cash—bonuses and rewards

—as well as in foodstuffs, quarters, hospitalization facilities, and trips to summer resorts, to the Volga, the Crimea, and the Caucasus. Thousands of medals and ribbons grace human breasts, each carrying with it certain rights and privileges. But most important of all is advancement up the administrative ladder, the kind of success that gives a person inner satisfaction, a sense of dignity, a feeling of pride, for advancement signifies recognition of one's services by the omnipotent state.

A hierarchal society like that of Soviet Russia needs all this not less but more than any other. Rigid subordination, strict differentiation of rank, glorification of discipline—all the devices on which the old Prussian and Austrian idea of government service was based—find even greater application under the Soviet order: the chief of department and his subordinate; the army commander and the rank-and-filer; the general and the colonel; the director and the staff man; the secretary and the clerk; the people's commissar and the vice-commissar; the General Secretary and the member of the *Politbureau;* in the party apparatus, first secretary, second secretary, and third secretary; in the theater, "people's artist" and "distinguished artist."

Taken as a whole, however, the Soviet intelligentsia constitutes a great positive force. The progressive development of Russia now depends on its acquiring decisive influence in the political sphere.

Vague Programs

IF one may speak of the "class interests" of millions of government employees, these interests would appear to be of a dual character. Politically all these people, nonpartisans and Communists alike, dream of security, in their private and public lives, from unwarranted interference—security from arrest, purges, unjust demands, and demotion in rank. They find it intolerable that almost every family has some member who is being subjected to repression at home or is confined in a concentration camp; that one's every step is watched not only by superiors but also by someone else; that though someone is prying through one's office desk, one is not permitted to express astonishment; that one is held responsible for the mistakes of one's superiors; that no allowance is made for objective causes of failure to carry out instructions; that somewhere behind one's back, behind the wall, lists of suspects are being drawn up; that one is judged by a "fixed" court. What is truly unbearable is not so much the state of general lawlessness as a man's own inability to explain, to defend himself, to call things by their real names. Unbearable, too, is the fact that one cannot lead a quiet life even though one has not committed a single crime. And a quiet life is the dream of millions of average government employees after all the revolutionary upheavals and wars.

Since it is an amalgam of various political points of view, the new class of government employees cannot be considered to be wholly democratic in its political sentiments. The majority are people under forty years of age who have never known any form of rule other than stern dictatorship, and who are accustomed to associate democracy with all sorts of evil. Dissatisfied with this or that feature of the regime—particularly with the mass repressions—they cannot, without some ideological concert and group discussion, give concrete political expression to their sentiments. What they would like to have is a government based on law, not a police state. A government based on law is not necessarily a perfect democracy; history knows other examples. The prerequisites for great political programs have not yet come into being in Russia. Any outbreak that may occur will revolve round specific questions of limited significance; the deeper significance of any such outbreak will become clear only after the event.

In the economic sphere the new intelligentsia at first glance does not seem to disagree with the Communist system of universal state economy. The official press and scientific institutions never tire of asserting that every class of the population in favor of private property has been abolished in Russia, and that the restoration of capitalism, in whole or in part, has no supporters in a single social group. This claim rests on the fact that except for a few old people no one in Russia now desires a system of private trade and industry, and that no one is likely to express any such desire, either privately or publicly; but the situation is not so simple as all that.

There is a substantial difference in the attitudes of orthodox Communism and of the Soviet intelligentsia on the subject of the state versus private economy. The first regards the state economy as a boon to Russia and the rest of the world, in fact as the main bulwark of progress, for the attainment of which all else should be forgiven.

As far as the Soviet intelligentsia is concerned, the state economy is an established fact, but not a question of principle. The mass of government employees see no reason to prefer the state economy to a private economy where the latter seems more reasonable and economical. They do not possess that Communist enthusiasm which demanded the liquidation of every little private store even though the surrounding population was deprived, in consequence, of necessary commodities. Nor is there any mass enthusiasm for collectivized agriculture. On economic as on political questions, the intelligentsia has no clear program. Should a policy determined by the interests of this class gain the upper hand, it would have to follow new roads in the sphere of economics.

The same is true of many other Russian problems. On the question of religion, for example, Communist policy was in principle actively godless, deviating only from time to time toward neutrality. Most government employees, however, were never militantly antireligious. Many, perhaps the majority, considered religious marriage a necessary complement to civil registration, had their children baptized, and observed funeral rituals. The antireligious campaigns provoked their displeasure.

The attitude of the majority of government employees, even of party members, toward the Communist International has been very cool. They regarded the Comintern as representing a few hundreds or thousands of foreigners, "leeches and parasites," residing in Russia. The Hotel Lux in Moscow, which housed the Comintern, was the butt of nasty jokes and protests. The recent dissolution of the Comintern, brought about primarily by considerations of foreign policy, was at the same time a concession to these sentiments. The idea of world Communism, though not abandoned by the high party hierarchy, was never popular among the great masses of Soviet employees; it is now less in favor than ever.

In so far as Communist expansionism may yet influence the government's foreign policy, it will not meet with the approval of the Soviet intelligentsia. The military defense of Russia is

accepted as a matter of course, but any further plans and programs are not regarded as equally axiomatic. The Soviet intelligentsia, including even its Communist element, viewed very
coldly the Stalin-Hitler pact of 1939. This attitude may be
duplicated in connection with any further changes in foreign
policy. The attitude of the Soviet intelligentsia toward England has never corresponded to the traditional Communist
antagonism, which at times has been nothing short of hatred.

Such is the inarticulate, half-conscious program of the Soviet
intelligentsia. However modest and limited it may be, it differs radically from the attitude of the present regime. A government founded on law would mean especially the liberation
of the vast majority of prisoners from jails and concentration
camps and the abolition of forced-labor camps. The introduction of realism in economic policy would mean greater liberty
for the economic activities of the peasantry. These reforms
would put into effect what millions of Soviet citizens dream of
only silently.

In connection with this program, the Soviet intelligentsia—
and this is most important—reflects the hopes and interests of
every other class of the population. In comparison with the
general population, even the politically passive intelligentsia
represents an active group capable of initiative; the vagueness
of its aspirations is a model of clarity as compared with the lack
of political awareness of the lower classes. It may yet find an
opportunity to influence policy before other elements of the
population take their place on the political scene. The peculiar
role of the Russian intelligentsia as the focus of the political
needs of all classes of the population is by no means new in
Russia. On the contrary, it was this tradition that in the past
made the Russian intelligentsia a unique phenomenon in
world history.

Now it once more confronts the state power as the main embodiment of popular interests and sentiments. Having been
transformed from a small group of "old intellectuals" into a
class comprising many millions of government employees, and
having lost its onetime revolutionary fervor, it now reflects, in
its hopes and sentiments, the general urge for what might be
termed the end of the revolution.

It longs for a peaceful, wholesome life. It is being glorified
with slogans, lauded to the skies, honored with the titles of

heroes of labor, heroes of war, heroes of Socialist construction. But they themselves, these millions of employee-intellectuals, do not want to be heroes. They are tired of heroism, of stress and strain, of sacrifice and suffering, of persecution and war and death. They want to come home from work, relax, and play with their children. They do not want to have meetings and conferences every night; they want to sleep. They want to buy things without having to stand in queues, to read without being watched, to converse without fear, to love without danger, to obtain an apartment without having to play the sycophant. Two generations of Russians have not known the meaning of normal living. The people now on the scene want to live.

The ending of the revolution, after a quarter of a century of great experiments, transformations, and achievements; after wars, foreign and civil, unprecedented for Russia and the world; after countless sacrifices; after immeasurable sufferings, famines, epidemics, and unutterable misery; after repeated manifestations of extraordinary heroism and moral degradation; after the promulgation of great ideals and sweeping programs; after the imposition upon the nation of great lies and deceptions—after all this, the ending of the revolution would reflect the general need of the tortured, desperately tired people. The ending of the revolution would not involve a return to the past. Hardly anyone dreams of the restoration of old Russia. But the revolution must be ended. All that is beautiful in it, and all that is ugly, must be relegated to history.

In realizing this, the Soviet intelligentsia expresses the urge of virtually every class of the population.

The Communist Party and the Intelligentsia

THE normally energetic, dynamic, and persistent Communist party remains, like Hamlet, in a state of indecision before the problem of the intelligentsia. It has never been able to make up its mind whether to admit a sizable number of intellectuals into its midst and thereby lose its working-class character or to lose its grip on the machinery of the bureaucracy.

"The group of Communist employees," the Central Committee declared in 1927, "numbering hundreds of thousands in recent years, constitutes a barrier, because of its relative weight, to the altogether natural desire of the party to retain the dominant influence of those workers who are directly engaged in industry. On the other hand, there are too few party members in the directing force and employee personnel of the government apparatus; to strengthen Communist influence, it would be necessary to expend the membership in the party of government employees."

About 15 per cent of government employees are members of the Communist party. The majority, especially the most influential members of the party, live and work in close proximity to the mass of government employees. All share the everyday problems of Soviet life; there is a constant exchange of things and ideas between them. The party is always trying to indoctrinate the elements that surround it with its own ideas and to win them over to its side. The party exerts influence on its surroundings, on the mass of nonpartisan employees, but the surrounding social elements also influence the party. These elements, their needs, ideas, fears, and hopes, penetrate, in spite of all obstacles, into the great mass of party members, infect it, and tend to disorganize it. Thus, silently, does the class of government employees poison the party. True, it has no freedom of speech, no ideology, and no capacity for active resistance. Nevertheless it does resist, to a considerable extent, psychologically, passively. At times there ensues an apparent armistice, but never for long. Up to now the party has always managed, after making some concessions, to turn back to a former policy. But this, in turn, has tended to estrange the party from those whose labor built the national edifice. No real agreement has ever been possible; it remains impossible now.

Official reports and textbooks on the history of the Russian Communist party touch only lightly upon the role of the intelligentsia in the party. Formal statistics on this question have long ceased to be published. The newspapers print accounts of party meetings in the army, in plants, and in collectives. But nothing is said about the activities of party organizations in government institutions. Indeed, the facts do not fit into the framework of a "workers' party."

The first census of the Communist party membership, in 1922, showed that 8.2 per cent of Soviet employees belonged to the party. The highest percentage of Communists, 43.4, was in the GPU. Five years later another census disclosed 11.7 per cent of Communists among the intelligentsia, 6.1 per cent among the workers, and less than 1 per cent among the peasants.

But the 12 per cent of Communist employees in 1927 already included at that time the leading personalities of the Soviet state machine. The directors of all departments were all members of the party; all were people's commissars or vice-commissars, both in the central government and in each of the affiliated republics. The directing personnel in industry in the middle 'thirties was made up entirely of party members: between 95 and 100 per cent of the heads of enterprises and their immediate assistants, the directors of trusts and their immediate assistants.*

To the 15 per cent of Communists in the Soviet intelligentsia should be added about 10 per cent of Komsomol members.

Standards of Living

THE new intelligentsia is the highest class of Soviet society by virtue of its earnings and its standard of living, which are above those of any other class. Nevertheless there is a wide differentiation in earnings and living standards within the intelligentsia. There is a vast gap between the village teacher in some distant province and the Stalin laureate or ballerina

* A striking parallel between the quantitative growth of the party and the increase in the number of government employees is shown by the following figures:

Year	Number of Employable Intellectuals		Number of Party Members
1920	About 2,000,000		612,000
1929	4,600,000		1,532,000
1932	About 8,000,000	Before the purge	3,170,000
1939	9,600,000		3,200,000
1941	10–11,000,000		3,900,000

The increase in percentages over 1920 is as follows:

1920	100		100
1929	230		250
1932	400		518
1939	480		523
1941	500–550		637

in Moscow. This, however, does not alter the fact that a sense of unity exists among all elements of this class, from the lowest to the highest—a sense of unity more keenly felt than in any other country.

The earning capacity of intellectuals is lowest in the villages, where employees in administration, education, and rural economy are paid no better than industrial workers. The higher the administrative center, the higher the earnings. The average earnings of intellectuals are about twice the average of workers; particularly high are the earnings of engineers, which are many times those of workers. A few engineer groups earn several thousand rubles a month as compared with the average monthly wage of from three to four hundred rubles for workers.

Still higher are the earnings of picked groups of writers, actors, and scientists, who, in addition to their salaries of many thousands of rubles per month, receive all sorts of special grants, are given the use of automobiles, are occasionally exempted from paying taxes, etc. The higher aristocracy of Soviet society, consisting of artists, engineers, technicians, and some of the highest officials and comprising no more than twenty or thirty thousand persons, is the apex of the Soviet pyramid.* It is not entirely Communist; but its welfare depends closely upon its loyalty. Being in the forefront it is constantly watched. It is unqualifiedly devoted to the regime, with a devotion which relegates conviction and political opinions to second place.

---

* One criterion of the change is the increase in the number of domestic servants. At the beginning of the 'twenties, practically no one could afford to have a house servant, and the number of "domestic workers" (1,500,000 before the revolution) fell to 150,000 in 1923–24. Later it began to rise rapidly. By 1927 there were already 339,000 domestics, and the government's plans envisaged further increases: to 398,000 in 1929 and 406,000 in 1932 (see *The Five-Year Plan*, p. 17). In the latter part of the 'thirties, with the rapid rise of the new aristocracy and oligarchy, the number of domestic servants increased so greatly that official sources became silent on the subject.

Another criterion is the widespread growth of prostitution in recent years, particularly in Moscow. The cities had previously been cleared of prostitutes, who had been exiled to distant concentration camps. But in recent years prostitution has actually been legalized, particularly in hotels and restaurants allotted for the use of important officials from the provinces. Hundreds of prostitutes serve in the NKVD, which frequently uses them in keeping watch on visitors. "The abolition of prostitution in the land of the Soviets" is a myth unfortunately cultivated by ill-informed newspapermen.

Fixed monthly salaries are not the only source of income for many, particularly those employed in the economic field. All sorts of bonuses—for economy, for efficiency, for quality, etc.—increase incomes very considerably. Rewards frequently take the form of lower vacation costs and trips to vacation resorts.

But all salaries and incomes-in-kind combined leave the standard of living of most of the intelligentsia extremely low in comparison with living standards in the United States or western Europe. Even those few Soviet employees who earned as much as 2,000 rubles a month at the beginning of the war lived no better than Americans earning $20 a week.

Despite the inner differentiation, the class of government employees has a keen sense of solidarity; its differentiation from the "common man" has reached an extreme completely unknown in the United States. The bourgeois-intellectual origin of some, the snobbishness of others—parvenu elements that have sprung from peasants and workers—weariness from many years of privation, of imposed impoverishment, followed by the government's encouragement in the middle 'thirties to "live merrily"—all this has resulted in the development of hierarchical forms known only to medieval feudal society. Not to mix with "the people," to have fine clothes and fine furniture, to own a victrola and a radio, to ride in "soft" railway cars regularly used only by government employees, to enjoy vacations in "rest homes" as distinguished from the places frequented by workers, to eat in restaurants operated for the special use of Soviet employees—all this serves to give them a sense of superiority. Even in theaters, all the orchestra seats are filled by people in uniform, military and civil, while the old workers' shirts, *kosovorotki,* at one time in the front rows, have been banished to the rear of the gallery.

All this suggests a marked reaction against the epoch of the *kosovorotki* and the *uravnilovka,* like the revenge for the years of imposed privations. The encouragement by the government of these changes is officially explained in economic terms: as a reward for valuable services. The "happy life" enjoyed by some is designed to encourage others to follow their example.

The intelligentsia has not been able to satisfy its basic political aspirations. But one thing it has won is the right to a decent living for the small number of its elite.

Future Development and Differentiation

THE process of formation of new classes had not yet been completed when the war broke out. It will go on after the war. The fate of the higher classes, in particular, will depend, as heretofore, upon the course of inner political development, to wit:

1. If, after the war, the political system remains unchanged and retains the basic principles of an all-powerful state economy, the evolution of the higher class will proceed along the road of hierarchism. This development would mean the widening of the gulf dividing the members of the higher class from those performing physical labor. The transition of lower elements to higher levels would become more and more difficult. The expansion of hierarchism would imply an inner differentiation of the higher class into groups and subgroups, and their advancement up the social ladder would be circumscribed by rigid rules of government service.

In 1940 the Soviet Government had already issued a series of edicts making advancement for lower ranks more difficult, such as introducing tuition fees in higher educational institutions, rules prohibiting workers from changing their jobs without previous approval of the authorities, and so on. These edicts were prompted by economic considerations: the mass exodus of workers into the rank of Soviet employees had long been painfully felt in industry. The imposition of these rules had been postponed because they violated many principles previously laid down, but the war necessitated the abandonment of traditions. After the war the same considerations will operate even more strongly, for hundreds of thousands of workers have died in battle or been wounded, and industry will find it difficult to satisfy its demand for manpower.

The latter process will be furthered by the new system of ranks and uniforms. At present the rigid hierarchy of uniforms has been applied, outside of the army, to the diplomatic service, railway employees, and the courts. But this is only a beginning, and it may be assumed that the system will gradually be expanded to other branches of the government service. The decrees regulating the hierarchy of ranks divide the mass of government employees into classes, differentiating rigidly be-

tween the various grades, prescribing the order of advancement in the service, the time to be served at each stage, and the
use of a high-sounding title for each grade. Thus, prosecuting
officers are divided into eleven grades. The chief prosecutor of
the USSR is referred to as the "Actual State Councillor of Justice." The chief of the transportation system bears the title of
"Director-General of Lines of Communication."

At the same time, uniforms have been introduced for all
grades, similar to those in the armed services; there are shoulder straps, service bars, stars, etc. The psychological basis of
this phenomenon is the fanatical urge of hundreds of thousands who have risen from the lower classes to obtain the
maximum of security in their new positions, by receiving those
outward attributes of rank which may serve as their legal
charter. The same is true of orders, medals, and badges of distinction—all of which today play a greater part in Russia than
in any other country.

2. If political developments result in changed economic
principles—if, for example, freedom of small business is restored—the new small tradesmen and petty industrialists will
arise from the ranks of the same higher class. Thousands of
employees now working as salesmen in state-owned stores or
performing duties on the lower levels of the industrial machine will leave the government service; former store managers, for instance, will become independent owners.

The employees in question possess great practical knowledge, versatility, and the necessary minimum education; many
are greedy beyond description. These people will seize the new
positions before any elements from the ranks of the workers
and peasants have a chance to come forward and become a new
class of small tradesmen and capitalists. The more room the
state permits for private initiative, the greater will be the numbers that break away from the class of government employees
and the more rapid will be the formation of a new commercial-
industrial class.

3. If, theoretically speaking, the capitalist economy should
be restored, with private heavy industry, trade, and banks, the
new capitalist class would emerge wholly from the ranks of
government employees. Only from these ranks could come the
cadres of businessmen, promoters, directors, pioneers of foreign trade, department store owners, and bankers. The great

scope developed by Soviet industry was the product of human imagination; this imagination, in this theoretical case, would serve the cause of private economy.

4. Under all the varied courses of possible development, the new higher class will thus be preserved and will become the reservoir for all sorts of conceivable new social formations.

The present upper class will remain at the head of the nation, with changes of one kind or another, for a long time. It will continue to show differentiations, to develop, to learn, to change its political attire; eventually it may even drive political regimes from power and put others in their place. It may divide into parties. But it will stand for Russia in the eyes of the world.

IX

The Working Class

IT is usually assumed that the revolution destroyed or decimated only the propertied classes of old Russia. In reality, however, this applies also, though in a different sense, to the Russian industrial and agricultural workers. The working class that now exists in Russia, or rather the Russian working class as it existed prior to June, 1941, must be thought of as something entirely new. It came into being during the revolutionary period, and is to be sharply distinguished from its earlier counterpart. Workers of the prerevolutionary period and members of former workers' families constitute but a small minority, probably less than 10 per cent of the contemporary Russian working class. This is a fact of cardinal importance.

It must be remembered that the industrial workers constituted, in a political sense, the most important part of Russia's former working population. For various reasons, the agricultural workers, as well as the relatively small number employed in petty industry, played a small role in comparison with the workers in plants and factories. After their famous march to the Winter Palace in 1905, the industrial workers of St. Petersburg, as it then was called, gave the signal for the first revolution. The wave of strikes in 1905 culminated in barricade battles in sections of Moscow inhabited by industrial workers. The labor conflict and the suppression of the strike in the Siberian gold fields in 1912 were events of great political significance, and marked a turning point in history. Finally, it may be said that both the revolution of March, 1917, and the November revolution would have been impossible but for the intense political activity of the Russian workers, especially in the two capitals. Neither the mutinies in the army nor the agrarian disorders could have amounted to much or resulted in the victory of the new government without the impetus derived from the political movement of the workers.

On the eve of the first World War, however, industrial

and railroad workers in Russia numbered only about 3,500,-
000. To be sure, there were some 3,000,000 part-time agricultural laborers, and several million in trade and business offices,
but the industrial workers constituted the heart of the Russian
working class. Women workers were not very active politically,
and, if we exclude apprentices and minors along with them,
we come to the conclusion that what has been called the Russian labor movement before the revolution comprised about
2,500,000 workers. This was only 2 per cent of the adult population of old Russia.

Of these 2,500,000 human beings, a great many went to war
in 1914–16. Some were killed, others wounded, and still others
went back to their native villages after demobilization. Thousands of workers were drafted into the armies of the civil war
between 1918 and 1920; their mobilization assumed considerable proportions because the new regime, for political reasons,
preferred to mobilize workers rather than peasants, whom it
did not trust. Hundreds of thousands of workers were sent to
the front, and many never came back to their jobs. Industrial
production was declining, there were no raw materials, cities
were starving. All those who had any ties with the villages—
and most of the Russian workers were of peasant stock—tried
to leave the cities, particularly because the division of the land
was under way, and workers were eager to help their families
in the villages get their share. The wars, hunger, and the industrial depression thus combined to drive workers from the
plants and sharply reduced their numbers.

Of the total number of workers in the prerevolutionary period, only half remained in 1921–22, and even these were only
partly employed. By that time, according to certain statistics,
industry had declined 83 per cent. Its revival, begun in the
'twenties, brought new elements into the plants and factories,
in addition to the old workers, including former independent
artisans, employees in small trade, former minor government
employees, members of the old police force, and young people.
But the dissolution of the old working class continued.

This process was accentuated by the influx of many workers
into the ranks of the newly developing economic and administrative bureaucracy. This phenomenon assumed a mass character. In line with official ideology, the Soviet press and literature of the period exalted the spiritual and moral qualities of

the workers: the working man was the symbol of all that was lofty and great. The worker's courage and heroism, the worker's heart and the worker's soul, proletarian culture and proletarian art—all this filled the columns of the Soviet press and inspired Soviet orators. Many poets and writers who had scarcely set foot in an industrial plant sang the praises of the worker in all sincerity, though their knowledge of these people was altogether theoretical; others joined in the exaltation in order to be in step. This worship of the worker, which was essentially self-praise on the part of the regime, continued for about ten or fifteen years.

Meanwhile the real workers, who had experienced on their own backs what factory labor was like in Russia, were deserting the plants by the tens of thousands, the very same plants where the new human beings of the poets' songs were being forged. New managers were needed to replace the old and their number grew in proportion to the inexperience of the newcomers. The new administrative economic staffs, with their many divisions scattered all over the country, required additional human material, some of which was supplied from workers in the same industries. The trade unions were developing rapidly into a great state apparatus. The same thing was true of the Communist party machine, whose network reached into every nook and corner. A new administrative organization was being set up in the villages, and many of the new posts were being filled by workers.

Hundreds of thousands of vacancies became available, with able, shrewd people, particularly workers, rushing to fill them, whose social origin constituted an additional, substantial recommendation for the new jobs. Of the million former workers who remained in industry at the beginning of the 'twenties, hundreds of thousands soon moved up the social ladder.

Many of the children of the former workers sought to escape the hardships of industrial labor. Free education enabled workers to send their children into the engineering and teaching professions, to military schools, and into scientific fields. Thousands of girls took business courses or became saleswomen; many went into medicine or teaching. The end of the 'twenties brought the first mass graduations of young people from educational institutions, men and women who had never worked in industry; and, beginning with the 'thirties, this new type of Soviet intellectual was to be seen everywhere. The old workers were dying off, satisfied to know that their children were facing a better life than their own, not troubled by the question whether this was true Communism.

At the same time, however, the economic chaos was being overcome, and the number of new workers was increasing. By 1927 the number of industrial workers had been restored to the prerevolutionary figure of 2,600,000; in 1930 it was 3,670,-000; and by 1935 it had doubled, reaching the figure of 5,620,-000. Before the outbreak of the war it had increased to 8,000,-000.

Along with these millions of new workers, there were probably no more than a few hundred thousand of the old ones. The government, although it was in possession of the pertinent data, refrained from publishing the complete figures, for it sought to create the impression of the continuity of the Russian labor movement. It wanted to have it believed that the working class responsible for the revolution of 1917 had continued to function as the main foundation of the new regime. The few workers of the old category who remained at their jobs were the least capable element, devoid of initiative: even before the revolution they had been considered on the whole a backward, docile group.

Why No Labor Movement in Russia?

THE source from which the millions of new workers were recruited was the old Russian reservoir which in the past had supplied the Russian mercantile class, the army, and all former cadres of workers—the virtually limitless reservoir of the peasantry. During the eight years from 1928 through 1935 the cities absorbed 17,686,000 men and women who had come from the villages, or about 2,000,000 persons annually. The urban population, which was 28,000,000 in 1929, increased to 56,000,000 within ten years.

Without this great new labor force, there could not have been any successful industrialization. For a period of ten years, an endless procession of trains filled to capacity carried this mass of labor in unprecedented numbers from the villages to the cities. Neither Europe nor America had ever known such

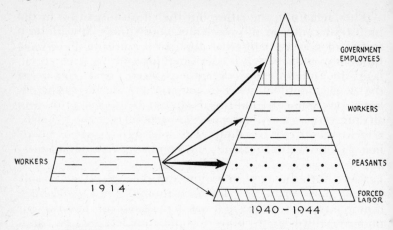

an intensive mass migration. It was as if some giant pump had lifted millions of human beings from their ancient habitats and moved them hundreds or thousands of miles to plants and public works of which they had never even heard before. Most of the new workers migrated to the cities voluntarily, hoping to find better working conditions. In the two famine years of 1931 and 1932 some 7,000,000 people went to the cities. More or less compulsory enlistment of peasants in industry played a substantial part in this migration during the years immediately preceding the present war. In 1940, for example, a new law mobilized a large part of Russia's peasant youth for training in technical schools by obliging the collectives to supply 400,000 boys and girls annually.

This was how the new Russian working class was formed. There were, of course, other elements in this great tide, such as former domestics who now moved into industry and the remainder of the former unemployed. But these urban reserves were soon exhausted, and had been completely used up by about 1933, which marked the beginning of the second Five-Year Plan. The new Russian working class constituted essentially a part of the peasantry transported to the cities for employment in plants and factories.* Many a memory and hope bound them, and continued to bind them, to the villages.

---

* In 1933–34 a trade-union investigation produced some interesting figures. The metallurgical industry disclosed that the percentage of former peasants or

They remain in the cities, but their transformation in the industrial cauldron is proceeding very slowly; it will be a matter of decades before the process is complete. They have brought to the cities all the characteristics of the Russian village, the paradoxically contradictory, enigmatic features of the "Russian soul," so mysterious to the outside world. Boundless subservience to fate, amazingly low living standards, and an endless capacity for enduring privation have been the characteristics of these people who have formed the mainstay of first-class armies, as well as the solid foundations of monarchies and dictatorships. And, coupled with this, there have been periodic outbursts of the wrath of millions, cruel and bloody peasant uprisings, with their sudden terrible vengeance for humiliation and whippings, for oppression and poverty, for undernourishment, for years of famine. And later, after merciless suppression of such uprisings, have followed periods of pacification. There have been heroic self-sacrifice and silent submission; mutiny and obedience; revolt and loyalty; the village community, *obshchina,* and cunning individual calculation; anticlericalism and religious devotion. The rational West always regarded all this as the extreme of the irrational.

It is not surprising, therefore, that until 1905 the Russian peasantry had never been able to develop the forms of life, habits, and action which have characterized the American worker and farmer, and the workers of western Europe; the capacity for systematic, consistent building of their own organizations, from month to month, from year to year, without stormy disturbances followed by apathy, without sweeping upheavals followed by loss of faith in themselves. How could the Russian peasants ever have developed any such characteristics? Having emerged from serfdom at about the time of the abolition of Negro slavery in the United States, they had only found themselves caught in the toils of a rigid police system.

This also explains the tardiness of the old prerevolutionary working class in making its appearance on the social scene. That working class was composed primarily of former peasants who had migrated to the cities with the development of Russian industry during the fifty years preceding the revolu-

children of peasants employed before 1917 was 31 as against 62 per cent in 1931–32. In the flour-mill industry, the comparative percentages were 48 in 1917 and 72 in 1931–32. In the building trades the respective figures were 56 and 78.

tion. Those workers, too, bore uncomplainingly the burden of poverty and dirt. There were no trade unions of any kind, for their existence would have been impossible, before the first revolution. Collective action by the workers was inconceivable, strikes were illegal and were punished by mass whippings and bloody suppression. It required much heroism to register any protest on economic questions. Very few were capable of displaying such courage. Before 1895 even sporadic, short-lived strikes were rare events. They grew more frequent later, but only the year 1905 brought the first great strike wave that swept the whole country.

Only then did the Russian worker begin to develop the characteristics that mark trade-union and political labor organizations and that require a relatively high degree of urban culture. This was facilitated, in addition to the experience gained in the cities, by the influx of thousands of intellectuals into the young Russian labor movement, with their enthusiastic faith in the liberating mission of the working class. The small group of intellectual élite born of this development supplied the leaders who, in the period between the two revolutions, 1905–17, built the first solid trade unions in the face of police repression, and founded all sorts of workers' relief organizations and educational institutions. Those twelve years constituted the only period when Russia had any genuine trade unions. Heroic efforts and a great deal of idealism were required to build them, and hundreds of persons spent a total of thousands of years in prison for this experiment in the Europeanization of the Russian peasant-worker.

The new postrevolutionary working class, which also sprang from the peasantry, was not a continuation of the old. Like the old it brought with it to the cities subservience and loyalty to the powers that be, long-concealed discontent, the tendency to be satisfied with little, and no knowledge of, or feeling for, social organization. The molding of this mass in the industrial cauldron was an exceedingly slow process, particularly because it no longer had the coöperation and encouragement of idealistic intellectuals and also because the more capable elements of the new workers, distinguished by some measure of originality, speedily left the ranks in an effort to gain advancement in the economic scale. For them, roads were opened for advancement, without any collective improvement of the general level of life. The relatively high pay enjoyed by the more skilled made the idea of any collective action, so far as they were concerned, seem quixotic and foolishly altruistic.

This is one reason why the development of a labor movement has proved impossible under the Soviet regime. There have been outbursts of revolt in factories, of the kind known before, marked by primitive anger and passion. These outbursts, easily suppressed, have been scarcely noticed by the country as a whole; indeed, they have been nothing more than sporadic phenomena. There is still a great deal of dissatisfaction among the workers, but it has taken the form of a dull, chronic pain.

Another reason why the revolution has failed to develop a new labor movement must be sought in the peculiar qualities that have marked the new Russian working class.

In all countries, and under all conditions, the most active workers in the labor movement have been adult men; the role of women, as members of unions and particularly as initiators and leaders, has been comparatively limited, and even less important has been the role of minors. Women constitute about 15 per cent of industrial workers in the United States (24 per cent of the total labor force), and 20 to 30 per cent in western Europe.

The situation in prerevolutionary Russia was to a certain extent analogous. Before the first World War, adult men made up 62 per cent of the workers, women 27 per cent, and minors 11 per cent. On the eve of the second World War, the composition of the industrial workers was quite different. Women numbered about 40 per cent in industry, while young workers (below 23) numbered 35 to 40 per cent of the men. Thus adult men constituted from 35 to 40 per cent. In 1937 there were approximately 7,800,000 workers employed in Russian heavy industry, but of these only 3,000,000 or fewer were adult men.

This relatively active part of the working class thus grew rather slowly. It bore no relation to the generally known figures showing the fantastic increase in population of the cities (100 per cent in twelve years), the increase in production (fivefold in twenty years), and the increase in the total number of wage earners. While the general mass of industrial labor increased from 300 to 400 per cent, the number of adult male workers grew very slowly. Even before the present war, the Russian working class consisted for the most part of women and youths.

The Standard of Living

THIS thoroughgoing transformation of the Russian working class during the period of the revolution makes a comparison of earnings under the old and new regimes almost pointless. The whole matter is political rather than economic in character. Of political significance is the question: What benefits have been derived from the social reconstruction by the class that enjoyed special privileges during the first period of that reconstruction? This question has played a vital part in the conflict of parties in Russia, and particularly in the factional struggle within the Communist party.

There are two answers, both official. The first explains why real wages for the Russian workers could not be raised in the 'thirties. It calls attention to the fact that Russia's unprecedentedly speedy industrialization required tremendous efforts on the part of a poor nation and called for sacrifice of immediate welfare for the sake of the future. It recalls also the need of military expenditures, which increased greatly in the 'thirties, using up immense sources that could have been employed to better advantage. Guns and tractors instead of butter, electrical stations instead of meat—such was the explanation, an explanation not without some measure of truth.

But along with this explanation we have assertions from the same sources that claim an unprecedented increase in earnings, not only of individuals, but of the whole laboring mass. Allegedly Russia has achieved the impossible: a simultaneous expansion of industrial investment and of military-industrial preparedness, coupled with an improvement in the workers' standard of living.

According to official statistics, wage scales, which had fallen very low at the beginning of the 'twenties, reached the prewar level in the second half of the 'twenties. In 1930 Stalin reported to the party congress that "real wages have already risen 167 per cent, in comparison with the prewar period." In 1934 he reported that wage scales again had risen, on an average, from

991 to 1,519 rubles per year. This meant that by 1934 they had already reached two and a half times their prewar level. Judging by official figures, wages continued to rise after that period. According to Molotov, "real wages doubled during the second Five-Year Plan [i.e., from 1933 through 1937]." If we combine the data given by Stalin and Molotov, we may conclude that wages had increased 450 per cent by 1938, as compared with prewar scales. Finally, a further increase of 35 per cent was contemplated under the third Five-Year Plan (i.e., before 1943). Thus, if we are to credit the official figures, real wages at the beginning of the second World War were five times as great as those which prevailed on the eve of the first World War.

If this miracle were true, it would justify a great deal of what has occurred under Communism. It would mean that millions of men who had barely subsisted under the old regime, and millions of new workers who had flocked from the villages to the cities after the revolution, attained within the short period of fifteen or twenty years a level of material well-being such as had never been enjoyed either by the workers of western Europe or by those of the United States, the highest paid in the world. If it were true that the wage scales of the Russian workers had increased fivefold by the outbreak of the second World War, as compared with prerevolutionary levels, it could not be denied that Russia had caught up with and overtaken the capitalist nations.

The fact, however, is that these claims are sheer propaganda. It is well known that any estimate of real wages is not a mere arithmetical process, and that all such statistics are likely to be unreliable, particularly under conditions of violent price fluctuations in times of inflation.

Not only were prices rising rapidly in Russia during the 'thirties but the same commodities commanded a variety of prices, depending on whether they were bought in the state coöperative stores, in the open market, or elsewhere. Contradictory conclusions may be drawn in any price studies under such conditions, according to the figures used. Moreover, official statistics included in the calculation of wages the benefits of social services, which are usually excluded in any wage computations: social insurance against illness, the cost of lectures provided by the government, maintenance of clubs, and other things;* this was referred to as the "socialized portion of wages." The workers, however, might easily have preferred to receive cash instead of lectures and similar things. It was by such methods that official statistics yielded their optimistic conclusions.

For purposes not of propaganda but of real work, however, the state adopted a very different procedure. Every ruble that could possibly be saved had to be devoted to expansion of the basic capital of the Soviet economy. According to this concept the Soviet State has the right to demand from its workers the maximum of sacrifice for the sake of their future well-being. In fixing wage scales it pays the workers only as much as it considers absolutely necessary. The Soviet Government has no intention of generally raising living standards until the program of reconstruction is completed, and until the "Americanization" of Russia permits a reduction in the tempo of economic accumulation and thus makes possible the increase of real wages to unprecedented levels. Such is the official concept. Whatever one may think of the ultimate aim sought, this concept, at any rate, expresses more correctly the official policy on the wage question than does the propaganda concerning the fivefold enrichment of the Russian workers during the twelve-year period under discussion.

One of the best-informed and most objective of Russian economists, Professor Sergei Prokopovich, came to some interesting conclusions.† He found that during the period of the first Five-Year Plan (1928–32) "there was less per capita production of foodstuffs and consumer goods than before the war"; thus, "wages at the end of the first Five-Year Plan were below prewar scales." He found that "in the course of the years 1935–39 real wages gradually went up"; however, the average real wage of workers and employees at the end of the 'thirties was "below the prewar level and below the level of the last years of the NEP," i.e., 1927–29. "The war in central and western Europe [from 1939 to 1941, when Russia was not a belligerent] produced another fall in real wages."

---

* Funds for "cultural services" alone covered 39 per cent of wages in 1933 and 35 per cent in 1935.

† Professor Prokopovich published a bulletin in Prague until 1939; since the outbreak of the war his *Quarterly Bulletin* is being published in Switzerland, in English.

The British economist Leonard Hubbard comes to the same conclusions, but, in calling attention to the very great differentiations in wages, he points out that the wages of Stakhanovites were ten times as great as the average. His conclusion is that the real wages of Stakhanovites were higher than wage scales in 1913, but the lower categories of workers received not more, and possibly less, than they did on the eve of the first World War.

Indeed, the new Russian workers are divided into many groups, with all the local economic differentiations that constitute the difference between poverty and sufficiency. Many a dramatic struggle revolved round this question during the first fifteen years of the revolution, many a utopia perished in the course of these conflicts, and many a person was "liquidated" for trying to preserve some semblance of equalitarian relations, to prevent the lower grades of workers from falling too low, and the higher categories from developing into a "labor aristocracy." These Communists of the old school could not understand why it was necessary to have a revolution only to return later to the old system of unequal wages and to restore the higher class of wage earners whom the Communists of all countries had detested as a manifestation of the "capitalist corruption" of the workers.

What triumphed in the end, as is well known, was that "realism" which has subjected everything to the task of expanding industrial production. Under the prevailing conditions of poverty, higher earnings naturally provided the strongest incentive to better, more productive work. For this reason, piecework became the prevailing system, and, what is more important, the wage scales set by the state for the skilled began to exceed many times the scales of the lower, unskilled workers. The distance between maximum and minimum wages was intentionally and systematically widened. This soon led to the development of that class of workers which, under Soviet conditions, is repeating the history of the "labor aristocracy" of England and other countries at the end of the nineteenth century. The Stakhanovites who make up this aristocracy, though not very numerous, are at the present time the most virile, determined and skilful of all the workers in Russia. Not only are the wages of the Stakhanovites many times larger than those of the rest of the workers, but they also enjoy many special privileges and advantages. We need only refer to summer "rest homes" and sanatoria, to which Stakhanovites have a priority.

In general, it may be said that the wages of workers and other employees had risen considerably in the 'twenties after the years of famine and civil war and the first period of the NEP; later, beginning with 1930, they fell considerably during the period of collectivization and the first Five-Year Plan; and they began to rise again about 1935, but the increase was uneven for the various categories of workers and other employees. At the end of the 'thirties the higher, more skilled groups, as well as limited circles of Soviet "specialists," had attained and even passed the prewar level, while the lower mass of workers and other employees had at the most reached the prewar level, which, incidentally, constituted a considerable improvement over the early 'thirties.

THE best criterion of the standard of living of workers in all countries is the extent to which female labor is used, especially that of married women and mothers. Factory work is hard on women in general, resulting, as it does, in a higher degree of illness and other burdens; it is particularly hard on married women and mothers. Under ordinary circumstances only necessity drives the wife of a worker and the mother of a family to take a job. Work in a plant or factory involves neglect of the home; obviously it means that children must remain without their mother for many hours.

Housekeeping in Russia takes up much more time than in other countries. An interesting study of the time required for this purpose by the wife of a worker was made at the beginning of the 'thirties. It was shown, for example, that a woman wage earner can donate less than a quarter of the time to caring for her children that a housewife who is not earning wages can give. The former spends 470 hours in preparing food, the latter 997 hours. The former stands in line for purchases 152 hours, the latter 182 hours.

Especially interesting are the figures showing how the worker's home and clothing suffer when the woman of the house has to go to work; the nonwage-earning housewife devotes 228 hours to the care of the home and the family clothing, while the wage earner spends only 110 hours, or half as much time. In addition, work in the little family garden, so necessary and so widespread in Russia, demands much effort, too much for a woman burdened with factory labor as well as with housekeeping. For mothers of small children the necessity of working in a plant is frequently a personal tragedy.

So much ideological nonsense has been uttered on the subject of female labor that it has become difficult to grasp the elementary facts. Many journalists and travelers have pictured with great enthusiasm the expansion of female labor in Russia; they often represent it as a great achievement. "Women are guaranteed equality of opportunity, but they have also to accept the responsibilities . . . The changed position of women in the Russian social structure was wholly good, both for them and for the country: crèches, nurses in uniform . . ."

These phrases are but unvarnished repetitions of what the writers have been told by Moscow guides, and parallel official declarations. "The woman works on a basis of equality with the man, both in industry and in the collectives," writes Sautin, chief Soviet statistician. "Such are the brilliant results."

No, factory work by women does not constitute, contrary to the opinion of many, any degree of progress. For most women it does not mean participation in social life. Their employment, to any great extent, is the consequence either of extraordinary political events, such as war, or of extreme poverty. Most ardent advocates of female labor have no conception of the pain and struggle which it entails for the mother of a family. Many writers who have visited Soviet Russia point to the network of day nurseries where small children are kept all day long; Soviet journals frequently take pride in the number of such nurseries. But this relatively cheap institution, found in some measure in almost every country, cannot possibly serve as a substitute for the home. It is particularly widespread in Russia not because of the nature of the Soviet economy but solely because female labor is nowhere so common as in Russia. The wide use of government-operated eating places is no more inspiring. Of course, these are necessary when the wife works in a factory, but she and her family never cease to dream of having their own home in the true sense of the word. Therefore, the percentage of working wives and mothers among higher social elements is much smaller than among Soviet workers.

The number of female workers in Russian industry at

the beginning of this century was about 400,000 or about
18 per cent of the total of industrial workers. As in all countries, the number grew rapidly until the first World War, and
reached 635,000 in 1913. Under the Soviet regime, female
labor expanded to proportions unprecedented in any country.
There were 28 per cent of women in industry in the 'twenties,
but in 1933 they numbered 1,826,000, or 35 per cent, and in
1935, 2,727,000, or 38.3 per cent.* There are no official figures
on the growth of female labor during the next six years until
the outbreak of the war. Even if the increase was not very great,
it is certain that the percentage of women workers in Soviet
industry immediately before the war was more than 40.

During the period 1941–44, according to official figures, the
percentage of women in industry exceeded 70. However, this
has no relation to any preceding data. The percentage of
women workers will naturally decline after the war, but, in
view of the tremendous loss of life at the front, it will probably
remain somewhere between 45 and 50.

But even in peacetime the percentage of female workers had
already reached 40 to 42 per cent. There are no figures to show
the number of married female workers. However, the total
number of women workers, running into millions, indicates
in itself how large the percentage of wives and mothers must
be. Another indication is afforded by the ages of these workers.
At the beginning of the 'thirties, 80 out of every 100 women
workers were more than 20 years old, while 60 were 24 or over.
It may be fairly assumed that married women predominate
in the general mass of female workers.

The percentage of female workers in Russia is higher than
in any other European country or in the United States; except
for China, it is probably the highest in the world. The United
States presents the opposite extreme; western Europe occupies
an intermediate position. Similar significance attaches to the
unprecedented increase in the employment of minors in Soviet
Russia.

These facts throw more light than any statistical tables could
on the question of the standards of living and wages of the
workers. The mere physical existence of the workers is possible

* In 1923, 404,000, or 28 per cent; in 1927, 700,000, or 28.2 per cent; in 1928,
769,000, or 28.6 per cent.

only because the number of breadwinners in each family is now greater than before; this constitutes the principal means of defense against inadequate wages. The number of non-workers in each family has declined considerably.* Only by increasing female labor and that of minors is it possible to exist at all.

The Workers and the Communist Party

IN the light of the aforementioned facts, it is easy to imagine the relations existing between the working mass and the Communist party. The majority of workers, particularly those in the lower brackets, take no interest whatever in the party. Neither the discontented nor the obedient, loyal workers feel that they can derive any benefit from membership in the party.

But the top layer, which strives for advancement and has some reason to hope for success, derives marked advantages from party affiliation. Every plant has groups of workers who are released from their jobs, temporarily or indefinitely, for such tasks as organizing plant clubs, for "cultural-educational work," for the business of the plant committee, and so on. There are hundreds of workers who perform governmental or quasi-governmental functions—in the *Osoviakhim* (Defense against Gas War) or collecting membership dues. Finally there are the Stakhanovites and "distinguished people," who have already moved forward. They are in the forefront; they find the party membership card useful and sometimes necessary, for it serves to open many doors.

The party, in its turn, follows a similar line of reasoning. It has no need for the millions of average workers, except perhaps as evidence, for propaganda purposes, of its tie with the working class; this was especially true in the periods of struggle against the opposition. What the party now requires is the inclusion of the more active elements in its ranks. Even if these remain at the bench, they are carefully husbanded, their activities are watched, and they are utilized for various forms of activity as need arises.

* Official statistics on this point reveal the following facts: In 1930 there were 2.05 dependents for each worker in a family; in 1934, 1.66; and in 1935, 1.59.

In sum, about three quarters of the workers are nonpartisans, about 15 per cent are in the Komsomol, and only 10 per cent or less belong to the party. The party has long refrained from publishing data concerning this question; but the fact is that the percentage of Communists among the workers has not increased.

An occupational census taken in 1933, at the end of the first Five-Year Plan, disclosed that the proportion of all members of the Russian Communist party and of candidates for membership among the workers, including apprentices, ranged from 8.4 per cent in the ceramics industry to 17 per cent in the machine industry. In the metallurgical industry the percentage was 13.9, in the building trades 6. The percentage of men was double that of women. In the Komsomol, however, men made up 13.8 per cent and women 18.6 per cent.

During the eight years between 1933 and Russia's involvement in the war, the number of workers doubled. During those eight years the working mass was expanded largely by the influx of peasant elements, the newcomers into the party having worked as peasants only a short time before. These worker-peasants showed no greater enthusiasm for joining the party than the other groups.

THUS the Russian working class represents an entirely new, very large, and rapidly expanded social class. The peculiarities of the Russian working class are the recent peasant origin of a considerable majority and the inevitable retention of the habits, traditions, and memories of the Russian village; a very low wage scale for the majority; the rise of a top layer with good earning capacity; a deep cleavage between the higher and lower elements. In addition there are the opportunities for the advancement of the docile; the helplessness of the mass; a network of "informants" in every shop and plant.

The result of these conditions is a vast social passivity, the absence of any kind of open or illegal organization, and, finally, a readiness on the part of the great majority to carry out orders and instructions in the economic and political fields.

The Communist party has no fear of great political difficulties or danger from the workers. It is quite right as far as the threat of the rise of any hostile political movement is concerned. The first signal for any such movement will not come from the workers. But any political movement that might arise in other social strata would find a sympathetic response among many Russian workers discontented with the low standard of living, the unbridled power and control exercised by plant officials, and the unlimited power of the police in private life.

X

The Peasantry

"Right" and "Left" Communism

FOR no other class in Russia have the consequences of the revolutionary upheavals been so tragic and disappointing as for the peasantry. This is true of their material comfort as well as their political aspirations. After the first decade of revolution, at the end of the 'twenties, it became apparent that the NEP experiment, a private trade system within a Communist state, had already yielded all it could. After its potentialities had been exhausted, a new turn in Soviet policy became imminent. Two roads were open. For several years the "Leftists" had advocated a great program of industrialization and collectivization; a fight against the "class enemies" still remaining, namely, the kulaks; and an integral program of Communism. The "Rightists," with Bukharin and Rykov at their head, continued to advocate private enterprise for the peasantry for the next period, and were prepared for new economic concessions. The government—Stalin —had to decide which way to go. It was a decision fraught with destiny.

The introduction of the NEP had brought a degree of pacification in the villages; the peasant uprisings ceased. Because of the primitive production methods of Russian agriculture, the peasant economy was being restored more speedily than that of industry. The new food tax on agriculture provided considerable foodstuffs for the cities, complemented by private trade.

The economic revival of agriculture was accompanied by a process of social differentiation among the peasants. Some peasants rented their holdings and moved to the cities, others rented more land and expanded their operations. The leasing or renting of agricultural implements and machinery became a growing practice. The sons of large families left their homes to take jobs as agricultural laborers, while other peasants became their "capitalist" employers. Some had bad crops; others, having sold their products profitably in the market, returned from the cities with articles of "luxury" and added a second or third cow to their inventory.

All this was "within the law" but very dangerous. The members of the party and the Komsomol looked with animosity upon the new "capitalist" tribe, and the less opportunity the law gave them to combat this capitalist breed, the greater became their urge for a change in policy. "This is not what we fought the revolution for!" What was worse, the majority of the peasants, fearing a new antipeasant maneuver, refrained from expanding their economy. Having restored it more or less to the prewar level, they had acquired a modest measure of security as far as their own immediate needs were concerned, plus a small surplus for disposal in the market, tax payments, and so on. To have gone beyond that would have meant rising from the status of *seredniaki*—middle peasants—to that of kulaks, and exposing themselves to possible reprisals in the event of a political shift. In many places the peasants feared to sow too much, or to increase the number of their cattle; they purposely divided their land among their children in order not to be thought to have too much property. In this way the number of peasant households artificially increased from 16,000,000 at the beginning of the revolution to 25,000,-000 in the middle 'twenties.

Thus the economic development of the villages was greatly limited by political conditions. The area of grain cultivation, which had fallen from 232 million acres in 1913 to 163 million in 1922, rose speedily under the NEP to 232 million in 1926. At that point, however, it remained stationary: the acreage was 232 million in 1927 and 227 million in 1928. The crop yield likewise remained stationary: in 1926 it was 76.8 million tons; in 1927, 72.3 million; and in 1929, 71.7 million.

The NEP could not last: either the peasantry would break through the outer political crust of the new order to create a new political system more compatible with its character and needs, or, in the event of the peasants' failure to mobilize the forces necessary to achieve this, the existing political regime was bound to remold the peasantry, transforming it from a class of private owners into an element of state economy.

The first-named course was essentially the program of the Rightists. To be sure, the "Right Opposition" was not a peasant party; both in its ideology and in its policy, it was a group within the Communist party whose leaders had been Lenin's close lieutenants and regarded themselves as representatives of the working class. But, paradoxically enough, it was in the persons of these and other "working class representatives," that the peasants' hopes for a liberation from their new yoke found their last expression. The Right Opposition termed the policy of collectivization "military-feudal" in character; it issued warnings against its severe economic consequences. It opposed the mass extermination of the so-called kulaks. It considered individual peasant economy the key to the reconstruction of agriculture.

What the Right Opposition wanted was a great expansion of private agriculture—a road that every noncommunist government would choose. It did not consciously fear the growth of a peasant capitalism with all its implications for a Communist state.

The Leftists, on the contrary, were strongly opposed to any new concessions to the peasant. A huge industrialization was point one on their program, and they saw no other sources for new industrial funds than the village. To this end a reconstruction of the peasant economy and the creation of collective farms were necessary. Trotsky, Zinoviev, and Preobrazhensky were the exponents of this movement.

Stalin decided for the program of the Left. It was the only program in harmony with orthodox Communism, with its militant anticapitalism, its traditional fear of the small peasant, its traditional preference for a great agricultural economy, and finally with its attitude of indifference to the fate of individuals, especially millions of "private owners."

"Petty economy," wrote Lenin, "gives birth to capitalism and to the bourgeoisie—constantly, daily, hourly, in elemental fashion and on a mass scale." "If we continue, as before, to maintain small economies, we shall inevitably be threatened with destruction," for "agricultural economy under the system of commodity production cannot free mankind from mass poverty and oppression."

"Because of Russia's economic backwardness, the division

of land [confiscated from the large landowners] has predomi-
nated; while the retention of [so-called Soviet agricultural]
economies was the rare exception," wrote Lenin in his *Theses
on the Agrarian Question,* prepared for the guidance of the
Communist International in 1920. "For most of the advanced
capitalist countries, the Comintern recognizes as the right
policy the preservation of large agricultural economies and the
establishment of *sovkhozy* of the Russian type."

There was no difference between the positions of Lenin and
Stalin on this point. "Is the restoration of capitalism possible
in our country?" asked Stalin in 1928. "Yes," he replied, "it is
possible. This may seem strange, but small production gives
birth to capitalism and to the bourgeoisie, especially under
the conditions of the NEP."

This theory exaggerated the importance of a large agricultural economy, even in its capitalist forms. Until his death
Lenin adhered to this idea; the wish was father to the thought.
He declared that in Soviet Russia "the peasantry was the last
capitalist class."

When the food crisis came at the end of the 'twenties, Stalin
drew the following conclusion from his theory: "The task is
to transform the USSR . . . into a land of large agricultural
economy, furnishing the market with a high percentage of its
produce." The old prerevolutionary view of the peasantry as
a reservoir of food supplies and raw materials was suddenly
again coming to the fore by means of new formulas and slogans.

"The rate of expansion of commodity grain production,"
said Stalin, "is lower than that of our increased grain requirements. Industry is growing. The cities are growing. The different regions are growing. Yet, production of commodity grain
is growing at an extremely slow tempo."*

Despite his hatred of Trotskyism, Stalin maintained that
"the greatest danger confronting us comes from the Right."
Indeed, in setting up the collectives, Stalin was in reality put-
ting into effect a plank of the Trotskyite program; he justified

* According to Soviet statistics, before the first World War, the landlords and
well-to-do peasants supplied the market with an average of fifteen million tons
of grain annually. Now the landlords had vanished, while the number of well-
to-do peasants and the size of their establishments had been reduced. In consequence, at the end of the 'twenties, the amount of grain reaching the market
from these "capitalist" sources was only two million tons.

this before the perplexed party by saying that no adequate forces had been available to wage a war with the kulaks when Trotsky demanded it.

"In 1926–27," Stalin declared, "the Zinoviev-Trotsky opposition had sought to impose upon the party a policy of immediate offensive against the kulaks. Was it possible for us to undertake such an offensive with any hope of success five or even three years ago? No, it was not!" And the fact that the establishment of the collectives involved the extermination of part of the peasantry failed to impress Stalin. "What's bad about it?" he asked. "Why not apply extraordinary measures against the kulaks if it is all right to arrest hundreds of speculators in the cities and exile them to the Turukhansk region?" He denounced the Right Faction as pursuing a "liberal bourgeois policy."

The establishment of the kolkhoz system in the course of three or four years and the transformation of Russian peasants into members of collectives constituted the most radical upheaval known in history. Its effects were more profound and distressing than the expropriation of the propertied classes in 1918–20. There were, however, instances of resistance to an extent and in forms of which neither Russia nor the outside world had any adequate conception. The Soviet press, of course, did not report them, and the cities heard only fragmentary reports of riots, of their suppression, of mass exile. As a matter of fact, there were a great many uprisings embracing whole regions, revolts, ruthlessly suppressed by GPU troops. Tanks were let loose upon the peasants, whole villages burned to the ground and even bombed by government planes. The execution of captured rebels was resorted to with the object of intimidating and terrorizing the population, and was therefore of a mass character. But even where uprisings did not take place, the authorities systematically exiled kulaks, that is, better situated peasants, the term being applied also to many of the politically more conscious, more intelligent peasants apt to express protest. They were exiled to the far north and distant east, chiefly to Siberia. The instructions from Moscow demanded the complete "liquidation of the kulaks as a class." These, with their families, numbered in 1928, according to official statistics, 5,859,000 human beings. Some day we may learn how many of them were exiled; perhaps all were.

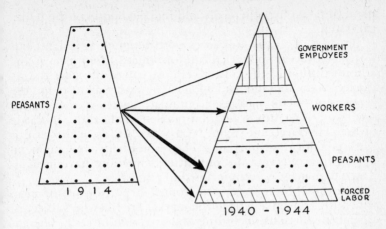

The reaction of the peasantry did not always take the form of uprisings. Even more threatening, perhaps, was their passive resistance. Under the new policy, the peasants were required to hand over to the collectives their livestock and implements; they preferred, however, to kill the cattle, sell the meat, or consume it themselves. In many instances, moreover, they wrecked their own equipment. The number of cattle, which had risen in the 'twenties, fell between 1929 and 1934 from 30.4 million to 19.5, the number of horses from 34.6 million to 15.6 million, etc. As a consequence of the general disorganization (and in part because of unfavorable weather), wheat production in 1931 declined 17 per cent. Since the state insisted on collecting its own share first, there was a terrible famine in many agricultural regions, with millions of dead.

The new system had taken definite shape by the middle of the 'thirties.

The Kolkhoz

ACCORDING to its rules, a kolkhoz is essentially a coöperative society, in which each individual participates with his own labor. Theoretically, the collective governs itself, introduces new machinery as it pleases, sells its grain on the free market, and, as circumstances permit, may earn considerable money. The collective contains the seeds of capitalist development, if taken hypothetically and independently of the political system.

But first of all the kolkhozes were designed as instruments for the extraction of agricultural products. From its crop the administration of the collective must pay to the state the required taxes in kind and money; it must pay also for the services of tractor stations, accumulate necessary reserves for seeds and other funds, retain a portion for feeding the cattle of the collective, and so on. Nearly two thirds of the crop is consumed for these purposes. The rest is divided among members of the collective, but only after deductions have been allotted to managers, technicians, and others.

The cash proceeds derived from that portion of the crop which the collective sells in the market are likewise subject to various deductions, including taxes payable in cash. The administrative personnel must also be paid from these proceeds. From the sum thus received by the individual peasant, he pays an income tax of 10 per cent, as well as other levies. In 1937, the most profitable year enjoyed by agriculture, members of the collectives received 48 per cent of the collectives' receipts, the remaining 52 per cent having been used to cover various expenditures.* From the 48 per cent, the peasant has to pay at least 8 per cent in taxes, leaving him 40 per cent. This 40 per cent is further reduced by the fact that, in buying goods for his own use, the peasant must pay sales taxes amounting to more than 50 per cent of the prices he is obliged to pay. Such is the balance sheet of peasant labor in the collectives.

The part played by the collectives as an instrument for the extraction of agricultural products is stressed in the minds of the peasants by the enormous apparatus of officialdom functioning in the villages. Neither Russia nor any other country had ever had such a huge swarm of officials. According to official statistics, there were 384,389 chairmen and vice-chairmen of collectives in 1938, 248,390 bookkeepers, and 232,421 chairmen of inspection committees. The whole personnel numbered nearly 1,000,000. In addition, there were 1,530,000 chauffeurs and mechanics employed at tractor stations. The total number of employees paid out of the peasants' labor was

* A decree promulgated in 1937 required that at least 60 per cent of the cash income be divided among the members of the collectives. It is not known whether this decree has been applied.

about 2,500,000. This, of course, did not include employees outside the economic administrative apparatus in the villages, such as treasury officials, police, teachers, and so on.

It is easily understood why the peasant pays more attention to his own small individual holding than to the business of the collective: small though it may be, it serves as an important foundation for his existence. Nearly 70 per cent of all cattle in the Soviet Union were to be found in these meager holdings. But even the 10 per cent of the grain crop produced by these holdings constitutes a tremendous help to the peasants.

At first the government had no intention whatever of permitting the peasants to retain any land for their own use; later, after the famine of 1933, came a concession, formally recognized in 1934–35. But the amount of land granted for private use was kept down to a minimum, from one quarter to one half of a hectare.* Within a few years, however, these small holdings, into which the peasants had begun to put their labor, became not only a part of the source of food for their personal use but, in part, the mainspring of supplies for the cities; paradoxically, these small plots furnished, within three or four years, a quarter of the country's agricultural production.

Before the outbreak of the war (1937–38) the average member of a kolkhoz put in 47 per cent of his labor hours in the kolkhoz, 33 per cent in his private plot or away from home, and the rest in his household. Millions of peasants began to avoid working in the collectives. In 1937, according to official figures, 13,100,000 peasants worked less than fifty days a year in their collectives, and, of this number, 4,600,000 did not work a single day.

For this reason new repressions were hurled against the individual peasant holdings in 1939. It was discovered that in some districts such holdings had expanded to the "gigantic" size of three hectares, and that in others some peasants employed in collectives had two private holdings, while others were selling theirs. Orders were then issued limiting the right to such holdings and the right to keep cattle; at the same time, and quite naturally, the state increased its demands upon the members of the collectives. In some districts every peasant was

* 1 hectare = 2.471 acres.

required to work in his collective not less than sixty days a year; in others not less than eighty days. Failure to meet these requirements entailed the loss of all the peasant's rights, including the right to his own holding. This compulsory labor minimum showed that the system of dividing the product of the collectives in proportion to each peasant's labor was inadequate, and that compulsory labor was an added necessity.

From the peasants' point of view, the collectives are a tremendous pump for draining the product of their labor through many channels; while the machine and tractor stations, with their political divisions, party cells, and propaganda activities, represent a state apparatus for political and police control over the villages.

Old Wine in New Bottles

THE establishment of this system was novel to the point of being sensational. The government had counted on speedy acceptance of the new conditions by the peasantry because of the marvels of technical progress introduced in the collectives. Critics, both in Russia and abroad, expected a catastrophe in Russian agriculture. It soon became apparent, however, that both the government and the critics had been mistaken, for they had failed to take into consideration certain old and tried methods known throughout Russian history, which were retained in the Communist system of agriculture.

To be sure, the peasants had long been accustomed to use the primitive plow and to fertilize the soil with manure. Now, they had suddenly come into contact with the wonders of foreign machinery, and in such quantities as were unknown to the best-ordered landed estates of old Russia, or even to the most efficiently regulated farms of western Europe. But behind the new brilliant façade of mechanized agriculture, there was a noticeable revival of old traditions.

It was this tradition that the Rightist leaders had in mind when they called the kolkhoz system a revival of the feudal-military economy or the old serf system.

Throughout Russian history, the peasant had enjoyed but a few brief moments as a free proprietor—thirty to fifty-five years, beginning with the 'sixties, in some cases with the 'eighties, of the last century, and until 1918. Before that, continuing for centuries, social relations in the villages followed this pattern: the majority of peasants were obliged to work for landlords; most of the land belonged to the latter, the peasants controlling only a portion. The peasants were compelled to work a certain number of days a week, in most cases three of six working days, on the landlord's estate. They lived only from the labor on their own land, and their objective was to reduce the amount of unpaid labor they were required to perform for the landlord.

This type of *corvée* labor on the landlords' estates was called *barshchina*. Another form of bondage was the *obrok* system; the *obrok* was a compulsory cash payment of the peasant to the landlord.

Peasant labor was compulsory, and the peasant was a serf. At the base of these economic relations was the state's need of a great army and of manpower, most of which, from the sixteenth to the eighteenth centuries, could be supplied only by the peasantry, the estates of the landed nobility serving as organizational centers.

Even after the emancipation of the serfs under Alexander II in 1861, the system of *barshchina* continued in some places for about twenty years, the peasants being required to work thirty-five to forty days each year on the estates. This system was abolished in 1883. What remained in many places until the revolution were the forms of share-cropping known as *otrabotki* and *ispolshchina*, as well as various other types of burdensome tenantry.

Characteristic of all these forms of peasant-landlord relations was the peasant's obligation to work for the landlord either without pay or in return for the lesser share of the product. For centuries Russia lived under this system; the nation expanded, grew more powerful, and achieved many a military success. But the foundation remained unchanged, and attempts at reform, undertaken from time to time, were unsuccessful.

The peasants themselves tolerated this economic regime for many generations, though not without complaint or efforts at resistance. In the seventeenth and eighteenth centuries great uprisings took place, sweeping entire regions, in addition to many local mutinies. In the middle of the nineteenth century the number of local revolts grew from year to year until the end of the 'fifties. All these mutinies were suppressed by local forces or by the army, which was itself composed of peasants.

For the regime of a vast country these sporadic outbreaks presented no real danger. They never threatened to develop into one united political movement, which presupposes determination and some degree of continuity. They were merely isolated protests against individual manifestations of cruelty, exploitation, and injustice—protests which died down as fast as they occurred and were soon succeeded by the same state of unquestioning obedience and submission to fate.

For the peasantry the system of collectives meant a return, in many respects, to the old order. To be sure, the private landlord was no more; instead there was the state-master; serfdom had vanished, and there were many other distinctions. History knows no perfect analogies. But there are also elements of the old in the new situation of the peasantry: a large economy, which requires "hands" and which the peasants give their labor to; the obligation to work diligently, without attempting to shirk one's duty; outside domination of one's household and labor; a pay system dictated from above; and, finally, the right to own a small plot of land. The small plot is one's own bit of land—small, to be sure, but precious. The collectives have been pictured as the most modern achievement of the twentieth century. But their chief elements are derived—and not accidentally—from the hoary past. "A feudal-military system," said the Right leaders to Stalin.

Of course, Soviet policy has not followed the old track because it deliberately wanted to revive the old Russian customs; on the contrary, the Soviet regime considers its policy extremely progressive. But there is small choice between economic systems, especially in questions involving the interrelationship of state and peasantry. Having repudiated the satanic principle of individual economy because of its inherent capitalist potentialities, but at the same time being in need of constantly increasing quantities of the peasants' products, the Soviet State really had no other way than to amalgamate the peasants into great administrative-economic units and to make labor compulsory. At the same time it was compelled to reduce the private holdings of each peasant to a minimum, in order not to lose his labor on the big landed estate known as the collective; and the hidden conflict between the state and the members of the collectives has continued uninterruptedly over the issue of the peasants' right to their own holdings and their obligation to work in the collectives.

The "Millionaires"

A SIGNIFICANT social differentiation among the peasantry has been taking place since the middle of the 'thirties. First, a growing differentiation among the kolkhozes became discernible, and, second, a differentiation among the members of each kolkhoz.

Differences in the achievements of the kolkhozes were a natural consequence of differences in the fertility of their soil, in the quantity of land at their disposal, in their produce, in prices and other market conditions. They were the outcome of the long history of Russia's colonization, and similar to the former prerevolutionary differentiation between the peasantry of the crowded poor regions of central and western Russia and the more recently populated provinces of the south and east. The sown area of an average kolkhoz amounted to 131 hectares in the Leningrad region, 273 in the Moscow region, 781 in the Ukraine, 1,414 in the Azov–Black Sea province, and 1,931 in the Saratov region. A prosperous kolkhoz does not, however, necessarily mean that its members are prosperous.

More significant is the second line of development, the differentiation among members of the kolkhozes, and the polarization of their poor and well-to-do elements. This evolution, which had naturally started before this war, has been accelerated by it. A member of a fortunate kolkhoz, working with his wife and three or four sons on the kolkhoz farm as well as on his own plot of land, has greater opportunities than, say, a poor widow. If a city lies nearby he has a free market to sell a part of his products—sometimes at fancy prices. He is not a kulak in the strict sense, since he is a member of a collective and does not hire labor; but if he is as clever and capable as a member of the liquidated class, he slowly climbs up the social ladder.

However, before the war these opportunities were limited. A few years ago it was only rarely that a peasant possessed such an excess of products as to emerge as a "rich *kolkhoznik.*" The war and inflation have changed all that. Now a peasant visiting a city market with fifty pounds of lard and a cartload of potatoes returns home with fifty thousand rubles or more. The peasant who possesses a few hundred thousand rubles in paper money is therefore no longer a rarity, although the "millionaires" who have been much publicized are not yet numerous. A further rise in prices in the free market may accelerate this process.

The upper stratum of the peasantry may be thought of as belonging socially to the upper classes of Soviet society. However, unlike the well-to-do elements of the cities, they play no part in the formation of public opinion and exercise no political influence. It may be that in their hearts they dream of other political conditions, that they fear the possible consequences of their comparative prosperity, and that they would prefer private enterprise to the present system. But their secret thoughts are of no real consequence at the present time.

The Communist Party in the Village

IT is not difficult to understand why the peasants have played so insignificant a role in the Communist movement throughout the history of the Soviet regime.

In 1926 statistics of a party census showed that Communist peasants engaged solely in agricultural work were almost nonexistent. In the whole of the Ukraine there were only 10,240; in Byelorussia, 1,350; and in all Great Russia, 51,000.

The beginning of collectivization was marked, on the one hand, by the dispatching from the cities of many thousands of party and Komsomol members for the purpose of setting up the new economic organization, and, on the other, by intensified recruiting of party members in the villages. New state institutions were being set up in the villages, offices with masses of employees, and these were naturally filled, as far as possible, by members of the party and the Komsomol. As for the collectives, they numbered more than 200,000. Wherever possible, their chairmen were Communists. This was true also of the machine-tractor stations.

For this reason the number of party members in the villages

increased from 404,000 in 1930 to 790,000 in 1934. But this did not at all signify any rush of the peasants into the Communist organizations. On the contrary, Lazar Kaganovich reported to the party congress in 1934 that "50 per cent of the collectives had no Communists at all."

This complaint was repeated time and again. Two years later it was reported to the conference of the Komsomol that it had no organizations in 149,000 collectives.

At the 1939 party congress, the last before the war, Andreyev reported that "in 243,000 collectives there were 12,000 party groups with a total membership of 153,000"; that some collectives had only Komsomol groups but no party groups; and that "in more than 100,000 collectives there were neither party nor Komsomol groups." Some of his figures astonished even the pessimists. In Byelorussia, for example, there were 9,665 collectives but only 44 party groups with a membership of 614; in the Vologda region there were 5,970 collectives but only 31 party groups, with a membership of 442; in the Perm region there were 3,314 collectives with 16 party groups and 274 members. Another delegate reported that in the Yaroslav region there were 36,000 party members but that only 2,500 were peasants.

In the Moscow region, a third delegate reported, there were about 250,000 Communists, but of the 6,556 collectives in this large region only 304, or 1.4 per cent, had any party units, while only 25 per cent of the collectives boasted units of the Komsomol. In 1938 the party had 27,000 candidates for membership, of whom only 334 came from collectives. A delegate from Leningrad reported that his party organization had admitted 28,217 members from the end of 1936 to March, 1939, but that of this number only 1,177 had come from the collectives.

Notwithstanding the intense efforts subsequently made to recruit party members, the results in the villages were insignificant. A year and a half later, the official organ of the *Komsomol* again complained that "in 90,000 collectives there were no Komsomol organizations." Immediately before the war, in the spring of 1941, the official organ, *Partiinoye Stroitelstvo,* reported that there were only 610,000 party members in the villages, or 19 per cent of the entire party membership.

Thus, after a quarter of a century, about 5 per cent of the

urban population belonged to the party (not counting the Komsomol), while in the villages the ratio was 5 per 1,000; even this included the administrative apparatus of the state. The peasantry continued to stand aloof.

This was the reply of the Russian village to the claim that the kolkhoz peasants had reconciled themselves to the new system.

The War

THE wartime policy of the government, as far as agriculture and the peasantry are concerned, was a direct continuation of the prewar system. Many expected that the Soviet Government would call on the private initiative of the farmers and that a "realistic" encouragement of their private economy, particularly in the devastated and liberated areas, would follow. The aim of such a reversal could lie in a real reconciliation with rural Russia, a kind of new NEP in a war and postwar world. These expectations were soon shattered.

The government left no doubt that it is determined to travel the old roads. It was natural that the obligatory grain deliveries of the kolkhozes and the private economies as well were doubled; but the discrimination against private economy was discernible. Private peasants in the liberated areas* were now obligated to deliver 30 per cent more products than the neighboring kolkhozes (before the war the difference amounted to between 5 and 10 per cent according to the decree of 1933). Animals, which were returned to southern and western areas after the expulsion of the Germans, went almost exclusively to kolkhozes, although private cattle, for example, exceeded the collective ownership by 50 per cent before the war. A decree provided for further increase of the number of kolkhoz cattle at the cost of private economies.

Obligatory work in the kolkhozes has been augmented since 1942. Before the war it amounted to 60 to 80 work days a year; but in 1942 the minimum was fixed at 100 to 150 days. Youths 12 to 16 years of age were made liable to work at least 50 days. People violating this decree had to bear the consequences:

* A number of kolkhozes have been divided up by the Germans.

namely, first, prosecution; second, the loss of all their kolkhoz privileges; and third, the loss of their plots.

All these decrees aimed at the restoration and strengthening of the kolkhozes and at further curtailment of private economy for the war and postwar period. Sometimes a paradoxical situation would arise. The collective economy is generally based on machines, tractor stations, repair shops, supply by industry, not to mention a steady supply of gasoline. This complicated system was disturbed when the automobile industry had to concentrate on war material, when gasoline transport was upset, and when workers were drafted for army service. The situation in the great area liberated from the invasion was naturally worst of all.

To a great extent agriculture had to return to old and at times primitive devices, since even horses were mobilized. Manual labor and work with horses and cattle more and more took the place of machines. Small economies were better adapted to the new conditions. Peasants worked on their plots, and workers and employees created millions of small subsidiary gardens of their own. However, the government adhered to its policy.

In future it may have to revise its course if things get worse. It is not impossible, after all, that some encouragement will be given to individual farming. If such measures are taken, they will be dictated by expediency, as a temporary policy, with the object of restoring the kolkhoz system in full force as soon as private initiative has helped it to traverse the first hard period after the war.

THESE conditions have been strongly reflected in the attitude of the peasantry toward the war. But this attitude, at first glance, was paradoxically contradictory, almost incomprehensible.

The army, which was rapidly expanded after 1939, absorbing nearly the total adult male population, was from 70 to 80 per cent peasant in composition. It fought bravely, enduring without complaint unheard-of privations. The peasants who remained at home, however, reacted differently to the military situation. When the German troops invaded Byelorussia, and particularly the Ukraine, the peasants in the villages hoped for some improvement in living conditions under the regime of

the invaders; they thought the Germans would probably dis-
solve the "Bolshevik collectives." Reliable information now
available, though incomplete, indicates that at the beginning
of the war, especially in the south, there was little manifestation of patriotism. This was the period, extending to the middle of 1942, when the Germans had made their farthest ad-
vances and had won their greatest successes. It was during this
period, too (June–December, 1941), that Stalin made his first
attacks on those in Soviet Russia who doubted the army's ability to cope with the situation.

At the same time, the behavior of the Germans in the occupied territories of Russia had begun to shatter the peasants'
hopes. The seizure of grain, meats, and fats from the peasants;
the many cases of violence, rape, and murder committed by the
Germans; and the disappointment suffered by some Ukrainian intellectuals who had hoped for the establishment of an
autonomous Ukraine under a German protectorate brought
disillusionment. It also became abundantly clear that the
Germans had no intention of abolishing the collectives. They
soon perceived their value as a means of draining food supplies from the villages; knowing little of Russian village life,
they preferred to deal not with millions of small economic
units but with large agricultural organizations. They drove
thousands of peasants and masses of cattle from the villages,
while being unable to provide the Russian villages with machines and gasoline. Only in rare instances, by way of rewarding individual villages for acts of collaboration, did they grant
special permission to break up collectives into individual
holdings. Such occasions of division of land were marked by
great celebrations, prayer meetings, military music, and other
signs of general rejoicing.

Some pro-German illusions that might have existed in the
minds of peasants in occupied territories were quickly shattered, while in the unoccupied regions, particularly in the
east and in Asia, there was experienced the beginning of that
typical wartime prosperity which is tantamount to impoverishment: a rise in the prices of foodstuffs sold in the "free
market," with corresponding huge profits. Even before the
war, peasants were permitted by law to sell their meat, milk,
butter, and lard in the cities. This trade had been small in
comparison with that conducted by the state, but in view of

the terrific wartime shortages it assumed significance for the elements of the population that could pay high prices.

Prices increased with the catastrophic speed that character-izes periods of food shortage. City dwellers would hasten to offer hundreds and thousands of rubles for lard, meats, and potatoes; others, less prosperous, were frequently compelled to sell their clothing and domestic furnishings in illegal city markets at high prices in order to buy food. Peasants who went to the cities with small supplies of their products would return home with thousands of rubles in their pockets.

Who was the winner in this competition between city and village? The urban population was naturally irritated by the peasants' "avarice." "The villages are waxing rich on the mis-ery of the people," the cities complained.

The peasants were amassing huge quantities of paper rubles. At times they understood the unreality of this wealth: "we give the cities goods and get paid in worthless paper"; at other times they made purchases with this money, but there was little to buy. The government endeavored to reassure them by pointing out that the state, which would continue to dispose of the bulk of commodities after the war, would sell to them at stable, relatively low prices, and that the peasants would be able to buy these goods in large quantities with their accumu-lated money, thus making a large profit. But such arguments were unconvincing in the light of the hard experience gained in Russian and other European inflations in the past.

The peasants were also urged to invest their accumulated savings in government loans, and huge amounts flowed into the State Treasury, accompanied by letters expressing devo-tion to Stalin. All this was pictured as a purely voluntary pa-triotic campaign. Letters from peasant millionaires were pub-lished in the Soviet press as manifestations of peasant patriot-ism.

At the same time, the collectives continued to supply the cities and the army to the extent of their ability; in many cases they did so beyond their means. Whenever the government was confronted with instances of extreme need, the respective divisions of the party's committees would call upon its organi-zations in the villages to launch a campaign of patriotic offer-ings for the cities in the guise of voluntary contributions.

Such has been the strange picture of peasant activities during the war: self-sacrifice on the part of peasants in uniform; doubt and frequent hesitation on the part of their people at home; the delivery of large supplies to the cities and the army, both by collectives and individuals; the investment of part of the money in bonds for the benefit of the state.

Viewed as a whole, the picture may seem incongruous, but such it is. The peasantry remains what it has always been—the chief material source of great armies and supplies. As ever, it gives to the state, without adequate compensation, its labor, its products, and its sons. They fight, as ever, loyally and magnificently. But, as was the case for centuries, the peasantry remains deprived of its own independent political or other organizations. There have been many stormy outbreaks of protest, but they have all died down, and obediently, silently, and frequently against its own interests, the peasantry continues to meet all the demands of the state.

SHOULD Russia experience any great domestic upheavals in the near future, the peasantry will not initiate them. It has at present neither the strength nor the ability nor the experience for any political initiative. The most it can do is to throw the weight of its influence on the side of an opposition movement after an upheaval, though without playing any independent role. New upheavals would be certain to affect the villages and lead to the restoration of an individual peasant economy in place of collectives. A new division of the land would become inevitable in the event of violent political clashes, and regardless of the programs put forward by the conflicting elements.

But should developments take a less violent form, without a popular revolution or counterrevolution, events in the villages would take a different turn. Under such circumstances the state would retain its authority, and its requirements would continue to play an important role. The development of the agricultural economy would then proceed along evolutionary lines—through gradual expansion, for example, of individual peasant holdings at the expense of the collectives, the lowering of prices of commodities manufactured in the cities, the reduction of taxes, and granting the peasants the right to expand their activities in any direction. The final effect would be the same, as in the first instance—a redistribution of land.

The interests of the peasantry, however silent and obedient though it may be, are bound to assert themselves very loudly in any political crisis. It will long continue to make up the most numerous section of the Russian people. And the economic requirements of the state and nation demand the speediest possible solution of the problem presented by Russia's hundred million pariahs.

XI

Forced Labor

IT is indeed extraordinary that one should feel obliged to begin a chapter about a numerous social class of a great country by demonstrating that it exists and constitutes one of the most important factors in the development of the nation's economy in general and of its industry in particular. But the conscious blindness of some and the false information disseminated by others have contributed to the fact that this class remains a mystery to many readers. To be sure many books and personal memoirs have been written on the subject but there are, of course, no official data. Much that is pertinent has been mentioned in the past two or three years by American and British correspondents. For example, here is what Quentin Reynolds wrote in 1942 in *Only the Stars Are Neutral:*

"A few miles outside of Kuibyshev we passed one of the big concentration camps reserved for political prisoners. Beyond that we saw a long line of them working on a new road. There were about 800 of them . . . On their faces there was no sign of hope. A few soldiers with rifles guarded them carelessly, for there was no place for them to run. Steele and I looked at each other and winced . . . We winced, I think, because these 800 prisoners were women."

In 1943, upon his return from Russia, Wendell Willkie published a series of articles as well as his book. He refrained from saying anything very unfavorable to the Soviet Government; nevertheless, he recalled the astonishment he had felt when, after visiting some Russian cities, he had failed to find a concentration camp in the suburbs of Yakutsk, an exception to the rule:

"We drove into Yakutsk in a heavy black Soviet limousine. Between the airfield and the town we looked for the usual concentration camp we have seen in some other cities—half barbed wire fences, with sentry boxes at the corners. But there was none, or at least we never came across it."

Walter Graebner, an objective and accurate correspondent, reported in *Round Trip to Russia:*

"On the way we passed hundreds of . . . barracks inhabited by labor battalions and political prisoners. It is impossible to get any accurate reports as to the number of prisoners, why they were arrested, etc. In many places I noticed high roofed platforms, on which rifle-bearing guards stood to see that no one escaped."

In *Blind Date with Mars* Alice Moats tells of a conversation with a Soviet citizen, who said to her:

" 'Do you realize that as a result of the great purge, there is not one person in this country who has not either been locked up himself or has had some member of his family in a concentration camp? Right now there are some fifteen million people in work-camps and prisons!' Later a person in a position to obtain accurate figures set the number at twenty millions."

The English journalist, Philip Jordan, who calls his book *Russian Glory,* writes:

"It was at Ryazan that we saw something which, had I seen it at home, would have filled me with indignation and disgust, but which, because its victims seemed not to care or to object, was no concern of mine. Standing beside our train was a long line of flat cars intercepted here and there by barren prison vans. On the flat track opposite our window were perhaps thirty women guarded by an NKVD man with a tommy-gun. They were squatting like dummies there, and had not moved for hours, for against their exposed flanks the first snows of winter had driven, and there they now rested. One of the women had a baby in her arms . . . The others were monoliths of sorrow hatched rudely out of some shabby but enduring stone. There was something terrible about them. They looked like the last inhabitants of a world they could remember to have once been populated by a race of happy men who existed no longer."

The correspondent of the *New York Herald Tribune,* Walter Kerr, tells in his book, *The Russian Army,* of the reception received in Murmansk by the large convoy in which he arrived in Russia:

"As we came alongside the pier we saw hundreds of Russian workmen waiting to unlash the planes from our decks and to hoist the tanks from our holds.

" 'Let's give them a cheer!' shouted one of our Scotsmen, and after the men had cheered they stared in amazement at the blank, disinterested faces of the Russians on the dock. There was perhaps a half minute of awful silence, and then the mouth of the Scotsman hardened and he screamed out, 'All right. Go to hell then!' And he turned his back and went below, followed by the rest of the crew. A few hours later we found out why the Russians had failed to acknowledge the cheer. They were prison laborers, far from their homes, guarded by police with rifles and fixed bayonets. I suppose they did not care whether any country sends supplies to Russia."

The British economist Leonard Hubbard, who has studied labor conditions in Russia, remarks:

"The quantity of labor at the disposal of the GPU in their various convict camps throughout the USSR ran into millions . . . The use of convict labor in the '30s has certain similarities with the use of serf and forced labor by Peter I."

Hubbard estimates the number of prisoners in Soviet concentration camps at "millions." There are, of course, no accurate figures. Those we have are subject to violent fluctuations. Reports current in Soviet Russia place the number at 15 to 20 million. These reports are the sources of Miss Moats's information cited above. But neither the Russian people nor those abroad can possibly have a clear idea of the situation. The subject is veiled in deep secrecy.

The late Polish Socialist Victor Alter spent about two years in Soviet jails as a political prisoner. He was released through the amnesty granted to Poles in 1941 and lived in Kuibyshev for several months before his execution in December of the same year. Alter was intensely interested in the subject of concentration camp prisoners. He concluded that their number was between 8 and 12 million. On the other hand, a person who until recently had been an inmate of a concentration camp in northern European Russia, writes in a report as yet unpublished:

"Soviet officials contradicted sharply the statement that the figure [of prisoners] was above 20 million, but they did not object to a figure within the limit of 20 million." Finally, as serious a publication as *The Nineteenth Century and After* has placed the figure, on the basis of its Russian sources, at 10 to 18 million, in 1944.

The American engineer John Littlepage, who was employed by the Soviet Gold Trust in Siberia for a period of ten years, until 1937, estimated the number of forced-labor workers as "from one to five million," and stated that "the recent purges, which affected hundreds of thousands of persons, undoubtedly added to the labor army."

Boris Souvarine, French authority on Russia, in his biography of Stalin, estimated the number of prisoners in concentration camps at 5 million, exclusive of forced-labor groups such as "inhabitants of isolation camps and the exiles." As of 1937, he declared, "15 million condemned in the various categories would probably be the number most in accord with the facts."

The official census returns for 1937 have not been published at all, and of the returns for 1939 only a few summarized figures appeared. They include, naturally, no indication as to the labor camps. In statistical tables these inmates, as well as all other groups of exiled or deported people, are registered just as "Wage Earners" in addition to officials and free workers. From 1934 to 1939 members of this wage-earners group, with their families, allegedly increased at a rate which even in the Soviet Union is impossible: from 45 to 84 million. The veil has not been lifted so far, but there can hardly be any doubt that the inclusion of all deported people in the great class of wage earners in 1939 is partly responsible for the statistical miracle.

At any rate, whatever the actual number of workers under the forced labor system may be, it is equivalent to the population of a country like Yugoslavia, or Czechoslovakia, or the Argentine, and it is certainly not less than the population of Australia. The number of people subject to forced labor is not less and is probably greater than the total number of industrial workers at liberty in Russia.

Labor as an Instrument of Correction

THIS extraordinary historical phenomenon of the creation of a great social class by the methods of exile, imprisonment, and compulsion has had its ideological inception in high principles of humanity and love of one's neighbor. Faith in labor, in the enlightening effect of labor, in the correction of the human being through labor, in treatment of criminals by the therapeutic use of labor, the appeal of the all-embracing poetry of labor, gave rise to concepts in Soviet Russia which ultimately found expression in hard and bitter experience. One can think of no greater paradox than this transformation of the most advanced ideas of the science and morals of recent centuries into a cruel system of compulsory labor for millions.

The road to hell is paved with good intentions. The contemporary world is given to forgetting rapidly and it no longer remembers the furor and resentment provoked, before the revolution, by the soul-shattering description of life in Russian prisons and places of exile; few, indeed, remember George Kennan and his *Siberia and Exile,* the books of Emil Dillon, Peter Kropotkin, and the thousands of pamphlets and articles published in the world press concerning the sufferings, horrors, the barbarism practiced in Russian prisons. Until 1917 the question of the Russian penal regime occupied an increasingly prominent place in the political literature of the world, as the Russian revolutionary movement expanded and thousands of intellectuals, writers, and political leaders passed through the gates of Russian jails.

However, the number of prisoners in the old Russian *katorga* ("penal servitude") was much smaller than in the Correction Labor Camps today. In 1900–05 there were 15,000 such prisoners; in 1910, 28,742; in 1913, 32,757, with only 5,000 political prisoners.

All members of the Bolshevik old guard had experienced imprisonment, and like all other revolutionists, they had reached the firm conviction of the need of radical prison reform: abolition of the accursed *katorga,* of "prison companies"; the need of humane treatment of prisoners, as long as prisons remained necessary for a short "period of transition"; the recognition of the human rights and human dignity of prisoners. The principle generally accepted was "correction rather than punishment." And labor in prisons was considered to be the best means of correction. Systematic work, particularly for professional criminals, was regarded as good training for a useful social life, because it made possible the acquisition of new habits, of technical skills, and facilitated the criminal's transformation into a useful member of society. These ideas,

derived from the non-Communist science of the nineteenth
and twentieth centuries, had been incorporated in the general
ideology of Bolshevism, whose leaders wrote the word "labor"
in capital letters, a word that played the role of a universal
moral principle. The basic program of Bolshevism guaranteed
to all "the right to work," and only those who toiled were to
enjoy political rights: "He who toils not shall not eat."

The penal policy of Bolshevism constitutes perhaps the most
interesting monument of the early years of the Soviet regime:
it was a striking mixture of the cruel "Red terror" and liberal
concern for the "care of prisoners." Occasionally, innocent
people—even hundreds of them—were executed, but those who
escaped execution could reasonably hope to be released from
prison. The famous Cheka, which later developed into the all-
powerful OGPU, at first had no right of sentencing prisoners
but merely had the duty of conducting preliminary investiga-
tions; the sentences were imposed by special tribunals, which
as early as two months after Lenin's assumption of power had
received the right of condemning prisoners to "corrective
labor."

But the first years, judging by decrees and official instructions, were marked by the highest, most humane intentions.
According to instructions promulgated in 1918, a prisoner,
while "obliged to do physical labor," received compensation
commensurate with trade-union wage scales, including over-
time pay. The laws for the protection of working women and
minors, and for inspection of industrial plants were proclaimed applicable to prisons as well. Vocational training of
prisoners was made obligatory. It was forbidden to address
prisoners with the familiar "thou"; prisoners were permitted
to smoke; occasionally they were granted "leaves" and were
permitted to live in private quarters; finally, it was intended to
make wide use of the parole system.

"Punishment must be devoid of any semblance of torture
and must not subject the prisoner to useless and unnecessary
suffering," declared the Commissariat of Justice in a document
issued in the heat of the civil war, in December, 1919.

Concentration camps, first introduced in the autumn of
1918, were intended for "the counterrevolutionary bourgeoisie." But at the same time, the Communist Party Congress
(March, 1919) adopted a program calling for the replacement

of prisons by corrective establishments, reaffirming the principle that "labor is the chief method of correction and training." Recalling the French revolution and Voltaire—"make a man diligent and he will be honest"—the promulgated reforms called for abolition of "fetters, handcuffs, solitary confinement, deprivation of food, interviews through bars."

The criminal code of 1922, seeking to draw a contrast with the capitalist world, limited imprisonment to a maximum of ten years. This was more humane as compared not only with old Russia but with the most democratic countries. Regarding the United States, in particular, Soviet textbooks and lectures on criminology sought to expose the cruelties of its prisons and drew comparisons between the principles—the principles, to be sure, not the practice—of the American and Soviet penal systems. All this was sincere at that time: the Soviet leaders believed that the time was not far distant when crime would quickly decline in Russia, the prison population would be radically reduced, and the penal system would become the model for the entire world.

Meanwhile practice remained strangely remote from principle. The civil war had ended but the prison population grew from year to year, and rather rapidly. The police apparatus, political and criminal, was expanding and becoming more efficient; new types of punishable offenses made their appearance. In 1922 the prison population totaled 57,200; in 1927 it was 122,700. In 1929 it rose to 242,000. The number of administrative punishments imposed (i.e., without trial) increased sixfold from 1923 to 1926. The prisons became congested, for there was room for only 80,000 persons.

And with the end of the 'twenties the government entirely ceased publishing figures concerning the number of prisoners in jails and concentration camps.

Still greater was the disappointment with respect to education and training of prisoners. Neither resolutions of party congresses, nor articles in the press, nor the instructions of the Commissariat of Justice, nor direct court orders found any expression in practice. There were no workshops in most prisons and the few that did exist were without tools and equipment. Moreover, there was still much unemployment at the end of the 'twenties and any increase in prison labor naturally reduced the available job opportunities for the unemployed.

In some instances sentences of forced labor were carried out fictitiously: the prisoners remained at work at their former places of employment, spending their nights in jail, and were eventually released altogether because of the prison congestion. These privileges were not accorded to political prisoners, however.

According to official figures only a third of forced labor sentences were carried out at the end of the 'twenties, despite considerable efforts to put them into effect.

The First Labor Camps

THE first real Correction Labor Camp appeared in 1923 and soon became the model for many such camps. Modest in size, it was established on the Solovetsky Islands, in the White Sea. The inmates of the Archangel concentration camp were transferred to this new institution. Unlike most prisons, the Solovetsky camp was placed from the very beginning under the authority of the OGPU. It was shortly abbreviated to SLON—the Russian initials for "Northern Forced Labor Camps for Special Assignment." Its location in the far north had the advantage of requiring only a small guard, because escape was almost impossible, and the distance from all centers, especially those abroad, permitted the introduction of a rigorous regime which in an even harsher form became the rule in the 'thirties.

The Solovetsky camp had 6,000 prisoners in the middle 'twenties, a figure which remained stationary until 1926–27. Most of the prisoners were "politicals," i.e., members of non-Communist parties, priests and monks, professors, "nepmen," and many lawyers of nepmen. So-called "wreckers" appeared somewhat later, as did hunger strikers from other prisons, and "anecdotists," that is, persons exiled for spreading political anecdotes critical of the Soviet regime and its leaders. Then came many Trotskyites and other Communist dissidents. From 1928 on the number of "campers" increased rapidly to 30,000; soon the Solovetsky camp and adjacent annexes expanded, part of it toward the mainland. In 1929 the Northern Camp Administration embraced seven concentration camps, of which the Solovetsky camp was only one. The total population of these northern camps on May 1, 1930, was 662,257, according to N. Kiselev, a former OGPU official. This figure is confirmed from other sources.

At first the northern camps had no great economic significance, and originally they had no economic aims. Because of climatic conditions there was no agriculture on the Solovetsky Islands, the prisoners being occupied primarily in lumbering and fishing. But this type of forced labor no longer had any relation to the idyl prescribed by the Corrective Labor Code. Trade-union wage scales, the eight-hour day, and labor inspections no longer existed. In reality, it represented the revival of the old Russian system of hard penal labor under a cruel, uninhibited administrative regime. Food supplies from the mainland arrived irregularly and were always inadequate; in the matter of clothing the situation was even worse. The death rate through cold, disease, and suicides was very high. Kiselev reports 183,490 deaths for the five-year period of 1925–29. Particularly difficult was the situation of the comparatively small number of women. "I did not know a single woman [in the camps], unless she was old, who in the end had failed to give herself to the Chekists," writes Kiselev. "Otherwise, she would quickly and inevitably perish."

The years 1929–30, which divide the history of the Soviet regime as a whole into two parts in the sphere of policy, economics, and ideology, also mark a turning point in the history of the concentration camps. It was the period of the second revolution, and its reverberations were felt in the most remote human settlements. From the initial experimental labor camps of the 'twenties there developed a great class of forced labor at the beginning of the 'thirties.

Many factors contributed to this process. The vast program of industrialization, begun in 1928, required huge numbers of additional workers, such as industry did not have at its disposal. The construction of railways, highways, and canals, which constituted a very substantial element of the various Five-Year Plans, required millions of workers, largely unskilled. The production of lumber for export had to be stepped up considerably because of the decline in production of wheat and oil, formerly the chief commodities of Russian export, due to the mechanization and collectivization of agriculture. It was hard to enlist workers voluntarily for the difficult jobs of metal, mineral, and coal mining in the far north and east. New industrial centers were being built in the east, particularly in Asia—Magnitogorsk, Kuzbas, and so on. Everywhere there was the problem of recruiting masses of unskilled labor for the speedy construction of new cities. Finally, as part of the war-preparedness program, it was necessary to build new railway lines, many airdromes, barracks, thousands of miles of military roads, and much else. Where were the necessary labor forces for all this construction to be obtained in the face of the labor shortage in the expanding plants and factories?

But then came the collectivization of agriculture, which the government coupled directly with the "liquidation of the kulaks." This liquidation, as we have seen, meant the exile of millions of peasants from the villages to forced labor. The collectivization campaign continued for four to five years, from 1929 to 1934. The enormous network of Corrective Labor Camps developed precisely during that period. Built on the Solovetsky model, they now became an economic enterprise of first-class importance. Their boss, the OGPU, became the greatest employer in the USSR and in the world: not a single branch of heavy industry, not even the Commissariat of Heavy Industry or the Commissariat of Transport, commanded such an army of "hands" as was at the disposal of the OGPU at the beginning of the 'thirties.

To meet the problem of the increased need of labor power, the government passed new legislation and issued a number of new instructions. In 1928 the Soviet of People's Commissars intensified the "measures against hostile class elements." In November, 1929, it decided to alter radically the entire penal system, to abolish imprisonment in general as a means of punishment in favor of the system of Corrective Labor Institutions. The Soviet of People's Commissars ordered that all those "sentenced to deprivation of liberty for a period of more than three years be exiled to Corrective Labor Camps in distant parts of the USSR"; those sentenced to shorter terms were to be sent to Corrective Labor Colonies (reserved, as a lighter measure of punishment, "for toilers only"). Judges were strictly forbidden henceforth to mete out short prison sentences without hard labor.

The consequences made themselves felt immediately. In 1927 hard-labor sentences totaled 18.6 per cent; three years later they rose to 56.5 per cent. Short-term sentences in 1927 were 32.1 per cent; in 1930, 1.9 per cent. Limited deprivations of liberty amounted to 8 per cent in 1927, and only 2.6 per cent in 1930. Publication of the actual number of sentences was discontinued because of the enormous totals. The population of the forced labor camps grew rapidly.

The general political climate became intensely grim. In August, 1932, the government promulgated a law concerning the "protection of state property," characterized by unprecedented severity and directed principally against peasants who refused to turn over their property to collectives. The punishment prescribed for violations was either death or "deprivation of liberty for not less than ten years." This law was very widely applied, but the exact number of sentences remained unknown. In the midst of this stream of repressions, P. Postyshev declared in behalf of the Central Committee of the party at a congress of jurists in 1931, "We will retain our penal system in all its ruthlessness, our repressions, our measures of suppression against the class enemy."

In July, 1934, the former OGPU was transformed into the NKVD, under which there was organized immediately the Chief Administration of Corrective Labor Camps and Labor Settlements (GULAG), whose duty it was to administer the many growing forced labor camps. The NKVD was vested with the right "to order without trial expulsions, exile, and imprisonment in Corrective Labor Camps for a period of not more than five years." A year later the NKVD was given charge of the construction of all highways. To put the police in charge of highway construction may appear incomprehensible in the United States, but it was quite natural in Russia in that period.

Successful Development

THIS regime of ruthlessness operated in the same direction as the general trend of collectivization and industrialization. In 1928, as far as can be established, the class of forced labor was about 30,000; in 1930, about 650,000; and in 1934–35 it was probably between 5,000,000 and 6,000,000.

These numbers continued to grow, in some years quite rapidly. They included: first, ordinary criminals, formerly maintained in prisons; second, kulaks, whose numbers were particularly large between 1929 and 1934; third, participants in peasant mutinies, which at times had swept entire regions, and all of whose inhabitants suffered exile; fourth, "counterrevolutionists," i.e., members of non-Communist parties and sympathizers; fifth, Communist-oppositionists, who comprise a very large number of exiles, particularly in the period of the great purge of 1936–38; sixth, national groups, exiled as a whole as a preventive measure, such as Soviet citizens of Polish nationality in the middle 'thirties (after Poland's *rapprochement* with Germany);* this category also includes Germans (Soviet citizens) exiled from various regions of European Russia and Siberia, especially after the beginning of the Russo-German war.† Added to the categories of exiles mentioned were "socially hostile elements" in the newly occupied regions in 1939–40. Over 1,000,000 were exiled from eastern Poland and hundreds of thousands from the Baltic States and Bessarabia. In addition there was the systematic exile of the population residing along the frontiers, as on the Finnish border, and from many places along the Polish border; in other places, too, where fortifications were in the course of construction, tens of thousands of civilians were driven to the east and north.

In addition to these principal groups comprising the basic mass of forced labor, there were numbers of Chinese brought to the labor camps from the Far Eastern frontier, Greeks from the Crimea and the Black Sea region; Kazakhs, Uzbeks, Tadzhiks from central Asia; Turks and Armenians from the Turkish and Iranian borderlands; "speculators" (black-market traders), smugglers, persons guilty of misusing state funds, of whom there were many in the 'thirties; and finally many former employees of the OGPU-NKVD.

From all the foregoing it is apparent that there have been and are various categories of forced labor in Soviet Russia. Some have been condemned to direct exile; others are sentenced to Corrective Labor Camps; there are many groups sentenced not by the courts but exiled by way of precautionary action, such as those moved from frontier regions. Living conditions of the last category, that of the so-called "special mi-

---

* There were approximately 626,000 Poles in Soviet Russia, but it is not known whether all or only a part of this Polish population was exiled.

† Germans in the Soviet Union numbered 1,423,000.

grants" and "voluntary migrants," are much more tolerable than those of the first-mentioned group. Of the national groups, for example, exiled to the east after the occupation of the Baltic States and eastern Poland, about one third were sent as prisoners to labor camps, while the rest were domiciled, without sentence, in other camps. The "aristocrats" among those condemned to forced labor are not required to live in camps but may have their own private quarters, under strict supervision of the NKVD; frequently they are separated from their families. Because of the advantages they enjoy they come closer, however, to the class of free wage earners. At the opposite pole of the forced-labor system are the inmates of Correction Labor Camps in the north.

All of them constitute a gigantic reservoir of manpower for the Soviet economy.

The Five-Year Plans

THE great projects carried out during the period of the Five-Year Plans were executed on the basis of the experience obtained through the Solovetsky labor camp. In 1930 it was decided to build the gigantic White Sea–Baltic Canal, the project being entrusted to Henrikh Yagoda, the notorious chief of the OGPU (executed in 1938). The work began in November, 1931, and was completed in 1933–34; the number of workers employed in the concluding period—all of them recruited from the labor camps—was nearly 300,000. The canal is situated along the Finnish border; some of the workers managed to escape across that frontier, and, in the middle 'thirties, made public some descriptions of life in the labor camps; these writings, checked against one another, presented what seems to be a clear picture of the situation.

Thus, for example, a French engineer employed in Russia and sentenced to forced labor, having managed to escape across the Finnish border, published in the French magazine *Etudes* a detailed description of the conditions of life and work in the construction of the White Sea–Baltic Canal; his account coincides with many other descriptions.

"More than 200,000 prisoners were employed on the project," he writes. "More than 50,000 died during a period of a

year and a half. The work day was eleven hours. There were
no Sundays or any days of rest. Interruptions occurred only
during transfers of workers from one camp to another. The
work tasks were set very high, and food rations very low. Those
who carried out their prescribed task received 800 grams [29
ounces] of bread daily; those whose performance was only half
of the prescribed norm received 300 grams [11 ounces]. Besides bread, a watery soup and salt fish were the only foods.
Most of the work was done by hand, without mechanical appliances. Despite the terrible Karelian cold, prisoners were
forbidden to build camp fires: 'You can warm up by working!'
they were told. This camp was named by the prisoners 'Hell
of Ice.' I myself saw dead people who had been frozen with
axes or saws in their hands. From 25 to 30 men died daily in
winter. Responsibility for discipline was placed collectively
upon each company: if a prisoner escaped the rest were punished by extension of their terms of service. Those caught es-
caping were shot."

From a purely economic point of view the project was a success: the canal, 142 miles long, was completed on schedule,
including many dikes, locks, dams, etc. The cost was comparatively low—95,000,000 rubles—which is not surprising consid-
ering the form of labor employed. The canal was named the
Stalin Canal, and its official opening was marked by a great
celebration, widely publicized in the press. Some fifteen Soviet writers wrote enthusiastic articles, emphasizing the social
significance of the project in regard to the labor employed—
the transformation of criminals into useful members of society.
Some prisoners, particularly genuine criminals, spoke and
wrote about the beneficent effects they had experienced under
the fatherly influence of the OGPU—in the hope of obtaining
clemency. When Maxim Gorky visited the project, the prisoners assembled to greet him sang the following lines:

> We are prisoners of a free land
> Where there is neither suffering nor torture,
> We are not being punished, but reformed.
> This is no mystery, no secret.

And, indeed, 72,000 prisoners—all criminals—were amnes-
tied upon completion of the project.

The policy of "reforging" camp inmates became a promi-

nent theme of Soviet press propaganda; in reality, this was an
attempt to soothe the consciences of those who were compelled
to witness the monstrous expansion of forced labor in Soviet
Russia. The policy of "reforging" was put forward to justify
the severity of the system, the extremely difficult conditions of
life and work, and the actual revival of the old *katorga*. Camp
papers published for the benefit of the prisoners by the prisoners themselves bore the title "Reforging." "Our principle,"
wrote thieves and robbers, "is: We give everything, we demand
nothing." Also:

> Our slogan is—forget the past,
> Drop your former habits:
> Forget all dives and wine
> And drills and master keys:
> Get into the ranks of toiling men
> In the battle for the Five-Year Plan.

For the outside world and for the Russian public, in particular, this was to serve as a moral justification of the new institution.

Simultaneously with the construction of the White Sea–
Baltic Canal, and particularly after its completion, the government launched a number of other projects. Among these was
the Moscow-Volga Canal, technically a very complex under-
taking, with pumping stations, hydroelectric works, and river
depots. In 1932 this project was placed under the OGPU.
Construction began in 1933 and was completed in 1937. About
200,000 workers were employed. Upon completion of the
project, 55,000 prisoner-workers were released before expira-
tion of their terms in view of their successful "reforging."

At the same time (1923–33) other projects were under way
in the Vishera camps, in the Urals, where 300,000 workers
were employed. Other great projects were also under construction, including chemical works on the Berezina, the great
Siberian-Turkestan railroad, and the Baikal-Amur road. Construction was also under way in the Kuznetsk region in western Siberia, where a new industrial base was being established:
coal and iron mines were opened in an almost deserted area
without housing or workers; the population of this area grew
from 128,000 to 770,000 within a period of eight years. An

additional track of the trans-Siberian railroad was being laid
to meet the military needs of the Far East. The government's
task of establishing a separate supply system for the Far Eastern
armies to make them as independent as possible of European
industry required millions of hands. Added to all these projects were many others, including new mines, lumber mills,
military works. Toward the end of the 'thirties a network of
forced-labor camps embracing an enormous population was
spread over northern Russia, particularly in the Archangel,
Vologda, Olonetsk, and Kem areas, and the prisoners were employed on the great railroad construction from Kotlas to Vorkuta. There were also many camps in western and eastern
Siberia.

"The number of inmates in the concentration camps," it
was reported in September, 1938,* "has assumed astronomical
proportions. Gigantic works are under construction: for example, the Verkhne-Kolymsk road, extending from the Sea of
Okhotsk, is being built with bare hands, without any mechanical appliances. The center of this project is at Nogayev, where
there is a huge labor camp to which thousands upon thousands
have been exiled. People are dying there like flies, perishing
in various ways, without anyone knowing about it, for the sentences dooming victims to prison and labor camps carry with
them the notation: 'without right of correspondence.' This is
how they live under horrible conditions of boredom, bad food,
in complete isolation from the outside world, slowly dying
from weakness and exhaustion, hunger and constant thrashing
of the nerves. They are buried alive!"

During the war, that is, since June 22, 1941, the camps have
acquired an even greater significance. New buildings had to be
erected for evacuated plants; great works were under construction in Arctic and White Sea ports; railways were hurriedly
built in various sections of the country. All these projects were
not only carried out but—to the amazement of foreign observers—also completed quickly and according to plan. All this involved, of course, a heavy cost in human lives. But the work
was done, and this appeared to be the important thing. Those
who believe that success justifies the means may point to the
defeat of Germany as justification of the system of forced labor.

* *Sotsialisticheski Vestnik,* Paris, 1938, No. 24.

The Network of Labor Camps

THE class of forced labor is as essential to Soviet economy as are the free workers, collectivized peasants, and state employees. Without the armies of forced labor the state economy could not have attained the effectiveness which it had reached at the beginning of the war. Without them the army could not have been supplied. The social-economic system cannot exist without forced labor. One might as well expect a bridge to remain in use with half a frame. Such optimism would be justified if the mainspring of class formations in Russia emanated from the caprice of a supreme leader; the fact is, however, that the development of the huge class of forced labor in Soviet Russia arose not from the good or bad will of human beings but rather as a consequence of the specific principles upon which the Soviet State has been founded.

The economic basis for this phenomenon is simple enough. The gigantic program of investments required of millions of human beings that they contribute more values to the state than they were receiving; their daily labor had to produce a greater value than the value of the food, clothing, and shelter which they absorbed. The difference between the values they created and the values they used constituted the surplus utilized by the state for its construction purposes. To increase this surplus to a maximum has been the basic task of Soviet economy. If this sphere of Soviet economy were to be freely studied in the scientific works of Soviet economists or in Soviet universities, we would be told, in terms of Marxian economics, of the Soviet State's need of "surplus labor," that is of its requirement of large surpluses over the values consumed by the workers.

The lower their consumption the greater the surplus left to the state. But to reduce consumption below a minimum was considered irrational because of the consequent speedy decline in the productivity of labor. For this reason the system of labor introduced in the camps takes into consideration both factors: the need of encouraging the worker's interest by making food allotments conform strictly to his output and the need of making his labor as cheap as possible—an objective attainable only under conditions prevailing in prisons and forced-labor barracks.

From the economic point of view, the labor camps embrace a huge army of labor operating under severe discipline and this army can be moved rapidly and efficiently in any direction. A ← leading feature of the organization is the utter mercilessness displayed with regard to the individual. Added to this is the aversion felt by the workers for their tasks, for the officials, for the regime, a loathing perhaps akin to that displayed in the labor relations that existed on some colonial plantations a hundred years ago.

Material at our disposal makes it possible to draw a picture of the conditions under which the class of forced labor lives.

The camps on which we have information comprise only a part of the total. The list presented below is far from complete:

I. EUROPEAN RUSSIA, *Northern Regions*
(Chiefly lumber, fisheries, shipping, construction, mining)
North Dvina Camps, Administrative Center at Kotlas
North Pechora Camps, Administrative Center at Narian-Mar
Soroka Camps, Administrative Center at Piasetskaya
Onega Camps, Administrative Center at Piasetskaya
Kargopol Camps
Archangel Labor Camp, Administrative Center at Archangel
Kandalaksha and other camps of the Murmansk District

In the Komi Soviet Republic
(Chiefly coal, oil, iron, ore, copper, lumber, turf)
Pechora Camps, Administrative Center at Ust-Kozhva
Northern Railroad Camps, Administrative Center at Knyazhi Pogost
Ukhta Camps, Administrative Center at Ust-Ukhta
Vorkuta Camps, Administrative Center at Vorkuta
Ust-Vym Camps
Izhma Camps

On the Island of Novaya Zemlya (Arctic Ocean)
(Copper and other mining)
Several labor camps

On the Island of Vaigach (Arctic Ocean)
(Lead, zinc, fluor spar, etc.)
Several labor camps

II. EUROPEAN RUSSIA, *Eastern Regions*
(Chiefly construction of roads and railroads, lumber, mining)

KUIBYSHEV PROVINCE
Labor Camps of Bezymennaya, Administrative Center at Bezy-
mianka

MOLOTOV PROVINCE
Usol Camps, Administrative Center at Solikamsk

MORDVA SOVIET REPUBLIC
Potem Labor Camps, Administrative Center at Yavas

URAL REGION
Ivdel Camps, Administrative Center at Ivdel
Northern Ural Camps
Revda Camps

GORKI PROVINCE
Unzha Camps, Administrative Center at Sukhobezvodnaya

YAROSLAVL PROVINCE
Volga-stroi Camps, Administrative Center at Rybinsk

III. ASIATIC RUSSIA. *Western Siberia and Central Asia*

NOVOSIBIRSK PROVINCE
Labor Camps of Novosibirsk

OMSK PROVINCE
Labor Camps, Administrative Center at Omsk
Asir Camps

KAZAKHSTAN AND UZBEKISTAN
(Mining, construction, cotton, etc.)
Camps of Petropavlovsk, Administrative Center at Petropav-
lovsk
Karaganda Camps, Administrative Center at Dolinka
Tashkent Camps
Czardzhuy Camps
Several Correctional Labor Camps of the Uzbek SSR

IV. ASIATIC RUSSIA. *Central and Eastern Siberia and the Far East*

KRASNOYARSK PROVINCE
Camps of Narylsk, Administrative Center at Narylsk
Igarka Camps
Several camps to the north of the Port Dudinka at the estuary of
Yenisei

Camps of Krasnoyarsk, Administrative Center at Kansk
Ingash Labor Camps
Absagachev Labor Camps

YAKUTSK PROVINCE AND THE FAR EAST
    (Gold, coal, mining, construction)
Northeastern Camps, Administrative Center at Magadan
A network of Labor Camps in the northern Kolyma region, Administrative Center at Kolyma
Chukotka Camps, Administrative Center at Chukotka
Bering Camps
Lena Camps
Aldan Camps
Labor Camps on the Bureya River, Administrative Center at Izvestkovaya
Kamchatka Camps
Camps at the Port Nakhodka (near Vladivostok)
Labor Camp on Franz Josef Land

There are forty thousand and more prisoners in each of the bigger camps. They are divided into *lagpunkty* (concentration points), *lagkolonii* (concentration columns), and *lagtochki* (administrative centers).

Inmates characterized as kulaks, counterrevolutionists, mutineers, "socially detrimental elements" are regarded as capitalist elements; the "purely criminal" cannot, of course, be characterized as such. The criminal elements in the camps consist almost entirely of confirmed professionals of the criminal world, dubbed "thirty-fivers" (from Paragraph 35 of the Criminal Code). The official view concerning the various class groups in the labor camps is as follows:

"Class differentiation in the camp: hostility between 'thirty-fivers,' on one hand, and counterrevolutionists and kulaks, on the other. The 'thirty-fivers' insist that they are not opposed to the proletarian state . . . The kulaks, however, fear to be together with the thieves and do not consider them full-fledged humans. The 'thirty-fivers' are beginning to look upon the counterrevolutionists and kulaks as class enemies."*

For this reason the Camp Administration looks favorably upon the "thirty-fivers," from among whom overseers of the inmates are chosen. Among the professional criminals are

* Averbakh, *From Crime to Labor,* pp. 192–193.

many gangsters of great daring and initiative, natural leaders of criminal bands, called in prison slang *pakhans* and "Ivans"; eager to win the favor of the administration, they are prepared to do anything, without exception.

"This type of inmate yields the cadres of the commanding staff both in [prison] economy and educational activities. The administration relies upon this element for support" (Averbakh).

The Northeastern Camps of the Yakutsk Region are situated even farther to the north than famous Turukhansk, the most terrible place of exile of the prerevolutionary era. Those exiled to Franz Josef Land have no hope at all. This island had been entirely unpopulated until recently, and under the Soviet regime it was originally only a meteorological station. Not much better is the situation in the Kamchatka Camps or on Chukotka. Together with some camps in the extreme north of European Russia, this group constitutes the places of most severe imprisonment and forced labor. To these camps are sent delinquents from other camps, in accordance with OGPU instructions of November 28, 1933: "All chronic loafers, malingerers, and dissimulators are to be sent to distant northern camps."

Below is a description, here published for the first time, of one of the northern camps, given by a person who himself was an inmate:

"I was brought to the Labor Camp on the Onega River. There I found about 35,000 prisoners. Like all other camps this camp is a purely economic institution. The prisoners work on undertakings and are supposed to be paid for their work. Bread is the basis of their food. The size of the bread rations depends on the output of their work. They get a hot meal twice daily: between four and five in the morning and between eight and nine in the evening. During the day you don't get anything but hot water. Sugar is unknown. No fruit or vegetables were ever given to us. Up to the outbreak of the war the bread ration amounted to 900 grams (as a maximum during the war the ration was reduced to 650 grams). No clothing was provided for the work, no mattresses, no blankets or pillows. We used to sleep on the floor in barracks or on dirty bunks.

"Our work was in the forests near Archangel. We had to cut trees. In our camp there were several hundred women, to whom the same rules applied. The younger tried to make up the low salary by selling their bodies: there were many prostitutes among them. The price was 500 grams of bread.

"We had to work in our own clothing. After two or three weeks our suits were torn to pieces: the prisoners were half naked. The temperature was very low: even in June we had up to twenty-five degrees of Celsius below zero [−13° Fahrenheit]. After twelve to thirteen hours of work in the snow-covered forests, we used to return to the barracks thoroughly drenched. In the same rags we went to sleep: there was nothing to cover ourselves with. Very often these rags were stolen. And after such nights we had to get up in the mornings in the same rags, cold, frozen, half dead.

"The prisoners could not wash. Men did not shave. There was no time for it; there was no need for it. We used to work without respite. Sunday was also a working day. Even May 1 was a working day. The majority of brigades in my camp had no rest during the entire period I spent there.

"The great majority of the inmates were political prisoners, divided into two groups: one of them was 'spies,' the other 'socially dangerous elements.' The first group consisted mainly of people from national minorities. In my camp, for instance, there were 400 Greeks, old inhabitants of the Kerch region in the Crimea, who had suddenly been arrested in 1937–38— they were sentenced to five to eight years in labor camp. Russians and Ukrainians used to get ten years as dangerous elements. The reason for their arrests was usually the occupation of their parents (middle-class people, rich peasants, civil servants, intelligentsia, and . . . Communist-oppositionists). They will never leave those camps. The reason is that release in the USSR, after a sentence is served, can follow only if the NKVD in Moscow permits it. For 'socially dangerous elements' such permits never arrive, if a decision does come it prescribes another sentence for another period.

"The work is being done promiscuously—in day and night shifts: in subpolar conditions it makes no difference, as during the winter the day is only two to three hours long. Almost all prisoners are suffering from scurvy, loss of teeth.

"The penal labor camps are places of the greatest moral degradation: prostitution, thievery, swindles mark this struggle for existence."

The author of the report concludes as follows:

"A sad picture: slowly, almost invisibly the mass of silent, dirty men in torn clothing moves—going to work or returning from it. Every now and then someone in the crowd slips and falls on the snow or into the mud. Nobody stretches out a hand to the fallen: you have got to save your own energy. Only the guard helps with his rifle to get up."

And here is another description. It concerns the labor camps near Kolyma in eastern Siberia.

"In the Kolymsk region there are many separate camps, scattered over hundreds of miles. For this reason the names of the camps are given as 'On the 400th Kilometer,' 'On the 1,000th Kilometer,' 'On the 1,500th Kilometer,' and so on.* These camps are hidden in the mountains or are situated along the River Kolyma, in the distant Tundra, extending northward to the shores of the Arctic Ocean. It is very difficult to reach them, approach being possible only by water. In good summer weather it takes seven days from Vladivostok to get there, in stormy weather fifteen days, in winter even longer. Before the war, however, there was communication by air.

"Winter begins at the end of September. In the camp 'On the 1,500th Kilometer,' for example, there was snow one meter high on September 20. The temperature was minus forty and lower. The inmates, inadequately clothed, are dying in masses in such temperatures. They wear waistcoats of poor quality and trousers. At night they can cover themselves only if they have blankets of their own, and they wrap their heads in sacks. The two brothers M. died within five minutes of each other: they left their barracks in seventy degrees below zero and were almost instantly frozen.

"Russians are in the majority, but one also meets other nationalities—Germans, Greeks, Chinese, although these are few. I met an exceptionally large number of Poles of Russian citizenship, arrested merely on suspicion of espionage for Poland, or even without suspicion, as early as 1936–38.

* The mileage refers to the position of the camps along the course of the Kolyma River.

"To Kolyma they send political prisoners, serious offenders, those condemned to death and then pardoned: among the non-political prisoners there were murderers, thieves, burglars, prostitutes. Nonpolitical male and female offenders are as a rule put together with the political prisoners, whom they are allowed to order about and to whom they often 'administer justice,' since political prisoners, unlike the criminal offenders, do not enjoy the protection of the authorities.

"Very often the chiefs of individual camps are recruited from among former prisoners, and the prisoners, whether they are political or not, are being treated according to the caprice of the chief. For example, in the Camp of A., where I worked in the fish industry, the chief was a former petty criminal. He used to treat us better and was more considerate to the prisoners. On the other hand, in O., the chief, also a former prisoner, treated prisoners horribly.

"The conditions of work for men: twelve working hours a day. Those who do not complete their assigned tasks within this time remain at work until they do so. If the period over which someone failed to complete his task extends to over one week, he is considered guilty of deliberate sabotage. The prisoner is then locked in an isolation cell, and condemned to death without trial. These verdicts are signed by D., the 'battalion commissar'—in other words, the local chief of the NKVD. After the execution, the sentence is read to all the prisoners and posted on the refectory wall.

"Women's working hours: eleven hours, an hour's break for dinner counts as the twelfth hour. In the 'well run' camp in M., the best of the camps in Kolyma, the break for dinner lasted up to one and a half hours. Women prisoners are wakened at night if the exigencies of work require the bringing in of coal, cabbage, potatoes, firewood, no matter what the temperature may be—at night it is always very low; this extra work is demanded regardless of the number of hours worked in the daytime. Without taking into consideration the number of hours spent at work during such a night shift, the women are sent at daybreak to their normal work.

"In the camps of Bukhta Nakhodka [near Vladivostok] only people who worked were fed. As there were too many prisoners in that camp for the work available, a part of them, whether capable or incapable of working, were left behind in the barracks, where they were not given any food. Their overseers, recruited among the nonpolitical prisoners, collected money from those sent to work, thus making it possible for them to receive food. I arrived, for example, at Bukhta Nakhodka after a journey of sixty-one days in a railroad car of the NKVD, when we received only bread and water. The train was full, twelve to fifteen people in each compartment, lice everywhere; it was only possible to sit huddled up. A small space was always left free for those who wanted to stretch their legs (one at a time, in turn). There was no talk of food during the journey, although next door to us was the kitchen where food was being prepared for the guards and their commander. Even water was given to us only twice a day, in spite of the unbearable Siberian heat wave. Very often at some station or other our part of the train was simply sealed and moved to a siding, while the guards with their commanding officers went to the town for the whole day, leaving us without water and without any possibility of satisfying our physiological needs. Usually we were let out for this purpose three times a day if the convoy was good, and twice a day if they treated us badly.

"After this sort of a journey, lasting for sixty-one days, with some stop-offs, I arrived at Bukhta Nakhodka so weak that I was incapable of the smallest exertion. For this reason I was not sent to work, but as I was not working, I received no food. It was only owing to the help of an old Don Cossack (also a prisoner) that I managed to survive this part of my captivity.

"*Billeting conditions:*

"*Men.* In the '400 Kilometer Camp' the men made their own tents, covered with moss; in other camps there were wooden barracks, with crevices in the walls filled with moss, and leaking roofs. There were no sleeping accommodations, everybody slept on the floor, sometimes a few had a common bunk, if they were lucky. There were no blankets of any sort. Everybody was extremely cold. In the '400th km.,' which was considered an 'easy camp,' when the temperature fell more than forty-three below zero and there was a very strong wind work was suspended and the prisoners were allowed to take shelter in their tents or barracks. Their clothing was abominable.

"*Women.* It depended upon the camp. In Arman, for example, they lived in new, very damp barracks, which leaked so badly that when it rained the women used to hang a blanket above their heads, but even that device helped very little. The barracks were comparatively clean. There were no mattresses. Each woman had a wooden bunk and was given a large bag which could be filled with shavings. They received also pillow cases (if they had pillows of their own) and a rug. The air was so damp and stale, the fog so heavy, that the women often did not undress at night. Only once a week they changed their underwear in the bathhouse.

"In Magadan [the center of the Siberian Northeastern Camps] two women's camps exist, only two streets distant from each other. In the first, there are half-decayed wooden barracks, inside a ruin of wooden bunks, and a dilapidated fireplace in which things could hardly be warmed up. After sundown there was no lighting. . . .

"One of the women's camps in Magadan was run by two young women leaders from the NKVD, both very pretty, energetic and hellishly tough and wicked. It was a sort of exemplary camp, perhaps even a show camp. Situated in a large area at the foot of the mountain, it was surrounded by barbed wire and a palisade.

"The stocks of clothing consisted not of the normal prison clothes, but mostly of garments confiscated from prisoners or those left by the dead, and of parcels sent by the families to prisoners who had died. I was witness myself of confiscation of personal property from newly arrived prisoners. I was myself ordered to surrender my sweater and old woolen underwear.

"During the summer season prisoners doing field work were sent out of the camp for a few weeks for haymaking. They live in tents or usually just under canvas stretched across poles. Men and women live together. Women who in this condition kept to themselves and went to sleep separately were made fun of and teased by the prisoners.

"*Health, death rate:*

"The prisoners were extremely weakened, exhausted by their long imprisonment and heavy physical labor. Owing to the cold and dampness most of them suffer from kidney trouble. They also suffer from swelling of legs, open sores on legs, on arms, and around the ribs, as well as from scurvy. Many go blind. There are a great many cases of frostbite. Illnesses are spread because of the lack of recreation and any signs of civilized life. Many die of diarrhea [dysentery, a variety peculiar to that part of the world different from another type of dysentery, known in the north]; finally, people die from general exhaustion. How high the death rate is is difficult to ascertain, but I know from a prisoner who was in my company that in his camp he belonged to a special group whose duties consisted only of digging graves. Others told me that in the mountains where the soil was heavy and the temperature low, they did not dig graves, but just collected a number of corpses and left them in the snow, far from the camp. I heard similar accounts from other people from Kolyma.

"Women stood up to the new conditions relatively well. They suffered only from their sores on legs and arms. On the legs the sores continued as far as the lower parts of the abdomen. The sores are difficult to cure, and the discharge of pus goes on for months. The scurvy makes the skin on arms and on legs crack. The fingers bleed from hard work. These sores do not exempt one from work. With hands covered with sores from scurvy and with pus, they are obliged to pack herrings into barrels, wearing only linen gloves, or rather something resembling gloves.

"The woman-prisoner B. suffering from lung trouble was forced to wash floors in the barracks despite a serious cut on her hand; this caused blood-poisoning. The commandant did not exempt her from work, despite her fever of 39 [102° F.]. Only when she lost consciousness was she sent to Magadan to the hospital: 'to her funeral,' the commandant said when she left.

"In the hospitals physicians, even university professors, treat the patients; all of the physicians are prisoners themselves. There are no physicians in the camps, except imprisoned doctors."

IN recent years there have been reports of mutinies in the camps, particularly in the Kolyma region—mutinies which were mercilessly suppressed. Riots have also been reported among prisoners evacuated from the Kolsk Peninsula. Other reports spoke of the death of 800 prisoners in the tundras of Pechora in the winter of 1941–42, while 1,800 prisoners and

110 guards were reported to have perished in a prison train in February, 1941. There was a report of the sinking of prison barges in the White Sea with a loss of 7,000 lives.

The political prisoners employed at forced labor are naturally, as far as any interest in political questions can exist, in violent opposition to the existing regime, a sentiment which in time of war can easily develop into defeatism. The only hope of liberation these people may have rests upon the possibility of a domestic political upheaval or military defeat. They care little about who makes war on Soviet Russia. Any upheaval, any new regime appears to them to be preferable to a strong, stable government and its victory in the war. Indifference, inability to distinguish between methods of political struggle, readiness to try anything, including alliance with any enemy at home or abroad, emerge as the natural consequence of living conditions in the camps; and it is no accident that persons of Russian nationality who have managed to escape from these camps to other countries have often found their way into the camp of Russian Hitlerites.

This, of course, is hardly a reason for continuing to keep human beings in slavery. The longer this institution is preserved the greater will be the danger presented by the prisoners and deportees to any other, freer political system should the prisoners ever be restored to freedom.

XII

The Communist Party of the
Soviet Union

AT the beginning of the first Russian revolution (1905), the Bolshevik party numbered from five to eight thousand members. At present it has some five million party members, supplemented by more than seventeen million adherents of the Communist Youth League, a party auxiliary. From a paltry few thousand to more than twenty million is a considerable growth.

Paradoxical as it may sound, the fact is that the governing element of the party, numerically speaking, has remained about what it was some thirty years ago. The real party, in its Bolshevik conception, consists as before of a few thousand members.

It is very difficult for an American to grasp the peculiar Russian-Communist view of a party. An American party is a great entity united by common political opinions but leaving room, at the same time, for new ideas and new leaders. Every few years an American party may witness a contest that determines its leadership, shapes its program, and offers its voters an opportunity to set its policies and its fate in one direction or another. Such a party keeps its ear attuned to the wishes of its followers and the electorate, to what its local politicians report, to polls, to changes in sentiment in the various states and districts. All this is the exact opposite of the Bolshevik concept of a party. Yet unless this difference is kept in mind it is impossible to comprehend much that goes on in Russia.

We will come closer to the question if we draw an analogy between the Bolshevik party and the officer corps of an army. The rank-and-file soldiers, comprising at times millions of men, are merely the material in the hands of the commanders. A few thousand officers, trained from youth and making it their career, constitute the nucleus of a modern army, which, when necessary, is transformed, through mobilization, into a vast force of many millions. When this army is again contracted to a minimum the officer cadres may remain almost unaltered. The rebirth of the German army after Versailles became possible only because the army was given the right to maintain four thousand officers.

Such was always the Bolshevik concept of a party: an officer corps which organizes its army; not a party according to the American idea, which chooses its commanders. Soldiers do not choose their own generals.

The Bolshevik idea of a party is akin to the steel framework in modern architecture. The framework is erected first; then it is covered with bricks. Sometimes even the brickwork may be removed and a new building erected upon the old steel framework. To be sure, it is impossible to attain the objective without support from the masses, just as it is impossible to live in a structure consisting only of steel girders and rafters. But everything rests upon a framework. The party is the framework and the people are the necessary, but secondary, element.

At the beginning of the first revolution, in 1905, the Bolshevik party (at that time termed the Bolshevik fraction) consisted of a few thousand men and women, devoted to their cause. The great majority were not workers—in all probability there were more members from the ranks of the lesser nobility than manual laborers. As the revolution developed, however, tens of thousands flowed into the various revolutionary parties, including that of the Bolsheviks. When the revolution had attained its high point—October–December, 1905—these parties, among them the Bolsheviks, had enrolled masses of people, with scores of organizations and countless sympathizers. Then, with the end of 1906, came the reaction; the revolution was soon crushed, and the years from 1907 to 1917 marked the last stable period of the tsarist monarchy. The masses deserted the revolutionary parties, and the Bolshevik party was reduced, too. In March, 1917, the tide of popular support began to rise again, once more filling the readymade party mold with human material, and by October, 1917, the Bolshevik party was the strongest of all the Russian parties.

As Bolshevism conceives it, a party is not a popular mass, and a popular mass is not a party. A party is solid, constant, a backbone; while the people are unstable, changing, flesh and muscle. A party has a clear theory, a revolutionary conception; the people are subject to moods and hesitations. The party leads, the people follow. A party is a minority directing the majority. A party must not be too big; when it numbers millions it loses its stability and spiritual quality. It is possible to find a few thousand, perhaps a few score thousand firm, unbending enthusiasts, but millions cannot sustain this enthusiasm. From this flow all the difficulties of the present period, when the Bolshevik party has become an organization of millions.

At the dawn of the Bolshevik movement, when its foundations were being laid, no one could, of course, foresee this difficulty. The "people" to whom the small party appealed were, first and foremost, the industrial workers, who numbered in prerevolutionary Russia about two to three million. The Bolshevik leaders regarded them very dubiously. "An elemental labor movement," wrote Lenin, "can create and inevitably creates only trade unionism, and a trade-union policy of the working class is a bourgeois policy of the working class." The workers themselves, he wrote, cannot develop a Communist consciousness: "this can be brought only from outside."

By "outside" he meant a small party seeking to lead the workers but not necessarily consisting of workers. "The founders of modern scientific Socialism themselves, Marx and Engels, belonged to the bourgeois intelligentsia," wrote Lenin, just as the Communist movement* in Russia developed not as a movement of workers but as the "natural and inevitable result of the development of thought in the revolutionary-socialist intelligentsia." "Only from outside," he declared, emphasizing the word "outside," "is it possible to bring a new political consciousness to the workers."†

By "outside" Lenin meant an "organization of revolutionists essential to the carrying out of a political revolution." Such an organization "must embrace people whose profession consists of revolutionary activity." This profession must con-

* Lenin spoke in this instance of the Social Democratic movement, which, in present-day terminology, should be translated to mean the Communist movement.

† It must not be supposed, however, that Lenin placed particular hope in the intelligentsia. They were, for the most part, anti-Bolshevik even then, and adhered largely to the moderate parties. Lenin had in mind only the small group of Russian intellectuals whom he considered capable of forming the nucleus of an extreme revolutionary party.

stitute their only or most important occupation, and for this reason, said Lenin, the party "must not be too broad." It must be an organization of directors of the revolution. "Give us an organization of revolutionists and we will turn Russia upside down!" Lenin exclaimed.

Such a party, he taught, must work in deep secrecy and preserve the strictest discipline. Its various organs must carry out without question the instructions of the higher authorities. The entire structure was actually made up as follows: a small group constituted the Central Committee, which had at its disposal an apparatus of agents and representatives; the agents selected local and regional committees from among party members. The system of centralization was applied to an extreme degree, buttressed by rigid discipline. But while there were many changes, for various reasons, in the composition of the Central Committee, one man remained unsupplanted at the head of all party organizations, committees, and editorial offices from 1903 to 1923. That man was Lenin. It was he who actually picked the members of the Central Committee, thus being able, under the system of rigid centralism and discipline, to direct the entire party.

In this way, even at its beginning, the Bolshevik party structure led to the centralization of all leadership in the hands of its outstanding leader, while the small organization of revolutionists was the embryo of the *future state power*.*

The important role played by the party leader was accompanied by a worship of discipline unknown in any other party. Long before the various purges of the later period under the Soviet regime, the blind obedience expected from the party members was elevated to a high principle. The orders of the commander-in-chief must be implicitly obeyed. The intellectual life and ideological independence of the party members were considered much less important than unalterable, rigid discipline.

During that period—the period preceding the downfall of the tsarist regime, when the old foundations of the nation's political structure were being shaken—Russian youth was in-

* When Lenin put forward this concept, the young Trotsky remarked prophetically in 1904: "In Lenin's scheme, the party takes the place of the working class. The party organization displaces the party. The Central Committee displaces the party organization, and finally the Dictator displaces the Central Committee" (*Nashi Politicheskiya Zadachi*, p. 54).

clined to subject to criticism all traditions, without exception. Rebellious "nonrecognition of authority" was the symptom of the approaching storm; in place of the old authoritarianism there was criticism, respect for the "critically thinking individual," for spiritual and intellectual life. But Bolshevism fought these tendencies, taking the position that the authorities of the old world had to be overthrown, to be sure, but must be replaced immediately by new authorities; by new men, new ideas, to be followed without criticism, blindly, even without comprehension, perhaps, of the deeper, long-range aims of the leader.

For this reason, the Bolshevik party never required from the mass of its members any deep understanding of programs and principles: what was important was not so much the intellectual preparation on the part of the individual member as emotional devotion to and faith in the leaders.

Lenin's Party

AT the time of the downfall of the tsarist regime in 1917, the Bolshevik party was a small group. Officially, it claimed at that moment 23,000 members. In the new revolutionary atmosphere, however, the party's influence mounted rapidly among the workers and soldiers (because of its antiwar position—it was the only party opposed to the war) and within six months the membership leaped to 200,000.

That was the short period of Russian democracy, when the doors were opened wide for political debate and struggle; freedom of speech and assembly were fully utilized for its own purposes by the Bolshevik party, with its network of organizations covering the entire country and the entire front. In accordance with his general scheme, Lenin considered his task simple and natural: "Russia used to be ruled by 150,000 landlords," he wrote in August, 1917. "Why could not 240,000 Bolsheviks do the same job?"

At the time of the November revolution, as already indicated, the party had some 200,000 members.* In the next two

* Official party statistics subsequently revised this figure, giving the number of party members at the time of the November revolution as even below 100,000. However, this revised figure is rather doubtful.

years the party continued to grow, but slowly. First the Brest Litovsk peace served to cool the sympathies of many, and the subsequent civil war and armed conflict between the government and peasantry, which at moments had threatened to end in the overthrow of the government, slowed the influx of new members. In the spring of 1919 the party membership numbered 313,000.* Subsequently, however, after the liquidation of Allied intervention and on the eve of the collapse of the White armies, the influx was resumed. The number of party members at the Bolshevik Party Congress in 1920 had risen, according to official figures, to 612,000—an increase of almost 100 per cent, reflecting the victories of the Soviet regime.

Lenin's original scheme of party organization presupposed the creation of a small party of Communists, absolutely devoted to their cause, whereas, after the November revolution, the party was inundated by tens and, later, hundreds of thousands of people, who flocked to it from conviction, or from the desire to make a career, or from considerations of immediate material gain. The party swelled to huge proportions.† To be sure, it would have been possible to reduce its membership arbitrarily or simply to close the doors to new members. However, the great party mass now became the reservoir supplying thousands of people for the expanded apparatus of administration and state economy, and the admission of new members facilitated control of the state machinery. The party no longer resembled the staff of the commander-in-chief of a disciplined army. This was the period of a plethora of "intraparty discussions" on numerous questions, such as "the trade unions," "democratic centralism," "socialism in one country," the Chinese revolution, Trotskyism, industrialization projects, agrarian policy, the collectives, the left opposition, the right opposition, the degeneration and transformation of the bureaucracy, etc.

All this was contrary to the classic conception of what a

* This number did not include, however, many regions situated at that time behind the anti-Bolshevik fronts of the civil war.

† This growth affected its composition. In 1918 according to official party figures, workers constituted about 57 per cent of the party membership; in 1919, 48 per cent; in 1920, 44 per cent; and in 1921 only 41 per cent. Even more striking were the figures of new members who joined the party in these years: in 1917, 56 per cent of the newcomers were workers; in 1918, 40 per cent; in 1919, 38 per cent; in 1920, 33 per cent; in 1921, 30 per cent.

Bolshevik party should be. "The party is in a fever," declared Lenin angrily, obviously and properly concerned about the situation. But after his death the fever grew considerably worse. Only toward the end of the 'twenties, when political struggles in general came to a standstill, did a calm descend upon the party so far as its inner life and ideological activity were concerned.

Molding the Party

THROUGH purges extending over a period of two decades, 1,500,000 to 2,000,000 people have been expelled from the Communist party and the number of those who were refused admittance to the party was also very great. A party which at the beginning of the 'twenties numbered about 500,000 members subsequently expelled or refused admittance to numbers vastly greater than its former total membership.

At the base of this practice lay Lenin's old idea of a small Communist nucleus, whose task it was to organize whole peoples in military fashion in epochs of political storms. As we have seen, it was not the mass that was to impose its will upon the revolutionary leader but the leader who was to direct the mass. The people inside the party was something quite new. But inside or outside the party, the people remained merely the object of policy. It became necessary to regulate this intra-party popular mass, to remold the party as if the vast membership were so much clay, to give it the form best suitable to the realization of the aims of world Communism, the roads to the attainment of which were clear only to the small nucleus of leaders. The party had to remain an instrument in the hands of a chosen few, and this instrument, like every instrument, had to be constantly sharpened, ground, cleaned, and repaired.

The right of the leader to institute purges follows as the immediate conclusion from this conception.

The first general purge in the party occurred in 1921. Within a period of a few months nearly 30 per cent of the members were removed; of 585,000 members, 175,000 were expelled or found it wise to leave. This first experiment in the purge differed from subsequent ones in that almost none of the "purged" were arrested or made to suffer any other loss, most of them remaining at their former posts.

In 1925 the Central Committee again decided to remold the composition of the party within a period of two years: a minimum of 50 per cent of the membership was to consist of "workers-at-the-bench." By means of mass recruiting drives this was almost achieved by the end of the 'twenties, when 48 per cent of party members were workers. But this situation did not last long.

The general membership continued to grow as the growing state machinery required additional officials. In 1925 the figure had risen to 800,000, and in 1926 it was more than 1,000,000. In 1927 the number rose to 1,147,000, after a recruiting campaign instituted on the occasion of the tenth anniversary of the October revolution. Thus, in 1928, the party membership had expanded to 1,304,000. Finally, in 1930, a special "Lenin membership drive" was launched, resulting in the recruiting of 150,000 "candidates."

The second of the great purges took place in 1928. In the interval between the two there were smaller, partial purges, in 1924 and in 1926. In 1924 (after a not unusual outburst of party conflict marked by successes for Trotsky among students and in some organizations of government employees) the purges struck party cells in educational institutions and in government offices. In 1926 a purge was carried out in various rural party organizations. Roughly, the number of those expelled (and of those who left the party voluntarily, which was tantamount to expulsion) was as follows: in 1922, 45,000; in 1923 about 40,000; in 1924, 23,000; in 1925, 32,100; in 1926, 35,000; in 1927, 44,000; and in 1928—before the great purge—about 40,000. Thus, the number of those who were expelled or who left the party in the interval between the two great purges, or from 1922 to 1928, was approximately 260,000.

The end of the 'twenties was marked by bitter conflict between various party factions, and Stalin came out victorious. The great purge of 1929 was the natural consequence of this victory, being designed to strengthen the captured positions. The number of party members expelled was more than 160,000. Among those hit were the rural organizations, 15 per cent of whose members were driven from the party.

While expelling scores of thousands of old party members,

the party centers were forcing the admission of new ones. Despite the great purge the party membership continued to rise. In 1929 it was 1,532,000 and in 1930, 1,852,000.

Did this imply a growing solidarity of the population with the Communist party? The actuality, a process of historical significance, was much more complex.

For millions of people this process was not so much acceptance of Communism as the disappearance in the masses of the population of any spirit of militant resistance to the regime. After the defeat of all liberal and conservative parties, after all other parties had ceased to function for a decade, the Soviet regime had acquired a peculiar stability and endurance—it became "legitimate" in a historical and political sense.

By experience extending over many years, the Russian people were taught to accept the idea that this Soviet-Communist regime was strong and stable, that it was hopeless to struggle against it. In the realm of international relations this consciousness of its stability led to the recognition of the Soviet Government *de facto* and *de jure;* the process of recognition by various countries was extended over a period of ten to fifteen years. The average Russian, who had ceased to resist the Soviet Government by 1919–20, began to realize, long before foreign governments did so, the iron power and peculiar stability of the new regime. All capacity for resistance vanished. This was to be even more true of the younger generation, for whom a non-Soviet regime was now as much of an archaism as would be a journey on horseback from New York to Chicago.

Soon ideological debates in the party came to an end. Opposition groups were smashed, and as the Soviet regime had become identical with Communism, so Communism became identical with Stalinism. Membership in the party or in any of its auxiliary organizations became a certificate of loyalty; frequently it was an essential condition to admission to an important job in industry or in the government. Those who sought advancement had to pass through party offices if they wanted to avoid many obstacles. On the other hand, the party officials made it their business to seek out ambitious, prominent men and women and bring them into the party: writers, engineers, military people, students with honor records, successful Stakhanovites. These were the elements the party needed—the new "notables" of Russia. To be sure, the party continued at the same time to admit simple folk, rank-and-file workers and soldiers, but this had already assumed a decorative character, being designed to demonstrate the regime's "tie with the people" or to confer a reward for service to the Soviet fatherland.

No one took seriously the constitutional rights and liberties guaranteed in the Soviet constitutions, but the Bylaws of the Communist Party, that other constitution, did have a certain real value. The political rights enjoyed solely by party members included that of participating in decisions affecting current problems and an indirect right to determine the composition of the government. Elections to party conferences occasionally, in the 'twenties, took the form of genuine electoral contests. Party members at their meetings enjoyed a certain measure of freedom of speech. They had the right to bear arms. Arrest of a party member was inconceivable, except for extreme criminal offenses.

Subsequently, however, this constitution—the Party Bylaws —ceased to be observed. The political rights of party members disappeared with the liquidation of the opposition. Discussion of important questions at party meetings was abandoned, while the meetings became increasingly rare. From then on all voting at party meetings had to be unanimous. Thus, in this respect, too, in the matter of political rights, the distinction between the Communist and non-Communist masses disappeared. Henceforth a Communist could not only be expelled from the party but be arrested for political reasons. The hundreds of thousands of those expelled from the party, and, later, the arrested party members, gave evidence of the fact that the qualitative distinction between the party membership and nonparty mass had disappeared.

The consequence was the reëmergence of the old scheme: ten thousand devout Communists wielded the power in efforts to advance the Communist cause; behind them, with complete faith in their authority, without venturing to question or to criticize, marched several million people, displaying the emblems of the party and the Komsomol. All that was required of them was strict discipline and hard work. They constituted the transmission belts between the group of leaders and the vast bulk of the nonparty masses, who were supposed to toil in the sweat of their brows, in silent, patient expectation of the day when the sun, kindled by someone, would shine for them, too.

ALL the phenomena mentioned above had attained their full development in the 'thirties. Many of the processes described had reached their culmination. Party conferences or congresses, having lost their importance, having become parliaments without an opposition, were being convoked at increasingly rarer intervals. Although the 1927 congress decided that such party conclaves were to be convened at least every two years, three years elapsed before the next one. There was an interval of almost four years between the 1930 congress and the next. Finally there was but one other party congress during the period preceding the war—in March, 1939. More than five years will have passed before the next Congress of the Russian Communist Party is assembled, if it ever is.

The purge begun in 1933 continued for several years. Nearly two hundred thousand members were eliminated from the party in the first year. It was expected that the purge would be concluded by 1935, and the announcement of a forthcoming restoration of normal party life was actually made. However, this did not happen. A new purge was launched in 1935, and with the summer of 1936 began the greatest and most terrible of all party purges (it coincided with the changed international situation). This continued until 1938, and in the army and navy until 1939. Many hundreds of thousands of party members were expelled; thousands were arrested and executed.

After the conclusion of the purge, Stalin informed the party congress of 1939 that the party membership had decreased by 270,000 as compared with 1934. The total of party members and candidates at that time, in the winter of 1939, was 2,478,-000. In September–October, 1939, the party membership exceeded 3,000,000. A year later it was 3,700,000,* and, in the spring of 1941, before Russia was plunged into the war, the figure was approximately 3,900,000. During the war the

* This figure included the new Communist organizations in the regions annexed to Soviet Russia between September, 1939, and July, 1940.

party continued to expand. By autumn, 1943, it had 4,600,000 members. In the short span of two and a half years the two million members of 1939 had grown to almost five million.

Stalin and His Party

HOW can this development be reconciled with the traditional Bolshevik concept of the party as a small directing group of devoted, enlightened Communists organized to lead the great nonpolitical masses?

It must be remembered that Stalin shared fully Lenin's concept of the party. Stalin saw in the masses "inertia and political indifference":* according to Stalin the party cannot and therefore should not amalgamate with the people or with the workers. It must be a minority, a group, composed only of "the best elements"; it must move in advance of its class. The party, Stalin maintained, must be a "political leader."

"The party must be the advance guard of the working class. . . . The party must absorb all the best elements of the working class. The party cannot be a real party . . . if it cannot overcome the inertia and political indifference of an elemental movement. The party must stand in advance of the working class."

From this concept of the party Stalin's favorite analogy of a small general staff commanding an army of millions flows logically. "The party is the fighting staff of the proletariat," said Stalin. "The party must lead the proletariat into the offensive . . . and must direct the retreat if circumstances demand it."

Stalin continued to regard the working masses, even the millions within his own party, as an unstable human mass which could veer suddenly in the opposite direction; and he persisted in believing that the sole guaranty against its moving in a false direction lay in the enlightened Communist reason of the party leaders. His giving party cards to hundreds of thousands, bestowing party rights upon them, did not indicate any increase in his faith in the stability of the masses.

What Bolshevism once conceived as the principle that

* Stalin, *Lenin and Leninism*, Lectures 1924.

should govern the relationship between the small party and the people was now transformed into the governing principle operating within the party itself. The gigantic expansion of the party has transformed it into a huge body, but this party mass is not divided by an impenetrable gulf from the outside mass; both are politically dangerous, for both may "hesitate" in a moment of danger. The leaders remain the steel framework of the party structure.

Stalin's attitude toward this party mass was expressed quite recently, in 1937–39, when the apparently unimportant question of admission into the party was again under discussion. In 1934 it had been decided that only those candidates were to be admitted who, having passed a course of political education, had "mastered the program and constitution of the party."

"Every party member must master the basic principles of Marxism-Leninism," declared Kaganovitch, in those years the most powerful man next to Stalin, in explaining this requirement.*

Three years later Stalin came out against this principle. What was required, he maintained, was not "mastery" of the party program but merely its acceptance, as had been the case in Lenin's time. True knowledge and understanding must be assumed to reside only in the upper spheres, where Leninism has been "mastered." For the party at large, however, this was not to be obligatory.

The Party Bylaws were again altered in 1939 in accordance with Stalin's views.

Thus the party membership has been divided into two parts: those who have "mastered" the program and policy of Communism, and those who merely "accept" it. The first are the leaders; the second include the useful workers, administrators, engineers, economists—elements essential to the life of the country, useful in their respective districts as long as they act in accordance with instructions.

Stalin has always been conscious of this difference. He has defined the Stalinist concept of the party as follows: "Three or 4 thousand men of the high command—the generals of our

---

* At that time this proposal was, of course, supported by Stalin. During membership purges, such as this one, the leaders were looking for opportunities to get rid of many members, and failure to master the true teachings of Leninism was to serve as a point of indictment.

party. Then 30 to 40 thousand intermediate commanders: these constitute the officers' corps of our party. And further, 100 to 150 thousand of the leading elements of our party—these are, so to speak—the subaltern officers of the party."

Thus, according to Stalin's calculation, the governing elements of the party numbered 150 to 200 thousand members, no more than 10 per cent of the party membership of that year (1937), no more than 5 per cent of the present enrolment. Even so, one would hardly include all petty officers in the commanding elements of an army. Of the 30 to 40 thousand party directors (the middle category), fully one half are scattered throughout distant provinces, far from the main political center. They have no part in the formation of party opinion. Only about 10,000 to 15,000 comprise the heart of the Russian Communist party. These constitute the real party.

The Real Party

THIS party kernel, the successor to Lenin's organization of "professional revolutionists," has grown very slowly over a period of decades. As we have seen, the underground organization of the Bolsheviks at the beginning of the 1905 revolution comprised about 8,000 persons, and it had about 20,000 at the beginning of the second revolution in 1917. In 1922, when the party membership had already exceeded 500,000, Molotov placed the number of "active party workers" at 15,000.*

An official census of the party personnel in 1927, including party "generals" and "officers," disclosed the following figures: members of central, regional, and provincial committees, 3,500; minor leaders, 37,000.

Ten years later Stalin's report (just quoted) showed that the figures still held; there still were 30 to 40 thousand "generals and commanders." His report was a convincing proof of how slowly the party kernel was developing, as distinguished from the influx of the party mass.

---

* He gave the following figures: The Central Committee and its immediate associates in Moscow and in the provinces, 325 persons; these were the generals. Leading members in the provinces, about 2,000; party officials in the provinces and secretaries of individual cells, 13,000. These were the officers.

In 1939 Andrei Zhdanov presented the following report to the party congress giving the number of secretaries, i.e., of party employees, in charge of local organizations:

Secretaries and directors of regional and district divisions   843
Secretaries of lower party units   10,902

Total   11,745

The party core itself is divided into various gradations. The authority of the leader is undisputed, being far above that once enjoyed by Lenin. The scope of his power is unlimited, being much greater than that wielded by any Russian tsar.

After the leader, in point of influence, come the Politbureau and the administrative office of the Central Committee. The Politbureau is the party's real brain; it numbers 14 people* elected from among the 71 members of the Central Committee. Since Lenin's days the Politbureau has been practically the government of Russia. The administrative office of the Central Committee is subordinated to the Politbureau, but its importance is enormous. Its officials are not chosen by party conferences or congresses but hold office by appointment. Its importance is much greater than that of the small staff of executives and employees in the White House, or at 10 Downing Street. It is not analogous to a premier's office, for there is another institution performing that function under the chairman of the Soviet of People's Commissars. The executive office of the Central Committee is an all-embracing administrative apparatus impinging upon all phases of government activity. It assembles material for Stalin's speeches, for government and party declarations, and important resolutions. It collects data pertaining to every prominent member of the party, and maintains complicated statistical records. The fate of many party leaders and rank-and-filers has been decided on the basis of material collected in these offices.

This institution also prepares projects dealing with collectivization, industrialization, purges, shake-ups, projects which are subsequently approved or rejected, as the case may be. Ministers and other high government officials come to the office of the Central Committee for instructions, for many offi-

* Nine members and five "candidates."

cials in that office wield greater authority than do the people's commissars.

It should be kept in mind that the rank of minister (people's commissar) in the Soviet Union cannot be compared in importance with that of a cabinet member elsewhere. There are more than eight hundred people's commissars in Russia. Of these, only fifty reside in Moscow as commissars of the USSR or of the Russian Republic. Hundreds of others are people's commissars in the affiliated Soviet Republics. Only those people's commissars who also happen to be members of the Politbureau, men like Beria, Molotov, and a few others, occupy positions of great authority.

Thus, hundreds of ministers scattered all over the country are conscious of the watchful eye of the administrative office of the Central Committee in Moscow. In practice, and contrary to the Constitution, they are responsible not to their respective parliaments (Supreme Soviets) but directly and indirectly to some specific division in the administrative office of the Central Committee.

At the beginning of the 'twenties the office of the Central Committee comprised only 100 persons, including the minor personnel. In 1927 the figure was 650. This was subsequently reduced, and in 1929 the personnel numbered 375. Almost half of these were so-called "responsible workers." In the 'thirties the personnel was considerably expanded, but the exact number was kept secret. These "responsible workers," together with an administrative staff of from 300 to 500, constitute the brain trust of the Russian Communist party and of World Communism.

The office of the Central Committee consists of several divisions, each of which is charged with administering a special sphere of government or party activity. There are the Secret Division (later rechristened Special Division), the Distributive Division (later Division of Cadres), the Division of Schools (a Department of Education), the Division of Mass Campaigns (collectivization, public demonstrations, and so on), the Division of Propaganda and Agitation (press, radio, lectures), the Military Division, and several economic divisions.

Even the party hierarchs look upon this office with great respect not unmixed with fear. During the purges, for example, the awe-inspiring Revisional Committee, having investigated, as part of its duties, the personnel of the administrative office of the Central Committee, humbly characterized its members as follows:

"The apparatus of the Central Committee represents a firm, ideologically galvanized organization, composed of tried and theoretically accomplished Bolsheviks who have gone through the school of struggle against class enemies and their agents inside the party."

Thus the well-integrated and comparatively stable party leadership rests, like the cupola of a great edifice, upon several party columns: men of industry, leaders of agriculture, of education, of finance and trade. But among these columns there are two of primary importance: the Red Army and the NKVD.

The Komsomol

THE Communist Youth League is a specific Soviet phenomenon. This league has played a very important role throughout the entire history of the Soviet regime, and its development has been symptomatic of the evolution of Soviet society.

By virtue of its sphere of activity the Komsomol has been something more than an ordinary league of youth. It conscripted thousands of its members for fighting in the civil war, sent thousands of youths to work in plants and factories, and to wage political campaigns in the villages. Thousands of village offices were filled by Komsomol members, who also constituted a large percentage of the membership and officialdom of local Soviets. The Komsomol is a political organization, and has passed through all the phases of development which history has bestowed upon its older sister, the Communist party: the struggle of factions, expulsions, purges, arrests, executions; the obligation to hear long political reports and vote unanimous approval of the government's policy. Thus, the Komsomol is but another party organization, or rather an auxiliary mass organization, which the party utilizes for various purposes and to a very substantial degree.

According to its first constitution, members of the Komsomol were to be youths between the ages of 14 and 23. Very soon it became apparent, however, that many, having reached the latter age limit, remained in the Komsomol instead of transferring to the party or joining the mass of nonpartisans. At one time, some 30 per cent of the Komsomol's membership consisted of such elements, aged even 30 and more. The point is that the Communist party was very strict in sifting candidates for party membership; there were the frequent purges, and frequent cessations of admissions. Tens of thousands who desperately needed party membership cards preferred to be registered as youths, although in many cases they were men with large families and were approaching forty. The congress of the Komsomol in 1936 legalized this situation and set the age limits for Komsomol membership between 15 and 26. Members might remain in the organization beyond the age of 26, but they were to have only a voice but no vote. The limitation, however, did not make much difference.

Founded in 1918, the Komsomol at first grew at a slower pace than did the party. The first year showed a membership of about 22,000, and the year following 96,000. After that, like the party, and for the same reasons, it began to grow rapidly, reaching 500,000 members by 1920. Simultaneously with the first party purge, the membership of the Komsomol was cut in half; in 1922 it was 247,000.

Then came a very rapid expansion. In two years the membership increased fivefold, reaching 1,140,000 in January, 1925. By that time, the principal features of the new political situation had become apparent in the Komsomol—long before the appearance of analogous phenomena in the party.

Membership in the Komsomol had become the sole opportunity for advancement for young men and women, particularly for the youth of the cities. Schools and higher educational institutions, although offering free tuition, took into careful consideration the party affiliation of applicants for admission. Membership in the Komsomol became extremely useful—at times indispensable—for entrance into a university or technical school. Workers eager to help their children get on in life hastened to utilize the new opportunities; children of government employees and intellectuals naturally sought to complete their education; even from the villages thousands flocked into the schools. In addition to offering the advantages of facilitating schooling and higher education, the Komsomol promoted excursions, maintained social clubs, provided evening entertainments and dances. It arranged for visits to theaters and supplied books. In short, the social life of young folk centered around it, for no similar organizations were permitted to exist; and young men and women who, naturally, did not relish isolation from the world sought to join the Komsomol.

Unlike the party, the Komsomol set no great obstacles to admission of new members, except for government employees and intellectuals. There were no limitations for workers and peasants; but out of fear of an influx of oppositionist elements of the intelligentsia it was decided to create for employees and intellectuals, constituting at that time a grade "B" class of citizens, a special category of "candidates for the Komsomol"; for these there was instituted a probation period of a year and a half before they could be admitted to membership. For a long period there were about 100,000 such candidates.

In the cities the Komsomol was allotted a comparatively modest role, that of auxiliary to the party, and the reservoir of new material. In the villages its function was much more important. There, members of the Komsomol, individually and in groups, frequently wielded authority over the nonpartisan peasantry; often they acted by appointment (although formally by "election") as chairmen of village soviets. Of 63,000 village administrations in Soviet Russia, members of the Komsomol ran about 6,000.

Before very long the Komsomol also became the center of intense political struggle. The discussions which subsequently shook the party raged in equal measure at Komsomol meetings. At such meetings Trotsky often won great victories, and Zinoviev at one period scored tremendous successes. In Leningrad, Zinoviev's satrapy, the Komsomol prided itself upon being the most powerful workers' organization.

The intention was at first to include in the Komsomol all young workers, for the purpose of "buttressing the composition" of the organization. Zinoviev related proudly in 1925 that 50 per cent of all young workers in Leningrad had joined the organization; in 1927 the percentage had risen to 73. Although this plan, of course, entailed the danger of admitting large numbers of non-Communists and even anti-Communists, one must keep in mind that by the middle of the 'twenties the

Soviet regime had grown so strong and all other parties had been so completely crushed that the danger appeared to be very slight.

THE Komsomol continued to grow rapidly during the second decade of the Soviet regime, and overtook the party. Already in 1928 it had 2,070,000 members; in 1930 the membership rose to about 2,500,000; and in 1933 it mounted to 4,000,000. Like the party, the Komsomol halted its expansion at this point for several years.

By that time—the middle 'thirties—the position and function of the Komsomol had become fully established. Of its 4,000,000 members, some 700,000 were enrolled in higher and middle educational institutions. More than 100,000 were at work as teachers. More than 40 per cent were in the villages, and of these many were officials of state farms, and many others occupied administrative posts. About 1,000,000 were active in the collectives, combining their agricultural work with various functions of administration. Between 35 and 40 per cent of the organization consisted of young workers.

During this period, the central organs of the Komsomol stopped publishing statistics on its social composition in order to avoid the necessity of acknowledging its largely "nonproletarian" character. One could have cited, for example, the figures of new Komsomol members in the Moscow region for 1938–40. Of 208,522 such newcomers, workers represented only 36 per cent (76,000); government employees and students, 54 per cent (113,000); and peasant collectivists, less than 4 per cent (7,500). Thus at the end of the 'thirties, the Komsomol was no longer a "class," a "workers'" organization. There was no longer any need of regulating its composition artificially, for all members had become "loyal."

In 1936 Stalin decided to carry out an experiment which, if successful, was to be applied to other spheres. He determined to abolish all limitations of the admission of intellectuals to the Komsomol, of government employees and their children, and even of children of former capitalists and kulaks. On Stalin's personal orders, the congress of the Komsomol proclaimed the principle of equality for all who sought admission into the organization. The category of "candidates" henceforward was applied only to illiterates.

The growth of the Komsomol continued at an increased tempo. By 1939 the membership had reached 9,000,000; in 1940 it was 10,000,000; on the eve of the war in 1941 it was about 12,000,000.

At the outbreak of the Russo-German war there were about 40,000,000 persons of Komsomol age in Soviet Russia. Between 12,000,000 and 13,000,000 were in the cities, of whom 7,000,000 to 8,000,000, or 60 to 70 per cent, were in the Komsomol. Virtually the entire youth in many Soviet institutions, plants, educational institutions were Komsomol members. These were no longer the "advance guard" of youth but virtually the entire youth. At the same time, the Komsomol was shedding its old features of a militant, fighting organization.* It lost a great deal of its old Communist *élan,* and became a universal, workaday organization devoted to practical everyday needs, such as education, advancement in jobs, and preparation for military service. The only political note that remained was the publicly avowed loyalty to the regime, regardless of the policies it might pursue.

The Komsomol's organization constitutes a guaranty of loyalty and blind obedience. Each local group elects, of course, its executive committee; the committee selects its secretaries, who direct the affairs of the organization. But the secretaries —and this is the important feature—must be confirmed by higher authorities in the hierarchic scheme. Thus, for example, the secretary of a Komsomol village group must be approved by the district organization, i.e., by the district secretary of the Komsomol; but this district secretary must, in turn, have the approval of the regional secretary, whose existence depends upon approval of the secretary of the Central Committee. The secretary of the Central Committee of the Komsomol—"the Vozhd (Leader) of the Communist Youth"—is actually appointed by the Politbureau of the Communist party: the Politbureau considers in advance the composition of the Central Committee of the Komsomol, including the secretary. The Politbureau can decide on removal of its lead-

* At the outbreak of the war the so-called "Pioneers," ages from 11 to 15, were an organization of 8,000,000 to 9,000,000; in the cities virtually all adolescents of these ages belonged to this preparatory school for the Komsomol. There were also the *Oktiabriata* ("Little Octobrists") ages from 8 to 11, comprising about 4,000,000.

ing officials. The secretary of the Komsomol, appointed by the Politbureau and then elected unanimously by the Central Committee of the Komsomol, controls the regional secretaries, who, in turn, control the district and local secretaries, and so on down the line. At the same time, the Politbureau appoints one of its members to supervise Komsomol affairs. In the period immediately preceding the war this post was occupied by Andrei Zhdanov, one of Stalin's closest and most trusted lieutenants.

Thus, the direction of the Komsomol, founded formally on a democratic basis, proceeds actually in authoritarian fashion, from above downward. The Komsomol became a government institution administering the affairs of youth, as well as some other affairs. Nothing would change if the government should abolish by a stroke of the pen its bylaws with the congresses, elections, membership regulations; the central and local administrations would remain and would continue to perform their prescribed functions.

This process was accelerated with the outbreak of the war. Many millions were mobilized, particularly the village youth, which, as already noted, had been but little affected by the Komsomol organization. It now appeared useful to draw the peasant-soldiers into the organization, which was developing wide military-educational activity at the front. Now the Komsomol began to grow rapidly in the army, recruiting millions of soldiers.

The thin partition which continued to divide the Komsomol in the years immediately preceding the war from the non-Communist youth was imperceptibly removed during the tempestuous war period. At the end of 1943 the membership has reached 17,500,000. Whole sections of the new army—recruits as well as more seasoned soldiers—were incorporated in the organization. On the occasion of its twenty-fifth anniversary (October 29, 1943) the Komsomol addressed a greeting to the Central Committee of the Communist party signed by 17,320,000 men and women. The peculiar character of the Communist Youth League, its long battle against "backward youth," "religious prejudices," "peasant atavism," and "irresoluteness of the intelligentsia"—all this was no more. The type known to the world as a Komsomolets—the brazen, militant, swashbuckling fellow shaking his fist at the Pope of Rome and burning the effigies of "Kings and Churchills" in public squares—had become dissolved in the broad ocean of youth. Today a Komsomolets is a young Soviet citizen and, conversely, the young Soviet citizen is a Komsomolets.

The original social movement represented by the Komsomol, therefore, no longer exists. But the Komsomol organization remains: a network of committees, secretaries, organizers, who receive their instructions from above, from the highest authorities. The instructions pertain to schools, war work, and work in plants and Soviet institutions. Although they overlap the work of other government institutions, these organs continue to be considered essential because they are an additional means of assuring the loyalty of young citizens, of controlling their thoughts and conduct, of rewarding the worthy and punishing the guilty.

XIII

The Red Army and the NKVD

TWO kinds of armed forces have existed in Russia throughout the Soviet period: the army and the police. The police was a political force, the army was nonpolitical. The police was a tool of the party, the army was an object of its activity.

The history of the Soviet period, all the shifting policies and slogans, all turns and zigzags are reflected in the history of the Red Army. The main problem of the Russian revolution, the relationship of the people and the government, finds expression in the relationship of the army and the party, of the commanders and the NKVD. Persistent efforts to expand the "proletarian kernel" as a guaranty of the army's obedience; the creation of party organizations in the army, embracing chiefly the commanding staff; the efforts of the Komsomol to recruit young privates; lecture programs, operation of Communist "political grammar" schools, and publication of a score of newspapers mark the history of the Red Army. Other methods used were the frequent mysterious removals of officers, leapfrog promotions, and purges, small and great.

The two principal instruments used in keeping check on the army were the Political Administration and the NKVD. The Political Administration, a department of the party's Central Committee, operated through thousands of its civil officials (under their various titles, such as "political commissars," "military commissars," "political workers," "party organizers," and others). The activities of the NKVD often were secret, and the identity of many of its chiefs and thousands of informants was not known to the army. The party commissars and the NKVD worked of course in close collaboration.

Each of these elements developed rapidly in the past fifteen years. The Red Army and its officer corps grew in numbers and quality. The number of Communists among the officers was constantly increasing but so was the danger confronting the party in the army. The "political personnel" in the army was 14,000 in 1925 and increased to 34,000 in 1939. In 1925 it appeared that no outside control would be necessary once all the commanding posts were occupied by party members. In 1938, however, when this goal was achieved, the army was covered with an unparalleled network of control and punitive organizations. At the beginning of the 'twenties less than 2 per cent of the army rank and file belonged to Communist organizations, and the government had to keep close watch upon the "potential counterrevolutionists in uniform." In 1939 half of the army's and two thirds of the navy's rank and file were members of the party or of the Komsomol.* But the government, nevertheless, found itself compelled to keep an even more careful eye upon the armed services.

Not for a minute did the party leaders forget the history of Napoleon and Cromwell, and every conceivable political instrument was put to use to forestall the possibility of an analogous development in Russia—that is, the rise to political leadership of some revolutionary hero who would discard the revolutionary process with the aid of a revolutionary army.

After the revolutionary years, as popular political activity declined, the soldier mass became more obedient and politically amorphous. Its capacity for political initiative diminished and with this diminished also the threat to the security of the Soviet system emanating from the army rank and file.

What did appear dangerous, or potentially dangerous, were elements of the government-employed intellectuals. Red Army officers, "military intellectuals," were part of the large class of state officials. Whenever the government accentuated its policy against the Soviet intelligentsia, the relations between the regime and army officers reflected a similar tension.

Intellectuals in officers' uniform, even active members of the Communist party or "Old Bolsheviks" assigned to military posts, often used to become infected with the spirit of opposition after some years of work; at times they joined various opposition groups (in most instances the Right Opposition in the party), and they were frequently subjected to punishment.

* In 1939 Marshal Voroshilov declared that more than 50 per cent of the army rank and file belonged to the Communist party or the Communist Youth League. In the navy the percentage was 67.

One of the most talented Soviet military leaders, Marshal Tukhachevsky, at one time joined the Right Oppositionist circles of the Communist party. He was executed in 1937, together with seven other Soviet military leaders, when a conflict arose over the restoration of the hated "commissars" in the army.*

The great expansion of the Communist party did not make the established regime feel secure about the army any more than about the civil organization of the country. But the outward forms of conflict assumed other features. The army was no longer opposed to the party but to its only armed rival, the only other force possessing rifles, tanks, and military airplanes, to the institution that checks the army, reports on the army, purges the army, arrests army leaders for political motives—an institution occupying a position above the army, and which has an army of its own. This is the NKVD.

THE NKVD (formerly called Cheka and OGPU) is the purest Communist organization of all. Nowhere is the percentage of Communists so large, nowhere is the ratio of "nonpartisans" so low. All executives and nearly all employees of the NKVD are party members, carefully checked and sifted, clear of any oppositionist taint. Only the complete solidarity of the NKVD with the high party leadership makes possible the existence of the Soviet State; this constitutes the first prerequisite of its stability, a fact which permits of no deviations. The slightest ideological deviations, even suspicion of heresy on the part of a member of the NKVD, has invariably and inevitably led to his liquidation. The entire development of the Soviet State, from the romantic chaos of the early years to the confident stability of the latter period, has been closely bound with the strengthening and expansion of this institution.

In the past the OGPU, too, had been the scene of raging ideological differences, when groups of its agents in the corridors of this police fortress had engaged in heated discussions about Socialism in one country and the course of the Chinese

* More recently the American press has shown an inclination to accept the official Kremlin version concerning the alleged treason of Marshal Tukhachevsky and his executed colleagues, and to believe in their negotiations with Germany. Some rather dubious "experts" from Paris and Prague have strenuously propagated this legend.

revolution. There were many years when a party card had served as a guaranty against molestation by the GPU. But all this has long passed. At first singly, then in hundreds, later in many thousands, once privileged party members began moving under convoy across prison corridors and through transfer points into the forests and tundras of distant regions. All discussion about the Chinese revolution has long ceased and no longer does anyone at the Lubyanka Headquarters venture to differ with the powers-that-be in the Kremlin.

The small, weak Temporary Extraordinary Commission of 1917 (the original Cheka) has developed into a permanent institution, which has overtaken all others in its phenomenal growth, including the expansion of industry and the rate of collectivization. Only shamefacedness on the part of the regime prevents the publication of the facts and figures concerning this speedy and brilliant development. Bureaucracy and its red tape exist in other spheres of the regime but not in the NKVD; other Soviet institutions are charged frequently with lack of initiative, but there is plenty of initiative in the NKVD; in other institutions bustle and restlessness interfere with quick decisions, but the actions of the NKVD proceed always with lightning-like speed and are invariably productive.

The NKVD is not a political police in the ordinary sense of the word.

There is no economic enterprise outside of Russia, private or public, the scope of whose operations approaches the economic sweep of the NKVD. The network of schools administered by the NKVD would do honor in its size to any small country. Great "popular movements," such as the antireligious campaigns, have been carried out under the direction of the GPU and later of the NKVD. The NKVD constitutes the actual government of entire regions in the east, where the local authorities exercise but a shadowy authority. Unlike the practice in all other countries, all places of imprisonment in Russia are not within the jurisdiction of the ministry of justice but under the authority of the NKVD. This applies also to the various Corrective Labor Camps and Labor Colonies mentioned in Chapter XI. Many building projects, for example, such as the construction of highways, canals, etc., come under the authority of the NKVD. Its budgets have, therefore, been tremendous, increasing from 482,000,000 rubles in 1933 to

3,000,000,000 in 1937. Together with other projects (in particular the construction of highways and railroads) the figure has been as high as 4,000,000,000.

During the war period, 1941–44, other functions have been added to the NKVD. Contrary to the system in vogue in all other countries, all war prisoners are immediately transferred from the authority of the Red Army into the hands of the NKVD, and all war-prisoner camps are administered not by the military but by the police. For this reason, organizations of war prisoners, such as the Free Germany Committee or the Union of German Officers, are formed on the initiative of the NKVD, on orders, of course, of the higher authorities. All decisions taken by these German organizations and all their resolutions must pass the censorship of the NKVD. Finally, its wartime functions include the supervision of many military and engineering projects.

An important function of the NKVD is checking on the Red Army. This function is performed through the long-established Special Division, created solely for this purpose. All military commissars under their different titles, and other political officials attached to the armed forces are obliged to report regularly to the Special Division, either directly or through the so-called PUR—the Political Administration of the Red Army. Attached to the army for the purpose of watching the conduct of officers (at first former White officers and later all officers), these officials furnish the Special Division with information concerning sentiments in the army, current talk, and "conspiracies." Upon this information the Special Division carried out the purges in the army.

The NKVD has its own not inconsiderable army. At first this was termed Special Service Detachments (*Chon*). Later it was changed to Internal Security Troops (*Vokhr*) and Special Troops of the NKVD. These consist of troops selected not only for their physique but for their loyalty. Twenty years ago they comprised only a few thousand; during the peasant uprisings party members had to be used to augment their forces. To avoid this in the future, the size of the GPU army was expanded. At the end of the 'twenties, with the beginning of the collectivization in the villages, which was accompanied by widespread revolts, these troops were increased to 60,000. Official Moscow sources reported subsequently, over a period of

years, that the NKVD had an armed police of 58,900 men.*
These figures soon became obsolete, although officially Moscow continued to quote them for ten years, up to the outbreak
of the war. Foreign correspondents in 1936–37 estimated the
forces under command of the NKVD at 250,000. This figure,
given in reports passed by the censorship, is closer to the truth.
The NKVD forces constitute a real army, with their own officers, artillery, and even aviation. They are better paid than
the Red Army and their uniforms are more elegant.† The
famous secret weapon *Katusha* was not entrusted to the Red
Army, but whenever it was brought to the front or transported
back it was handled by the NKVD army. The privileges enjoyed are so great that during the war the NKVD army has
been sent to the front only in particular instances and for short
intervals. This army represents a revival in many respects of
the prerevolutionary Corps of Gendarmes, whose function was
also that of political security guards, and which during the
first World War had aroused so much resentment by its comfortable situation in the rear that with the outbreak of the
revolution the demand arose: "The gendarmes to the front!"
However, the gendarmes of that period comprised an insignificant force compared with the troops of the NKVD.

But the power of the NKVD does not rest merely upon these
outward attributes of authority. More significant, perhaps, are
its unseen tentacles, which embrace a larger number of people
than its army. Every member of the Communist party, no
matter where he may be working, is obliged to keep the NKVD
informed of everything he sees and hears that may be of interest. That this is no mere "moral obligation" has been demonstrated by the fate of hundreds of Communists who for reasons
of carelessness or because of humane considerations had failed
to report on their relatives. But in addition to the general obligation impressed upon the millions of party members, thousands of special Communist informers have the direct task of
gathering information on various aspects of social life and informing the NKVD; these operatives are present in every institution, office, plant, scientific society.

* Divided as follows: frontier guards, 28,150; frontier troops stationed in their
own home territories, 17,240; escort troops, 13,200.
† Only in 1943 were the NKVD troops ordered to put on the regular Red
Army uniform in order not to arouse resentment by their appearance.

Many thousands of nonpartisans perform the same function, diligently and without pay. These are persons who once had an unpleasant contact with the NKVD; they have been permitted to remain at liberty on condition of serving as regular informers; they are instructed to follow their usual occupations, without changing their mode of life in any way, to visit as usual their friends, schools, meetings, but to present reports about them. What is the number of such informers? Perhaps the NKVD itself does not know.

This army of spies presents a special problem. Their social position in the circle of their friends and acquaintances does not change when they become informers of the NKVD, although not infrequently those in whose circles they move become aware of their function; they cannot very well be excluded from these circles, first, because of fear of repression, and, secondly, because the matter is altogether an everyday phenomenon. The presence of informers in every nonpolitical group, at every entertainment, in every house committee is accepted as a matter of course. Thousands of these informers themselves undoubtedly dream of an opportunity of quitting their activity, of seeing the day when their shameful reports concerning their relatives and friends go up in flames. And, conversely, they would be horror-stricken if the archives were to be opened and their work given publicity. All this is material for some future Shakespeare.

Soviet scientists of world reputation, frequent participants in international congresses; writers whose works have been translated into many languages; suave and polite diplomats, Soviet pedagogues who teach the young the basic truths of morality; doctors with large practices; and many other figures of various degrees of importance would gladly give everything they own, down to the last shirt, if they could only destroy the handiwork of their sheer, animal cowardice. This might be called, in ordinary times and places, the moral degradation of some individuals; but how can the characterization be applied to a mass phenomenon? How can we expect heroism to be a mass phenomenon?

Both the volunteer informers and the paid squealers, the thousands of the victims and prospective victims, the purged and the expelled, the exiles and their families, all those who out of elemental fear of the NKVD will not venture to utter a word of criticism, desire what to them appears to be the impossible—the disappearance of this institution and its entire system.

Among these passionate dreamers Communists occupy a very prominent place. They have been painfully whipped in the last ten years, and the very name NKVD has filled them with no less terror than it has their nonpartisan associates. They, too, have opened the invitations to appear before the NKVD investigator with horror regardless of whether or not they knew themselves innocent; all that has yet been written about this drama is but a pale shadow of the truth. Communists, too, have been exiled by the thousands; they, too, have rotted in distant places; they, too, have been renounced by their wives and children. When permitted to remain at liberty, they, too, in shameful fear, have woven informers' tales about their chiefs and subordinates, their school friends, their intimates. And because of their diligence and enthusiasm, their pains and their services they quietly, sullenly, passionately hate the NKVD.

Such are also the sentiments of the rest of the population, civil and military. This has been true before and it is true now, in the midst of war. There is hardly a family that has not lost someone in the war; and there are few families who at one time or another have not paid their tribute to the Moloch NKVD. Some friends and relatives have stood under the hail of German bullets at the front, others have been imprisoned in concentration camps, where they died young of hunger and disease, toiling at forced labor. Some officers landed in the hell of German captivity, others were removed and demoted as a consequence of reports by the ubiquitous agents of the NKVD.

Many observers and very many Russian Communists have more than once expected a decisive conflict between the army and the NKVD; predictions of such a conflict have been heard even during the war. So far these expectations and predictions have proved unfounded; but the first fortress which may fall after the war as a consequence of the combined efforts of the army and the people, as soon as the first rays of spring begin to alter the rigorous landscape, will not be the party, not even the collectives, but the incomparable, majestic, unique monolith resting upon inhumanity, slavery, abomination, and death —the NKVD.

XIV

Conclusion

EVERY government wages war in its own way, depending upon its political character. The strategy, war economy, and aims of Hitler's Germany are different from those of the Kaiser's. Stalin's Russia wages war in a manner different from Imperial Russia and different, too, from that which would have been followed by any other Russian political regime. A political organism, like a living one, fights with the organs, muscles, and fangs that it has at its disposal.

Soviet policy in the war period represents a harmonious whole. It reflects a unity of military policy, internal and external. All parts are harmonized, each complements the other.

In its foreign policy the Soviet Government has defended itself with its own specific measures: first, by means of a pact with Germany, later by an alliance with the anti-German forces. Its foreign policy was amplified by political strategy—territorial expansion in the west in 1939–40. In national economy, it was supported by the vast industrial construction and, later, by the evacuation of some industrial units to the east; by centralization of the collectives as the source of food supply; by the millions impressed into forced labor for rapid execution of urgent economic plans and strategic works; finally, by the scorched-earth policy carried out before the advancing enemy. The complement in internal policy was a ruthless political system, marked by suppression of all opposition in the country as a whole, and particularly in the army.

The component parts were closely welded in this harmonious system. The result was the German retreat. It was a success of the combined forces of the nation's economy, of its armed strength, of the government's policy, and of the material aid received from outside. It is too early to determine the importance to be attributed to the last mentioned of these factors; the moment for that has not yet arrived. For the evaluation, however, of the wartime policy of the Soviet Government, one must take into account also the price paid in terms of losses suffered, for this will determine in large measure the future of the country.

Under any conditions the conquest of Russia was in general an impossibility. Russia is not Belgium, nor even France. She can be defeated, and, indeed, there have been many wars, both in the Soviet and non-Soviet periods, in which Russia was vanquished. But actual conquest of Russia, as it was planned in Berlin, was the fantasy of feverish minds. It would have been easier to drain the ocean with a pump than to conquer Russia.

The defense methods used by Russia would have been different under different political conditions. Another type of relations with Germany in peace and war stood open for Russia in the 'thirties: no pacts or neutrality, but a real alliance with France; in case of war, simultaneous action with the Western powers. In this situation Germany probably would not have destroyed the French Army or occupied the entire Russian south and wiped out a great part of Russia's military-economic achievements.

But this road of foreign and war policy was not the way of defense for the Soviet Government. So it had to wage alone a continental war between 1941 and 1944; a great portion of the industry developed in the south and west under the Five-Year Plans was destroyed so far as its utilization for war purposes was concerned, so that the enormous sacrifices made by the population over a period of years for the sake of industrial development were in large measure rendered useless from the viewpoint of national defense. Russia need not have lost the entire Ukraine, and the Kuban and Ukrainian fields would not have had to be abandoned to feed German troops. The war would not have lasted so long, if Europe had not fallen into Germany's hands; and the Allies would not have required almost three years to prepare for their invasion, while Russia suffered ruin.

The measure of the efficiency of the Soviet conduct of the war is Russia's sacrifices and losses. One element of the Soviet military system, inherited in part from Russian history but tremendously accentuated during the revolutionary period, has been its contempt for the life of the individual and for sacrifices in general. No one, including the Soviet Government, knows the actual losses in human life suffered by Russia in this war. These losses are not confined to those killed on the fields of battle but include people who perished in the evacuation of the civil population, those who died of epidemics and exhaustion and as labor slaves in Germany. But one thing we do know: never in history has any country suffered the war losses borne by Russia in this war. They are greater than the combined losses sustained by all belligerent countries in the first World War. They exceed considerably the losses suffered by all other countries in this war.

According to some sources Russia's losses are estimated at fifteen to twenty million human beings. A year ago a high official of the War Department in Washington estimated Russia's military losses at ten million. But the world will shudder when the final balance sheet of death becomes known in all its details: losses from disease, which in the last war were greater than losses on the battlefield; the ravages of typhus epidemics among the civil population from 1941 to 1944; deaths among the many millions evacuated from the west to the east; deaths from undernourishment and hunger among the city population and as a consequence of the exhausting labor of men, women, and children.

Germany will be defeated in this war, but Russia's losses will far exceed Germany's. If we are to believe the German figures, the number of Russian war prisoners is between four and five million. Their fate illustrates the degree of contempt for human life now prevailing not only in Russia. Russian prisoners are kept under much worse conditions than those of any other country. They get the very worst food, the most inadequate medical care, the most cruel treatment; as a consequence, their death rate is very high. The Soviet Government would not join the international convention concerning the treatment of war prisoners concluded in Geneva in 1929, and the International Red Cross therefore has no right and is not obliged to care for Russian prisoners in Germany. Accounts of their appalling condition are reaching the outside world. Their country has abandoned them to their fate, has washed its hands of these millions of her sons. Why?

By not joining the Geneva convention, the Soviet Government has retained a free hand in dealing with German war prisoners. In line with the rule established in 1918, they are placed under the jurisdiction of the NKVD; members of the Free Germany Committee, the Union of German Officers, and similar organizations are recruited from their midst. Papers are published for their benefit, they attend lectures, conferences are organized for them, and political cells are being established among them—all for the purpose of creating an organization to be used for Soviet political purposes in Germany after her defeat. This would of course have been impossible if some international organization had had the right to exercise control over the life of German prisoners in Russia. The Russian people are paying dearly for a few German-Soviet divisions of problematical value.

The scorched-earth policy has been another feature of the Soviet method of waging war. It, too, harmonized with the general system. It may be assumed that not every government would have followed such wholesale destruction of Russia's west and south from Narva to Stalingrad. As a consequence of this policy, cities have been destroyed, grain supplies burned, the population driven in part to the east, industry has been wrecked. And then the Germans completed the transformation of entire provinces into deserts.

The outside world is concerned not with Russian losses but only with victory over Germany. This is a natural though narrow viewpoint, a viewpoint accepted also by the many false "friends of Russia," who praise her accomplishments, her sacrifices, and the wisdom of her government. Behind this mask of enthusiasm is hidden not only indifference to the fate of the Russian people but, at times, something else: namely, the secret satisfaction that Russia will emerge from the war greatly weakened for purposes of postwar policy.

And this may be only too true. The trite phrase that "Russia will emerge from the war stronger than she was before" is ill-founded. The main source of every country's strength is not in its industry, which may be destroyed and rebuilt in a few years; not so much in its economy, railroads, money, and wealth—and still less in grandiloquent phrases. It is the population of a country, particularly its adult, healthy male population, which constitutes the main criterion of its power. This cannot be created as easily as bridges or electric stations. A generation must pass before the quantitative and, particularly, the qualitative loss of lives can be made good. In comparison with other countries Russia has suffered most severely in this respect.

The success of the Russian defense may be a warning to future would-be aggressors, but the losses Russia has suffered may be a source of encouragement to military adventurers. The relative weakening of Russia's military might as a consequence of these losses is not a guaranty of peace or of a moderate and peaceful foreign policy of her government. Only a change in the general concept of the international relations of Europe's greatest nation can safeguard a durable peace.

The whole world will be grateful to Russia for her help and her sacrifices in this war. But the Russia of the future will have no reason to be thankful to the Soviet Government of today for its specific methods of waging war and for its wartime foreign policy.

The entire country will remember these methods when streams of human beings begin to move across its distances after the end of hostilities. They will come from German enslavement in search of new abodes, from war prison camps, exhausted, humiliated, and sullen. Millions will come from the east, from the regions of evacuation, after years of illness and crushing labor. And, finally, there will come the millions of troops from the fronts, who emotionally, intellectually, and physically will have experienced a great deal more in the years of war than would have been possible in decades of normal life. East and west will meet, north and south will come together. The legless, the armless, the invalids of war, the millions of widows and orphans will be for decades a feature of Russian cities and villages.

This is the dark but inescapable picture of the immediate future. This horrible poverty, these unheard-of privations inflicted upon the population do not in themselves constitute a guaranty of a wise foreign policy on the part of the government in the future, of abandonment of expansionism, any more than they are a guaranty of necessary internal reforms. Every political system has its own logic, while dynamic forces, once brought into action, continue to operate, as before. But the course of the war, the price of victory, and the postwar situation in Russia constitute the prologue to great internal changes, greater changes than some are inclined to expect.

Sources

FROM the large literature and abundant material on Soviet Russia only those sources are listed below which have been quoted or otherwise directly used in this book.

Chapter II. The Limits of Stalin's Realism

Lenin and Stalin as Political Realists:
Yevgeni Pashukanis, *Marx i Proletarskoye Gosudarstvo*, Moscow, 1933.
Emil Ludwig's interview with Stalin, December 13, 1931.
D. Manuilsky in *Bolshevik*, 1944, No. 1.

Communism and the State:
Lenin, *Works*, 2d ed., Vol. XIV², *Gosudarstvo i Revolutsiya* and *Uderzhat-li Bolsheviki Gosudarstvennuyu Vlast*.
—— *Works*, 3d ed., XVIII, 81 ff.; XXII, 291 ff.
Stalin, *Voprosy Leninizma*, 3d ed., pp. 702 ff.
Bukharin and Preobrazhensky, *Azbuka Kommunizma*, Saratov, 1920.

Stalin and His Party in the War:
Stalin's speeches, particularly July 3, 1941, May 1, 1942, November 7, 1943, and Stalin's Order of the Day, May 1, 1943, in Soviet War Documents, Washington, 1943.
A. Kursky in *Bolshevik*, October, 1943.
K. Kuznetsov in *Propagandist*, 1942, No. 9.
A. Fadeyev in *Propagandist*, 1943, No. 21.
New York Times, November 17, 1941, May 3 and 27, 1943, June 20, 1943, July 4, 1943, November 22, 1943, December 7, 1943, February 14, 1944.
Eve Curie, *Journey Among Warriors*, New York, 1943.

Marxism–Leninism in the War:
Nekotorye Voprosy Prepodavaniya Politicheskoi Ekonomii, in *Pod Znamenem Marxizma*, No. 7–8, 1943.
A. Makhanov in *Propagandist*, 1942, No. 3.
Leading article in *Propagandist*, 1942, No. 7–8.
G. Alexandrov in *Propagandist*, 1942, No. 19–20, and in No. 5, 1943.
Leading article in *Propagandist*, 1943, No. 11–12.

P. Pozdnyshev in *Propagandist*, 1943, No. 13.
Leading articles in *Propagandist*, 1943, Nos. 14 and 18.
M. Mitin in *Propagandist*, 1943, No. 19–20.
Leading articles in *Bolshevik*, 1943, Nos. 22 and 23–24.
Alexander Shcherbakov's Report, January 21, 1943, in *Propagandist*, 1943, No. 2.
Istoriya VKP, Kratki Kurs, Moscow, 1938.

Chapter III. The Devil's Name Is Trotsky

Bulleten Oppozitsii, 1929–1940, particularly Nos. 5–6, 75, 81, 82–83.
Trotsky, *Nashi Politicheskiya Zadachi,* Geneva, 1904.
Stalin, reports, December 27, 1929, and at the 16th Congress of the Communist Party, in his *Voprosy Leninizma*, 11th ed.
Trotsky, "If World War Comes Again," *Yale Review*, 1938, No. 4.
—— *Works,* Vol. XV, *Vseobshchaya Trudovaya Povinnost.*

Chapter IV. New Religious Policy

N. S. Timasheff, *Religion in Soviet Russia,* New York, 1942.
Stalin in *Izvestiya*, September 15, 1927.
New York Times, June 20 and September 25, 1943, August 12, 1944.
Izvestiya, February 16, 1930, September 5, 12 and 17, 1943, February 1 and April 6, 1944.
Komsomol i Antireligioznaya Propaganda, Moscow, 1937.
Christian Science Monitor, September 30, 1941.
Russian Orthodox Journal (in English), Philadelphia, March, 1943.
Neue Zürcher Zeitung, January 16, 1941.

Chapter V. The Soviet Concept of Foreign Policy

Stalin's speech of November 7, 1941.
S. Lozovsky in *Bolshevik*, July, 1941.
New York Times, July 23, 1942.
Stalin's reports at the 17th and 18th Congresses of the Communist Party, in his *Voprosy Leninizma*, 11th ed.
Farrin in *Voina i Rabochyi Klass,* September 15, 1943.

Chapter VI. The New Social Structure

Equality and Inequality:
Lenin, *Works,* 3d ed., XIX, 37 ff.; XX, 133 ff.; XXI, 233, 438; XXIV, 102, 185–186.

Decrees of the Soviet Government, November 12 and December
16, 1917.
Vserossyiskaya Konferentsiya RKP, 1922, *Bulleten*, Moscow, 1922.
Stalin, *Voprosy Leninizma*, 11th ed., pp. 462–495.
Mitin's speech at the 18th Congress of the Communist Party, in
Stenograficheskyi Otchet 18 S'yezda.
N. Bukharin in *Bolshevik*, 1925, No. 9–10.

The New Social Classes and Their Income:
The statistical yearbook, *Sotsialisticheskoye Selskoye Khozyaistvo*,
1939.
Statistical yearbooks, *Sotsialisticheskoye Stroitelstvo*, 1934, 1935,
1936, 1939.
Statistical yearbooks, *Trud*, 1934, 1936.
Professor S. N. Prokopovich's *Bulleten Ekonomicheskogo Kabi-
neta*, Praga, 1935–1938, and his *Quarterly Bulletin of Soviet-
Russian Economics*, Geneva, 1939–1943.
Gosplan, Kontrolnye Tsyfry, 1926–27, 1929–30.
Problemy Ekonomiki, 1940, No. 7, Pisarev, *K Itogam Perepisi.*
Voznesensky's Report at the Conference of the Communist Party
in *Bolshevik*, 1941, No. 34.
Gosplan, Narodno-Khozyaistvennyi Plan na 1936, Moscow.

Population Problems:
Wolf and Mebus, *Statisticheskyi Spravochnik po Ekonomicheskoi
Geografii*, Moscow, 1928.
Ts.S.U., Statisticheskyi Spravochnik, 1928.
Ts.S.U., Trudy, Vols. VIII, XVIII.
Sautin in *Bolshevik*, May, 1940.
League of Nations, *Future Population of Europe and of the Soviet
Union*, Geneva, 1944.
Pravda, April 17, 1938.
Stalin's speech, December 3, 1935, in his *Voprosy Leninizma.*
Izvestiya, April 29, 1940.
League of Nations, *Statistical Yearbooks.*
Sotsialisticheskoye Stroitelstvo, 1936, 1939.

Chapters VII and VIII. The New Upper Classes

Communism and the Intelligentsia:
Lenin, *Works*, 3d ed., X, 207 ff.
Stalin's speeches, June 23, 1931, January 7, 1933, November 25,
1936, in his *Voprosy Leninizma*, 11th ed.
—— report at the 18th Congress, in *Voprosy Leninizma.*

Kaganovich's report at the 17th Congress, in *Stenigraficheskyi Otchet 17 S'yezda.*

Molotov's speech at the 18th Congress, in *Stenografcheskyi Otchet.*

Resolutions of the Central Committee of the Communist Party, July, 1928, in *VKP v Rezolutsiyakh,* Vol. II, Moscow, 1940.

Vladimir Tchernavin, *I Speak for the Silent. Prisoners of the Soviets,* Boston, 1935.

Rapid Increase of the New Classes:
Gosplan, *Piatiletnyi Plan,* Vol. II, Moscow, 1930.
Sotsialisticheskoye Stroitelstvo, Moscow, 1934, 1935, 1936.
Ekonomika Sotsialisticheskoi Promyshlennosti, Moscow, 1940.

Chapter X. *The Peasantry*

Lenin, *Tezisy po Agrarnomu Voprosu,* 1920.
Pravda, May 20, 1940.
Stalin's speeches, May 28, 1928, October 19, 1928.
Stalin's report at the Plenary Meeting of the Central Committee, April, 1929, in *Voprosy Leninizma.*
Pravda, April 3, 1930.
Planovoye Khozyaistvo, 1938, No. 9, and 1939, Nos. 5, 7, 9.
Izvestiya, May 22, 1938, and March 29, 1941.
Plan, November, 1936.
Sotsialisticheskaya Rekonstruktsiya Selskovo Khozyaistva, 1940, No. 11–12.
Sotsialisticheskoye Zemledelie, December 22, 1938, June 5, 1940.
Altaiski, *Dokhody v Kolkhozakh,* 1937.
Kolkhozy vo Vtoroi Stalinskoi Pyatiletke, 1939.
Ekonomicheskyi Bulleten, Professor S. Prokopovich, 1935–1938.

The Peasants and the Communist Party:
18th Congress of the Communist Party, 1939, speeches by Patolichev, Andreyev, Mikhailov, Chernousov, and Shtykov.
Kaganovich's report at the 17th Congress.
10th Congress of the Komsomol, speeches by Kossior, Andreyev, and Kosarev.
Partiynoye Stroitelstvo, 1934, No. 1; 1937, No. 12; 1941, No. 6.

The Peasantry in War:
Bolshevik, Decrees of the Soviet Government, 1942, No. 7–8; 1943, Nos. 7–8, 15–16.
Information Bulletin of the Soviet Embassy, Washington, February 10, 1944.

Chapter XI. Forced Labor

I. L. Averbakh, *Ot Prestupleniya k Trudu,* Moscow, 1936.

J. Littlepage and D. Bess, *In Search of Soviet Gold,* New York, 1938.

John Scott, *Behind the Urals,* Boston, 1942.

S. Firin, *Itogi Belomorstroya,* Moscow, 1934.

Insarov, *Baltiysko-Belomorski Vodnyi Put,* Moscow, 1934.

Lilian Mowrer and Olga Kochanska, *Arrest and Exile,* New York, 1941.

Vladimir Tchernavin, *I Speak for the Silent. Prisoners of the Soviets,* Boston, 1935.

Tatiana Tchernavin, *Escape from the Soviets,* New York, 1934.

Boris Souvarine, *Stalin,* New York, 1939.

Leonard Hubbard, *Soviet Labor,* London, 1942.

Besedovski, *Den Klauen der Tscheka entronnen,* Leipzig, 1930.

Chapter XII. The Communist Party of the Soviet Union

Lenin, *Works,* 3d ed., XXV, 578 ff.

Stalin, "Ob Osnovakh Leninizma," in his *Voprosy Leninizma,* 1939.

Stalin's speech, March 3, 1937, in *Bolshevik,* 1937, No. 7.

VKP v Tsifrakh, published by the Central Committee of the Communist Party, twice a year until 1928.

Perepis RKP, published by the Central Committee, 1922.

Vserossyiskaya Konferentsiya RKP, Moscow, 1922.

A. Mitrofanov, *Itogi Chistki Partii,* Moscow, 1930.

Pravda, November 15, 1943.

Stenograficheskyi Otchet 16 S'yezda, reports by Vladimirsky and Kaganovich.

Stenograficheskyi Otchet 17 S'yezda, reports by Vladimirsky and Kaganovich.

Stenograficheskyi Otchet 18 S'yezda VKP, speeches of Zhdanov and Shatalin, and the report of the Mandate Commission.

Komsomol:

Molodezh SSSR, Moscow, 1936.

Balashov, *Komsomol za Desiat Let,* Moscow, 1928.

Sotsialisticheskoye Stroitelstvo, 1936.

O. Mishakova in *Propagandist,* 1943, No. 18.

S. Ostriakov, *Chto Trebuyet Komsomol ot Komsomoltsa,* Moscow, 1937.

Pravda, September 26, 1940, October 8, 1940, October 29, 1943.

Izvestiya, October 29, 1943.
Otchet 10 S'yezda Komsomola, Moscow, 1936, report by Kossior.
Chto Reshil 10 S'yezd Komsomola, Moscow, 1936.

Chapter XIII. The Red Army and the NKVD

Voroshilov, *Stat'i i Rechi,* Moscow, 1936.
Komplektovaniye Krasnoi Armii, Berlin, 1926.
Agabekov, *Cheka za Rabotoi,* Berlin, 1931.
E. Dumbadze, *Na Sluzhbe Cheka,* Paris, 1930.
Essad-bey, *OGPU,* New York, 1933.
W. G. Krivitsky, *In Stalin's Secret Service,* New York, 1939.
Report on Court Proceedings, Trial of N. Bukharin and Others,
    Moscow, 1938 (in English).
D. Fedotoff White, *The Growth of the Red Army,* Princeton,
    1944.

Index

3782